Kevin Doheny CSSp

NO HANDS BUT YOURS

Memoirs of a Missionary

To: Bríd

With my Love
& my Prayers.
God bless you & your
family

Kevin Doheny CSSp

VERITAS

First published 1997 by
Veritas Publications
7/8 Lower Abbey Street
Dublin 1

ISBN 1 85390 327 2

British Library Cataloguing
in Publication Data.
A catalogue record for
this book is available
from the British Library.

Cover design by Bill Bolger
Printed in the Republic of Ireland by Betaprint Ltd, Dublin

No Hands But Yours is dedicated to my brother, Father Michael, who was 'the voice of the Poor'. It is also dedicated to refugees, the world over. The royalties on the sales of the book will be given to Refugee Trust.

This crucifix in a Catholic church in Ovamboland, Namibia, was severely damaged during a bombing raid. It recalls a crucifix in Bavaria, similarly damaged during World War II, to which the parish priest has attached the legend 'I have no hands but yours'.

APPRECIATION

My sincere thanks to the many people who encouraged me and cajoled me into publishing my memoirs. I refer in particular to Frederick Forsyth, Father Martin Keane CSSp, Provincial Superior of the Holy Ghost Fathers, Teresa Osbourne, Miss Audrey Murray, Mother Teresa, Paul Harrison and many others.

Touching Other Lives

My life will touch a dozen lives,
Before this day is done,
Leave countless marks of good or ill,
Ere sets the evening sun.

So thus, the wish I always wish,
The prayer I ever pray,
Lord, may my life help other lives
It touches on the way.

'My Influence'
G. Knight

CONTENTS

FOREWORD

We met on a dusty track under the African sun some thirty years ago, a frustrated war correspondent confronting a harassed Irish priest.

The secessionist state of Biafra was at war with its huge neighbour Nigeria and the tide of that war was rolling towards us both. My job was to report it, his to shield his bewildered and frightened parishioners from its cruelty. I suppose we both succeeded in part, had some small effect.

Kevin Doheny, stemming from a humble farm in County Laois, had taken Holy Orders and volunteered as a missionary priest in West Africa. There, but for the fickle finger of the Lord, he might have lived out most of his life, an obscure parish priest tending his small flock, before retiring to a peaceful dotage at Kimmage.

But the sight of the children dying all around him fired his Irish passion, so that he spoke out to the media without reserve or temperance. It was enough to make him a marked man, and to ensure his expulsion when the victorious Nigerians eventually marched in.

Thus began his second and great odyssey, a commitment to bring relief and succour to the hungry, sick and displaced refugees everywhere. It was a journey that would take him a million miles, hustling donations from the pampered rich to bring food and shelter to those once called 'the wretched of the earth'.

When he has passed from among us there may well be no great statue, as for king or conqueror. But there will be many in the Developing World still alive, who would else be dead but for this son of Ireland and his tireless quest to serve his God.

Frederick Forsyth
Hertford, England, 1996

CHAPTER 1

MY JOURNEY BEGINS...

My hair is white and thin now, but when I was born in May 1925 I was the baby of the bunch. I had a very happy childhood, getting extra special treatment as the youngest of ten – a normal-sized family in the twenties.

My father, Michael, died when I was about eight months old, which left the entire responsibility of the family on the shoulders of my mother and my elder brother, Jack. The day my father died was the last day of Jack's formal education. On the afternoon of 12 February, he walked out of the Salesian College in Palaskenry in County Limerick and was faced with the wake and funeral of our dear father, and the responsibility of the 150-acre farm. There were a few cows to be milked and foddered, fields to be ploughed, crops to be sown, and the many other activities associated with a farm – a formidable task for a young lad of twelve. But Jack was also formidable in character.

Jack had no choice. He did what four generations of Dohenys had done before him. And from that time, his knowledge was to be of the soil beneath our feet, the life that stepped on it and sprang from it, and the skies that poured their precious rain and rousing rays of sunshine.

Running the farm at Ballinalacken, Ballinakill, County Laois, was a tremendous challenge for Jack. Whatever dreams the twelve-year-old boy might have entertained for his future were dashed. He had the task of producing food from the land. Even though the stony ground was only suitable for livestock and not tillage, he managed to grow enough potatoes, turnips, cabbage and other vegetables to sustain the family.

Jack was destined to be set apart from all his brothers and sisters for the rest of his life. He alone was to stay on the farm in Ireland, while we travelled the world. But while we dined with princes and presidents, the thought of Jack's solid plate of potatoes gave us all an earthy reminder of where our deep roots were.

Jack married a beautiful woman, Peg McDonald, who was a great help to him. Peg fitted into the family very well and took good care of my ageing mother till she died. They had five children, Michael, Ken, Mary, Nora and Seán.

Tom was in Italy when our father passed away, and received the sad news in a letter from my mother about a month later. Tom was fifteen years of age, and it must have been awful news to receive on his own, with no one to share his great loss.

We all quickly learned what struggle meant, and we tasted poverty early in life. It was a great blessing and I feel it kept us very united. Moreover, it was a good preparation for the years ahead, and it made us aware at a personal level of what poverty was really about.

We were supported by a tremendously generous extended family of aunts and uncles, cousins and loyal neighbours. Such support systems are still the backbone of so many Developing World countries. In many of today's urban western societies these duties are frequently ignored, and responsibilities are conveniently thrust onto the Nanny State.

My mother was a major influence in my early childhood. She was very religious, hard-working and devoted. She knew what love was and what suffering was. The loss of my father was a very painful trial at such an early age. The problem of rearing a large family alone had its difficult days.

I remember my mother as a fantastic person, whom we all loved. She rarely, if ever, punished us, but she could get us to do anything for her by praising us. As a family we worked together and supported each other, as life was hard. Our mother had to see that the groceries were bought and paid for every week in the difficult times of the twenties and thirties, during the economic war with Britain. Jack carried a major share of the burden, and did so brilliantly.

My mother had a deep faith and trust in the goodness of God. She never complained. She never turned a needy person away from the door. As a child she would send me out to a man working on the road, breaking stones, with a hot cup of tea and some bread, a welcome gift on a cold day. She also had a keen interest in the missions, and supported appeals annually, in a small way according to her means.

As a child I once threw a ten-shilling note (a small fortune in the twenties) into the fire. I was too small to know the value of money, and in fact I don't remember doing it at all, but was often reminded of my misdemeanour.

You can imagine what hardships my mother had to put up with from us from time to time. She had a major influence on all of us, and yet she never interfered with our decision-making.

We were poor, but never destitute. And none of us, as children, guessed that we were about to embark on a lifetime profession of poverty. Our suffering as children offered us an insight into the suffering of thousands around the world. Our understanding of rural poverty enabled us to identify closely with the people we were to share our lives with overseas. It gave us the insight to offer the best solutions to folk living in far worse conditions than we ever knew, such as the dreadful famines of Biafra and Ethiopia, and the permanent, desperate poverty of the streets of Calcutta. We had learned about poverty in the best school of all, in our home, and at an early age, and that learning experience never left us.

One by one we left the shores of Ireland. Tom, the eldest of the family, was the first. In 1928 he joined the Marist Brothers and travelled overland to Italy by train – a journey of five days. He studied there for two years before setting off for the tropical climate of faraway Ceylon (now Sri Lanka). He taught in Stella Maris College, Nogombo, for about six years, where he struggled to master the art of teaching, without any professional training.

From there he travelled yet further afield, to China. In those days, religious went to the missions for life. We didn't hear from him for about six years (1939-46). He was lost in the province of Tientsin when the communists took over in the late forties. It must have been a great source of suffering for my mother. She did not know whether he was alive or dead, with no letters coming from him until the Red Cross eventually got a note out from him to say he was safe and well. His subsequent letters were cheerful, as he could not risk telling the truth, but as principal of the college, he had been in prison on several occasions, answering all kinds of false allegations made against him. He was a member of the Legion of Mary, which did not help his cause in a country where religion was now regarded as the opium of the people. He was eventually expelled, and arrived home after an absence of about twenty-three years. He was very nervous as a result of his ordeal, but recovered quickly at home. However, he could not wait to go back to Hong

Kong, where he became principal of a new college being built in that city. He had left Ireland when I was three years of age and returned for my ordination to the priesthood. Tom has now been posted to Rome, after spending sixty-eight years in the Far East, fifteen years in Tientsin and forty-five in Hong Kong. He has incredible contacts, even with his past students, who keep in touch from all over the world.

Tom must have inspired us, for six years later Des followed him into the Marist Congregation.

Next was Michael, who got his secondary education in Blackrock College, Dublin, and from there joined the Holy Ghost Congregation, a missionary order. Michael was a major influence in my life, as I will explain later.

My sister Eileen chose another route – she took a job in Kilkenny in my Uncle Michael Moore's drapery shop. She married Paddy Kelly of Bennetstown, County Kilkenny, in 1950.

Maury chose to be a nun and joined the Congregation of the Little Sisters of the Assumption. Their charisma was to nurse the poor in their own homes, and they were the first to promote this form of apostolate. They would nurse sick mothers or fathers, do the housework, prepare the children for school etc. Maury spent most of her life in Ireland where she served in Dublin and Cork, and spent some time in England. She used her training to good advantage when Eily became terminally ill and she looked after the Kelly family, helping them over a difficult period, until Eily died.

Joe, born in 1924, was not cut out for formal education, but he was a born farmer and he helped Jack on the farm for many years. He was invaluable to Jack, as he had a great pair of skilled hands, and could do all kinds of repair and maintenance work.

Against this background I found myself trying to make up my own mind what I should do. After my primary education in Firoda National School, I was sent to Blackrock College, Dublin, a very religious institution from which Michael had graduated with distinction. By the grace of God, I followed Michael, almost ten years my senior, into the Holy Ghost Congregation, dedicated to the missions, founded to assist 'the most abandoned souls'. It was a decision I never regretted.

My decision to become a priest was based on a number of factors. My mother was a wonderful inspiration by her faith and her example, though she never mentioned the priesthood to me. Michael was also a major influence on me, as were Tom, Desmond and Maury as each entered religious life. We had excellent teachers in Firoda School, like Davie Maher and Susan McManus, and later Mr and Mrs John McGrath. Their Christian way of life, their example, their interest in the missions and devotion to their profession had a profound effect on us.

I joined the Congregation of the Holy Ghost and of the Immaculate Heart of Mary in 1943 in the novitiate in Kilshane, County Tipperary. Seventy-two of us joined the Congregation at that time. After the novitiate, on 9 September 1944, we travelled by train to Dublin to enter the scholasticate in Kimmage Manor, beginning the long pilgrimage of nine years of prayer and study for the priesthood.

Life in the seminary was very strict, very regimented. We were isolated from the world around us, sheltered from the problems of the world. As students, we had no access to the daily papers, or to football or hurling matches outside the seminary, though we did get a month's holidays in the summer, while we were studying philosophy, though not when we were studying theology. Many of us felt raw and perhaps inadequate at the end of our course, with such little knowledge of the outside world. In our final year of theology, after our ordination, our ministry was limited to saying Mass in some parishes on Sunday but we had no access to hospitals, to counselling the sick or the depressed. It was the system of seminary training at that time, which fortunately changed with the Second Vatican Council in the sixties. We had to fall back on our common sense and our wits for the answers to many human problems. We learned from experience and from making mistakes.

I did a BA in philosophy in UCD and spent three years in Trinidad, teaching and prefecting in St Mary's College, Port of Spain. This delightful experience was my first exposure to teaching in a multi-racial and multi-cultural society. It was a most interesting three years, and it gave me time to reflect on my future, and on my vocation. It was, nevertheless, a very busy time, with a full day's class and sports in the evenings. I was in charge of the tennis club, and built up the membership gradually. It was a secondary college of over a thousand students of differing colour, creed, ability and sporting activities. The boys were very friendly and open. I loved them, and enjoyed teaching them. We spent our holidays on the Island of Gasparee, indulging in swimming, boating, sailing and fishing. I was sorry to leave Trinidad in 1948, after three very happy years.

My time there was most informative, an ideal preparation for the tougher life I was to experience later. It reconfirmed me in my vocation. I was ordained a priest on 5 July 1953 in Clonliffe College, Dublin, by John Charles McQuaid CSSp, Archbishop of Dublin. About forty-three of us were ordained together that year. A year later we were ready for the missions and I was appointed to the diocese of Owerri in Nigeria by our provincial superior, Father Dan Murphy CSSp.

In November 1954 we assembled at the North Wall in Dublin to board a boat for Lagos, capital of Nigeria. It was a quiet departure, with no relatives present. My family would not dream of coming to see me off, as it was a long journey from Laois to Dublin and cost a lot of money, which was needed for more important things in the house or on the farm. Twelve of us were waved off by a number of confrères from Kimmage Manor, on our four-week journey to our new mission. We were full of enthusiasm and excitement, like greyhounds straining at the leash. Our excitement overshadowed our loneliness. We all had a lot of luggage, large tin trunks of books, clothes and a lot of unnecessary things.

We had packed all our theology notes, which I put into a store on arrival in Nigeria, when I was doing the Ibo language course. After about six months, when I went to take my tin box out of the store, it was nearly empty. White ants had come up under the floor and eaten all my theology notes, and they disappeared into the ground. I was so glad, as I would never have used them anyway – they were out of date, most of them unsuitable for the new world we had entered.

Our journey to Nigeria was interesting. We spent the best part of a day in Las Palmas, and tasted the Spanish culture briefly. Our next stop was Freetown, Sierra Leone, where we were met by Bishop Thomas Brosnahan, who entertained us at lunch with his many interesting stories of Nigeria, where he had been for several years before becoming Bishop of Freetown.

In Freetown docks, we were berthed beside another ship full of local people, men, women and children packed together like sardines on the open deck. My interest was acutely aroused at their great poverty, as I watched them being herded on the deck like animals, with no privacy, no space for anything but bodies. I realized that this was Africa, as I looked down on a scene that would become very familiar in later life, of frightened refugees and boat people fleeing for their lives.

We were met by Father George Lahiffe CSSp in Lagos. We spent two days bumping along in the back of a lorry on the dusty, pot-holed roads that led to our final destination, the new diocese of Owerri. I was brought to Okpala, where my brother Mike was waiting for me and all the latest news of home. It was a wonderful reunion.

CHAPTER 2

APPOINTMENT TO NIGERIA

My first missionary posting overseas – to Nigeria – was a bit awesome. In 1954 it took a full three weeks in a steamer to arrive in Nigeria, at Port Harcourt, and a further two days of overland travel to get to the Lower Niger area. I was appointed to the same diocese of Owerri as my brother Mike, under Bishop Joseph Whelan CSSp.

We had been instructed not to take too many personal effects, and I really didn't know quite what to expect. In those days Africa was a great deal further away than it is now. There were no scheduled flights to Owerri or even to the city of Port Harcourt in the south, post took many weeks to get to England or Ireland, and was very unreliable, and we had no phones. Everything was new, strange and sometimes mysterious.

The land was rich and densely populated, the roads were sometimes treacherous, the people most polite and welcoming, but different. I experienced a great sense of joy and pride, and we all felt a great bond with the missionaries who were there already, some of whom had worked there for fifty years or more.

This territory had been entrusted to the Holy Ghost Fathers for evangelisation. We had a history of missionary work in Nigeria dating back to about 1860. The first Holy Ghost missionaries to visit the country were Frenchmen, Fathers Lutz and Horne, and Brothers Hermas and Gotto. They arrived in Onitsha on 5 December 1885 – the first Catholic mission team to settle in Iboland on the east side of the Niger. Father Joseph Shanahan CSSp joined the team on 13 November 1902.

It was by a strange providence that Father Shanahan was assigned to Nigeria. He was a teacher in Rockwell College in the heart of Tipperary, dean of discipline and in charge of games. One simple incident occurred which was to change the course of his life, and the course of the history of Nigeria. It was a rugby match. Father Edward Leen who was in Rockwell describes what happened in *A Great Irish Missionary:*

The College rugby team, of which the Dean of Discipline was in charge, had a fixture in February 1902 with a Cork team. The venue was in Cork itself. At that time, the College team, in order to reach the south, had to make a long journey of fourteen miles by car to Limerick Junction. On this particular day the arrangements miscarried and when the players arrived at Limerick Junction, they found to their dismay that the train for Cork had left.

There were no motor cars in those days and the situation seemed desperate. The match was an important one. The followers of the game in Cork looked forward to it with eagerness and large crowds were expected. A telegram announcing the impasse evoked a reply that was a cry of consternation. The station master, on being consulted, said the only possible course was to charter a special train from Dublin, but of course that would involve considerable expense. With characteristic generosity of spirit Father Shanahan said that honour was involved in fulfilling an important engagement and expense could not be allowed to weigh against that.

The decision was taken. The wires were set going. The line was cleared. The driver, having nothing to handle but the engine, the tender, and saloon carriage for the football team, made a record run from Dublin to Limerick Junction, and from the Junction to Cork. Prompt to time, the Dean led his team on to the Mardyke field amidst roars of applause, for news of his sportsmanship had reached the grounds.

The Rockwell Team won the match and Father Shanahan was overwhelmed with congratulations on the victory and the generous decision that prepared the way for it. The home authorities did not share the enthusiasm of the sporting world. They were not to be blamed. The Dean's fund, which had to meet the expenses of a special train, had received a setback from which it did not recover for years.

The incident was an indication of the kind of man Father

Joseph Shanahan had become, a man who could make a decision, provide leadership, a man of his word, who would go to any lengths to honour a commitment. Financial considerations should not stand in the way. If a thing was worth doing, it should be done well, notwithstanding the expense.

Father Joseph Shanahan found himself on his way to Africa, where he had always longed to go. Rockwell College lost a great teacher, a gifted sportsman, a man of his word, a very hard worker, and a wonderful priest. Rockwell's loss was Africa's gain.

The Eastern Nigerian provinces were daunting, stretching for countless thousands of square kilometres of tropical rain-forest. Here and there, there was a township with a name, a large market-place where thousands of merchants would converge each week, to sell, to barter and to socialise. You could actually find your way around this huge country with the help of a map. The territory stretched from Abikaliki in the north, to Owerri and Port Harcourt in the south, and to Calabar in the east. Onitsha was a very important trading centre in the centre of the country, on the banks of the great and lordly Niger river. It was said that you could get anything from a needle to an anchor in the market in Onitsha. Prices started very high, but bargaining was an art with the locals, who had perfected it to a fine art. The Ibo people in particular were clever traders – they were sometimes called the Jews of West Africa.

On arrival by boat on the Niger river at Onitsha, Father Shanahan was met by the superior, Father Léon Alexandre Lejeune, who describes his impressions of the young Irish missionary:

> I shall never forget my first meeting with Father Shanahan there, on the banks of the lordly Niger. A massive, red-headed giant, with a flaming red beard covering half his chest, he was built on herculean lines. By birth he is a Norman, the blood of the Vikings ran in his veins, and certainly one needed no imagination to picture him at the head of a band of savage Norsemen. He welcomed me to Africa in a voice that thundered in my ears like the roar of a mighty cataract. 'Ho, ho, just the man I want. Young and fresh and strong. Well, there is plenty to do here for a strong man, mon ami'.

The place-names mean little to you, but half a century after I lived there, to me they still evoke sharp images – the hard sunlight at dawn, the awakening sounds of a village coming to life as the sun shafts its way across the thick forest of tropical palms, the bright colours breaking their way through the tall trees. Strange scenes as the brown dust permeates everything, and rises at the passage of the occasional vehicle or the herd of cattle on the dusty road.

Everything was strange, the food generally delicious, at other times inedible, always surprising. The yam was the staple food, the Nigerian potato. Cassava was also popular with the local people. Meat was a luxury. Mosquitoes abounded in the intense heat, which reached a hundred degrees Fahrenheit, with high humidity, especially near stagnant pools. At sundown they would eat you alive, especially the white people, whereas the local people seemed to be immune to them. Most missionaries experienced regular bouts of malaria.

Father Shanahan was appointed to Onitsha vicariate, the only vicariate in this vast region, and he was soon made Vicar General. He appealed in Ireland for secular priests to join hands with the Holy Ghost Fathers in spreading the faith in Iboland. Bishop Shanahan prayed much before making his decision, which turned out to be the key to his success. He decided to evangelise through education, which was very popular with the Ibos. So he set about establishing small bush schools in the main towns, and the children flocked into them in great numbers. He used the schools as catechetical centres, teaching religion to the children, who brought the faith home to their parents. The parents then came to attend classes, and quickly absorbed the Catholic faith, and after a course of two years' catechumenate they were baptised. Bishop Shanahan had set a fire alight and it spread rapidly through the country. He set the country on the move towards God, a movement that would increase in momentum as the years passed by.

Five priests from the 1930 ordination group in Maynooth volunteered for Nigeria. Maynooth was to become a major influence in Nigeria as each of these men would soon become a bishop or an important leader in the Church. The young men of destiny included Father James Moynagh, Father Thomas McGettrick, Canon C. Ryan, Father P .J. Costello and Father C. Plunkett. In 1934 Father James Moynagh was appointed Prefect

Apostolic of the newly formed Prefecture of Calabar, which included Calabar, Ogoja, Ikot Ekpene and Abikaliki. He was consecrated Bishop of Calabar in 1947. Father Thomas McGettrick became Bishop of Abikaliki some time later.

Being a bishop was an immense challenge, a responsibility which the men from Maynooth enjoyed, and so the Gospel spread with extraordinary speed among a very susceptible ethnic group – the Ibo people.

Bishop Shanahan proved to be a great leader, a very strong character, a man of his word, a sincere and clever man, whose policy of evangelisation worked very successfully. The Holy Spirit poured out abundant graces and blessings on the Ibo people, who came to listen but remained to pray. The Lord used Bishop Shanahan as an effective instrument to bring the Good News to a beautiful people.

Not only did they learn this strange doctrine, so new to them, but they helped to build schools to educate their children, and they participated in building the churches, which were rapidly expanding in numbers. They even supported the missionaries financially, so that the Church soon became self-reliant and independent. They contributed to the building of the priests' houses and provided vehicles for them so that they could visit the parishes, which were separated by huge distances. The local people provided 'chop' (food) for the missionaries as they visited the out-stations. The missionaries felt safe and welcome wherever they went. Of course they experienced difficulties in the beginning, such as ill-health due to the effect of mosquito bites, poor housing, lack of additional priests to support them, very long distances between stations, transport problems, poor roads, acute loneliness at times, a very difficult language to master, competition with the Protestant churches before the advent of ecumenism, and so on.

In 1948 Father Joseph Whelan was consecrated Bishop of Owerri. As the Church grew from strength to strength, and as time passed, the Holy Ghost Fathers increased in numbers until we were three hundred strong in 1967, the beginning of the Biafran war. Following our expulsion after the war, the numbers of missionaries had dropped to about five or six. It was the end of a golden age and never again would Nigeria see such a strong contingent of Irish missionaries, thank God. After all, the success of a missionary is his ability to do himself out of a job, and go elsewhere to start again at the bottom of the ladder.

My first missionary job was as Master of Novices of the Brothers of St Peter Claver, a local congregation started by the Holy Ghost Fathers in Uturu. I was in Uturu with Father Brendan Timon, the parish priest, for one very happy year, and it was a good introduction to the missions. Father Timon was a man of great experience, and knew the African mind very well. We also had a parish in Uturu, and it was good experience in pastoral care. I used to visit the parishioners in their poor homes, chat with them, and invite them to church. The response was wonderful, thanks to the grace of God.

I had responsibility for the formation of the brothers on the one hand and the administration of the sacraments to the parishioners during the weekends. The brothers numbered about sixty; some of them were trained catechists, others were being trained in simple skills – carpentry, book-binding, etc. Some were assigned to parishes around the diocese.

Father Timon was a talented man, gifted in music, a perfectionist with a high standard of performance, and a lively sense of humour. The parish and the brothers were very well organised under his direction.

Missionary life was a learning process for us, not just for a year or two, but on an ongoing basis, as is to be expected in a land which was strange to us, with a different culture and language. Palavers were common and did not always have to do with Church matters. One had to be ready for every kind of situation.

On one occasion in my first year, when Father Timon was away and I was in charge of the parish, two children got into a fight on their way home from school. One boy knocked out the other's tooth. The two villages of the respective boys came into the Mission to see if the priest could solve the problem. The villagers were very angry, shouting abuse at one another. I tried to calm them without much success.

Fortunately there was a priest staying with me at the time, on holidays. Father Michael Foley was very experienced, having been in Nigeria since 1928, about thirty-two years in all. He came from my home parish of Ballyragget, County Kilkenny – the Ballyouskill end of it. I decided to ask for his help. He listened patiently to both sides under a palm tree. Eventually he banged angrily on the table and gave his ultimatum:

> 'If I hear any more of the missing tooth,' he said, 'I will remove every tooth from every person here.'

He then took out his false teeth and showed them to everyone. The effect was electric. None of them had seen false teeth before. They took one quick look and ran for their lives. The missing tooth was never mentioned again. It shows what experience can do. Father Foley played on their superstitions and fears. Had the case been brought to court, the legal arguments could have gone on for years at great cost to the poor people, as often happened.

Bishop Whelan had invited the Marist Brothers into his diocese to take over Bishop Shanahan's secondary school in Orlu. Teaching was their charism and they excelled in this vocation. In 1956 the bishop asked them to take over the Congregation of the Brothers of St Peter Claver and merge them into the Marist Brothers, producing an international congregation of high standing. The Marist Brothers increased overnight by about sixty brothers in 1956, leaving me free for another posting.

The brothers taught me a lot about the Ibo way of life, their social and medical taboos, and value systems. One social taboo, for example, was about twins. A mother who gave birth to twins would be ashamed, and disgraced, and would allow the weaker one to die, or the female where one was a male. The male heir was very important to the family and the female was always the underdog. This was deeply ingrained in their culture. To overcome this way of thinking, the Church used to celebrate the birth of twins, and give a donation to the mother.

The Ibos, most of whom were pagans or animists, flocked into the Church in great numbers, and became fervent Christians, very strict and conservative. The children were hungry for education, and through the children the faith was brought home to the parents.

I felt sad leaving Uturu and the brothers after a very enjoyable year assisting a dedicated group of men to become good religious. I was assigned to Holy Ghost Teacher Training College, Umuahia, with Father Paddy Smith as principal. It was a new and enjoyable experience to work with teachers in training, all of whom were black. I was deeply involved with the students in sports, mainly athletics and football.

After one year in Umuahia I was transferred to Bishop Shanahan Teacher Training College, Orlu, where I worked for a period of three years with Father Con Holly as principal.

Father Holly taught me a lot. He was an excellent teacher, a classical scholar, a keen sportsman with a sharp sense of humour, and an ideal principal. We had a small parish to run during the weekends. Father Tim Connelly was also there for a short time, and was followed by Father Gus Lindsay. It was a happy assignment, a new experience, and good for the younger missionaries who were shifted around during their early days on the missions.

Many changes of assignment were great for experience. After seven years or so at the same post, one's performance became less and less effective.

I believe that if possible one should have a complete change in direction, or occupation, half-way through life. I got this change after the Biafran war, when I took a sabbatical and studied development in Swansea University for one year. I then changed from education to relief and development work – working for the poor. It was a very happy transition, as I felt I had little to give in education after being through the Biafran war. A strange but understandable revolution had taken place in my life. I was haunted by starvation, by hungry children and dying people calling out for help.

In 1959 I was appointed Director of St Peter Claver Junior Seminary in Okpala, where I remained for ten years until the war ended in January 1970. Life was very happy in Okpala for the first seven years, with Fathers Mike Frawley, Tom Maguire, Paddy Devine, Tommy Crean, Joe Murphy, Tommy McDonald and Sean Broderick – there were four of us on the staff at any one time. Father Theophilis Nwalozie was the first Ibo priest to be appointed to the staff and he was excellent. We had about three hundred seminarians and a parish to care for. Life was very busy, teaching classes in the seminary, supervising the construction of buildings to accommodate increasing numbers, and looking after the parish's three out-stations – Achara, Obokwe and Alulu. Relations between the Irish missionaries and the Ibo people were always good, but the war brought us very close together.

In 1960 Nigeria became independent from Britain amidst great jubilation and rejoicing. In 1966, however, there was growing political tension between the Ibos in the east and the Hausa in the north. The Yurabas in the west were rather quiet and accepted the status quo. After years of a certain stability under colonial rule, the administration was peaceful and there was discipline in the country. The power vacuum created by independence meant that the future became very uncertain. Local rivalries grew more heated as would-be leaders vied for control of the huge nation. Ethnic and tribal rivalries became more and more evident. Nobody wanted to be dominated, but each of the three ethnic groups had a different view of how the new nation should be ruled.

After the initial euphoria of independence had died down, there was little agreement on what should be done next. The Ibos were the most disgruntled. They had a name for being aggressive, shrewd traders, sometimes noted for their sharp practice in commerce, and this brought the crisis to boiling point. The situation did indeed boil over with the onslaught on the Ibos in the north in 1966, when an estimated thirty thousand were killed and many more wounded in the pogroms and ethnic cleansing which took place in Kano, Makurdi and other big centres where there was they were concentrated.

It was the prelude to the great disaster, the civil war which started in June of 1967.

CHAPTER 3

THE MEDIA IN BIAFRA

One of the first TV men I met in Biafra was Allan Hart, of the popular TV documentary programme *Panorama*. Allan was a real professional, a charming man whom I first encountered in Okpala. He made a wonderful film of the Biafran war, which moved not only the hearts of the public but governments as well. He did thorough research of his subject in advance, and was an excellent commentator and interviewer.

I gave Allan an interview on my perception of the Biafran situation, emphasising the widespread famine caused by the blockade around Biafra. Allan was a man of deep integrity, dedicated to uncovering the truth, as reporters should do. He later went to Iran where he exposed the problems of poverty in the midst of great wealth under the Shah. I met him later when he was making a remarkable and historic film on world poverty, *Five Minutes to Midnight*.

My international experiences have given me the highest regard for journalists and great admiration for their courage and integrity.

Mike Nicholson of ITV came to Biafra at the height of the war, but he and his crew, Alan Downs and Mike Doyle, were arrested by the Ministry of Information. The minister, Dr Eke, told him he could not make a film as he was a British spy. It was understandable, as Biafra was losing the war, while Great Britain was supplying the federal government with arms.

I came into the picture as Mike and his crew were being arrested and I pleaded that Mike should be allowed to make a film – it could only serve the cause of Biafra. The minister was adamant – Mike must go into detention until he left the country. I appealed to him, and eventually we came to a compromise. Mike and his crew could stay with me in the Catholic mission in Umuahia on condition that he would not move outside the house, that he would not take any film, and that he would be on the next plane out of Biafra. So I took Mike and his team into custody, back to my house, and locked them inside.

I then went to assist at the feeding programme. Thousands of people had collected around the mission looking for food. Next we had an air raid – the jets were overhead. I ran back into the house while the people scattered in great confusion. There was pandemonium. As I lay on the floor of the mission house, much to my horror I could hear the voice of Mike Nicholson giving a commentary on the attack. The planes swooped over the house in a roar of thunder, hitting the church and the house with rockets. They repeated the attack three times. A bomb struck an oil tanker on the railway, sending it up in flames.

When the planes left and the smoke died down, I went upstairs to see if Mike and his crew had survived the attack. They were all safe but shattered. They were stunned and could not speak.

Mike had set up his camera on the open balcony upstairs in the mission house and had filmed the whole attack. He had a scoop of great pictures, which he would never have got had he been given permission to film, even at the front. It was a brilliant piece of professional filming, and very good propaganda for Biafra, showing the indiscriminate nature of the bombing by the Nigerian air force. His problem with the Ministry of Information had turned out to his advantage. But now he had put me in a fix – what was I to do with the film he had taken? Should I turn it over to the Ministry of Information? I believed so much in Mike that I brought him and his camera crew to the airport that night and helped them to get their film back to London for broadcast the next day. I did this in the best interest of the Biafran people, who suffered so much from the federal bombing. Mike's film was a masterpiece on the real situation in Biafra. He destroyed the myth that no civilians were being bombed in Biafra, which was the propaganda being disseminated by the federal Nigerian government, and swallowed by the British government and the BBC for political reasons.

Mike Nicholson was ably assisted by Winston Churchill Junior, a journalist with *The Times*. Churchill came to Biafra to investigate whether the federal government was engaged in a policy of genocide against the Biafran people. He first went to Lagos, where the government denied these claims, assuring him that no civilians were attacked from the air or on the ground. He came to see me on this issue, and I thought that the best way to convince him was to take him on a trip with me around the neighbourhood. I brought him to see a bombed-out school in Ezenehitte, and a few other places hit by bombs. I don't know if I convinced him.

Winston was just about to leave for the airport when Father Ray Maher came to tell me of a terrible air attack on Ohafia market in Bende Division. Market day is an important part of life in Iboland, as it is in most of Africa. In Nigeria the market was held every eighth day, and the people would come from the surrounding area to a small town or village to sell, buy and barter their produce. Thousands would attend the bigger markets and it was a great social occasion as well. The market is an institution in Nigeria.

I asked Winston to postpone his departure and visit the scene of the attack. He readily agreed, and Ray Maher took him to the scene in Ohafia. He was shaken by what he witnessed. In an open market-place about 360 people had been killed by bombs in a mild attack. There was no way this market could have been mistaken for a military target. It could be seen clearly from the air. Churchill got the story and the message onto the front page of *The Times,* and it resulted in a debate in the House of Commons. It was very embarrassing for the British government.

I met Winston Churchill several times since. He wrote to me when he went up for a seat in Parliament for Stretford, near Manchester, asking me to help him in his election campaign, as the area was strongly Catholic. I mentioned this to my sister Maury, who informed me that one of the Little Sisters of the Assumption was in that constituency and was a great admirer of the Churchills. I wrote to this admirer and explained my problem. I presume she moved into action and Winston was successful in winning the seat. Winston wrote to me to thank me for my help.

Yes, these were great journalists whom I admired very much for their courage and bravery.

The greatest journalist was perhaps Frederick Forsyth. He was assigned by the BBC World Service to cover the Biafran war. He followed the Biafran front at very close quarters, and reported everything accurately. He even followed the Biafran army when it invaded the mid-west, and got as far as Oron. They were on their way to take Lagos, but stopped in Oron for some unknown reason.

Forsyth's reports angered the Labour government in Britain, and shortly afterwards he was dismissed by the BBC. He was forced to become a freelance journalist. He got down to writing a historical account of the war, and published his first book, *The Biafra Story – the making of an African Legend.* He believed in Biafra and in the leadership of Colonel Ojukwu. I met him many times in Biafra and we became close friends – he felt for the sufferings of the people.

Forsyth deplored the international intrigues taking place in the world, in which the Africans were the victims. He did not mince his words when he was interviewed. He kept close to the war front and would warn the missionaries in advance about when they should move, and we would inform the local people to be ready to evacuate. Fred, I'm sure, was responsible for saving many lives.

We trusted each other and Fred was always straight and to the point. Towards the end of the war he was falsely suspected of being a British spy, and in fact I was asked by the Ministry of Information what I thought of him. Naturally I defended him. Frederick knew he was under suspicion and one day he called me into his caravan to discuss the rumours. He told me he was under surveillance and could be picked up at any moment. He had written to his mother and had left the letter on a bookshelf. He would not post the letter, but asked me if I would check on it every day. If the letter was taken, it would be a signal to me that he had been picked up by Biafran security. He asked that I should immediately contact specific friends of his in the government and alert them. If nothing was done to release him, I should meet Colonel Ojukwu and campaign for his release. So I used to check his caravan as often as possible. Fred was not picked up, but left the country shortly before the end of the war. He trusted me with his life.

I met Fred in London after the war and he invited me to a meal. He had just got word that his novel had been accepted for publication. *The Day of the Jackal* became the first of his great novels and a bestseller. He has published many best-sellers – *The Dogs of War, The Odessa File, The Fourth Protocol, The Deceiver, The Negotiator, The Shepherd, No Comebacks, The Fist of God,* all of which sold over five million copies each. The *Dogs of War* is based on his Biafran experience and the immoral and obnoxious intrigues carried out against Developing World countries.

Frederick Forsyth is now a member of the Board of Trustees of the International Refugee Trust, and is of invaluable assistance to them. He is familiar with Developing World affairs, knows poverty at close quarters, and is an accurate analyst of world affairs. He was a close observer of political and current affairs and once wrote of the Holy Ghost Fathers and the missionaries in Biafra:

> There are no words to express, nor phrases in this language to convey the heroism of the priests of the Order of the Holy Ghost and the nuns of the Order of the Holy Rosary, both from Ireland. To have to see twenty tiny children brought in, in a state of advanced kwashiorkor, to know that you have enough relief food to give ten a chance of living while the others are completely beyond hope; to have to face this sort of thing day in and day out; to age ten years in as many months under the strain; to be bombed and strafed, dirty, tired and hungry and to keep on working, requires the kind of courage that is not given to most men who wear a chestful of ribbons.

Des Mullan came out from Ireland with photographer John O'Neill. Des was a journalist for the *Evening Herald* and the *Irish Independent*. I helped him as much as I could, got him to the war front, and brought him face-to-face with the massive starvation in the country.

CHAPTER 4

IN THE FACE OF GREAT DANGER

We had narrow escapes – God was looking after us. Sister Cecilia Thackaberry was the only Irish missionary killed during the two-year Biafran war. She was travelling down a long, straight stretch on the Elele/Owerri road with another sister when a jet pilot saw their car from the sky. He swooped down on them twice, the first time to have a close look. On his second round he fired a volley of shrapnel, which hit Sister Cecilia. The other sister was hiding in the bushes, away from her car. Sister Cecilia bled to death.

Bishop Whelan, commenting on her death, described it in some detail. I quote his report, dated 17 September 1969, in full:

> Mother Cecilia Thackaberry was killed a mile and a half from Villa Assumpta (her home) on the Port Harcourt road. Sister Elizabeth Murray of Nenagh was injured. The driver of the car was likewise killed and a nurse was slightly wounded when a Nigerian jet rocketed and strafed their car.
>
> Fathers, brothers and sisters work in the danger zones of Biafra and we often wondered at the miraculous escapes of our personnel. And now catastrophe strikes against all the laws of probability. There are twenty Holy Rosary Sisters and ninety Holy Ghost Fathers. Most of us have been under bombing, rocketing and strafing and we have, thank God, come through. There are only three Presentation Sisters and one of these was to become our first victim.
>
> Mother Cecilia and Sister Elizabeth were on their way to Mbirichi on the main Owerri-Port Harcourt road, to visit a sick baby. They saw a jet coming towards them and according to our usual custom, they stopped. The driver lay on a bank near the road; the sisters and the nurse walked into the bush and lay down together on sloping ground.
>
> The bush was thick growth of wild shrubs and they

could penetrate only about ten yards from the road. They were completely hidden but there was nothing to give them adequate covering. The jet returned from Owerri, rocketing as he went by. He turned and came back for a second attack, strafing the car. This time he passed near Owerri town, homeward bound.

After the attack, Sister Elizabeth asked Mother if she were alright. She replied that she had been hit as the plane returned for its second encounter. The other two dragged Mother back to the embankment. When they got up Mother was bleeding profusely – shrapnel had severed the artery at the elbow. She collapsed almost immediately and died from loss of blood. Sister Elizabeth had deep wounds in the thigh. The nurse escaped with minor injuries. The car, a Peugeot 403, was a shambles. A rocket had gone through the back window and exploded inside. The windscreen had many bullet holes.

Mother Cecilia came to Port Harcourt in October 1965 at the invitation of Most Rev. G. Okoye. When Port Harcourt fell in 1968 she and Sister Brendan (now Mother General of the English Sisters of the Presentation) took possession of the Holy Rosary Convent in Owerri. After the fall of Owerri she went home on leave. She insisted on returning and came back to Biafra in January of this year. For a while she served in a remote corner. Then she moved closer to Port Harcourt Diocese, first to Etche, and then at Owerri. A teacher's house in Owerri Girl's Secondary School was put at her disposal. It was a base for welfare work at stations on or near the Owerri-Port Harcourt road. She was well aware that this was a danger zone.

Before the fall of Owerri I preached a retreat to a group of sisters which included Mother Cecilia and Sister Brendan. Mother Cecilia was deeply interested in the things of God and sincerely interested in her work. A more spiritual and more apostolic soul I have seldom encountered. For our people her return was an act of great courage. Her presence among us was a source of inspiration and moral support. Her work was a valuable asset in a sector which had been devastated by war.

Tonight her remains were brought to the Chapel of the Holy Rosary Hospital, Emekuku. The funeral Mass was celebrated by Bishop Okoye at 8 o'clock on 18 September in the presence of His Grace, Archbishop Arinze of Onitsha and Bishop Whelan of Owerri. Bishop Okoye spoke on the text: 'Greater love than this no man has than a man that lays down his life for his friends' (John). At the graveside in Emekuku Mission the Administrator for Owerri Province conveyed the sympathy of His Excellency, the Head of State, to Mother Cecilia's fellow missionaries and the gratitude of the Biafran people to Mother Cecilia. She awaits the Resurrection, amid a group of missionaries who, like her, died at their posts. To Mother Brendan, the Superior General, and the whole province of the Presentation Sisters, especially to the two who remain with us, we offer our thanks for the good they have done for Biafra by the life and death of Mother Cecilia. We are sure that her example of a saintly apostolic life and a martyr's death will inspire many to embrace the missionary vocation.

✠ J.B. Whelan CSSp
Bishop of Owerri, 16 & 17 September 1969

Mother Cecilia was a sister of Father Thackaberry, the administrator of the Pro-Cathedral in Dublin, and she has a sister, Ignatius, in the Presentation Congregation, who was a missionary in Zambia. The death of Mother Cecilia brought home to us all the reality of war, our closeness to death, and the need for courage in our commitment to the people the Lord asked us to serve.

CHAPTER 5

GROUP CAPTAIN LEONARD CHESHIRE

One of the greatest blessings of my missionary life was to meet Leonard Cheshire, in Africa. When I went to Africa I could not look straight at a disabled person. I would see only the deformities. Cheshire taught me to look not at the disability, but at the person behind. Soon I no longer saw the deformities, and I was at ease in the midst of handicapped people.

I met Group Captain Leonard Cheshire in extraordinary circumstances, after a bombing raid in Umuahia. I had taken cover by lying in a dike on one side of the road, while Leonard had taken cover in the dike on the opposite side of the road. He had been looking for me. He approached me and asked, 'Are you Father Kevin Doheny?' I said 'Yes', and he said he had been recommended to see me, as I might be able to get him to the Head of State of Biafra, Colonel Ojukwu. Gradually he unfolded his mission, his reason for visiting Biafra. The British government had asked him to come to Biafra to establish peace between the warring sides. He came also to see the Cheshire Homes in Enugu and Port Harcourt, which was a good and genuine cover for his mission.

I arranged for Cheshire to meet Colonel Ojukwu. Afterwards, he told me that Ojukwu was prepared to go a long way towards achieving peace, and was willing to compromise on some very important issues.

Leonard Cheshire was one of the two British observers who witnessed the dropping of the atom bomb on Nagasaki in 1945. The other observer was William Penny. Cheshire described the dropping of the bomb in his book, *The Light of Many Suns*.

Up to this Leonard had been a daredevil pilot, but after witnessing this event he became very serious, and sought a way of bringing lasting peace to the world. His attention was drawn to the many destitute people, especially soldiers returning from the war-front. In many cases their homes were bombed out, or their families were killed, and they were left with nothing.

Cheshire tried a few schemes to rehabilitate these people, but he failed. He soon found himself with a large empty house and a huge pile of debts. It was then that Providence intervened. The matron of a local hospital told him that an old friend of his, a man named Arthur Dykes, was dying, and that the hospital could do no more for him. Leonard took Arthur home and cared for him until his death. Arthur Dykes played a real part in Leonard's conversion to Catholicism. Arthur was a lapsed Catholic, but as he approached death, he regained his faith by reading the Scriptures and praying. As he got weaker, he asked Leonard to read to him, and by so doing, Leonard gradually became interested in the Catholic faith. Following Arthur's death in 1948, Leonard pursued his new-found passion, and within a very short time he was received into the Catholic Church.

Arthur Dykes was significant also in that, without realising it, he was the first patient in a network of Homes that would become renowned the world over.

Gradually Leonard's house began to fill up with a strange variety of people – the disabled, the old, some TB cases and others. Leonard himself contracted TB and had to go into hospital. He then had to make provision for his patients, and was forced against his will to establish a committee to take over his work. As fortune would have it, when he came out of hospital, he decided to go elsewhere to start a second Home. And so the Cheshire Homes began to spread.

In 1955 Leonard Cheshire decided to go to India with about £100.00 in his pocket. Today there are some twenty-five Cheshire Homes in India, thanks to Providence guiding Cheshire all the way through.

Leonard Cheshire could charm the coldest of creatures, and it was almost impossible to say 'No' to him, as in my own case when he asked me to work for him in Africa. He had a magnetic personality which drew unexpected people into his vast organisation. He appealed to the Indian, the African, the Japanese, the Chinese, the Russian, all with equal success. He was a born leader, an attractive personality, a courageous worker and a highly respected man on the international scene. He had a lively and rather British sense of humour and loved to play practical jokes on his friends. When he would meet me, he would say with a big, warm smile: 'Have we met before, Father?'

Cheshire taught me many lessons. He introduced me to his Homes for disabled people, and to the great value of community development. I had studied community development and social administration in Swansea University, but my knowledge remained at the theoretical level. It was thanks to Cheshire that I learned the reality of community development, at grass roots level. I realised that community is very important to the African, who has a great respect for the extended family. As Julius Nyerere says:

> There is no such thing as an orphan in Africa. Each child has a near relative who looks after him/her as his/her own child.

So, I found it relatively easy to open twenty-five Cheshire Homes throughout the length and breadth of Africa, at the rate of about one per annum – faster than in many parts of the world. Cheshire Homes were second nature to the African, whose society has great respect for the elderly, and regards them as wise and trustworthy. Africans will usually consult with the oldest man in the village before making decisions. In fact, they have a special name for an elderly man. They are called Msay in Kenya, Shemagula in Ethiopia, and so on. But these titles mean more than just 'being old'. They mean 'full of experience and wisdom – the perfect man'.

Most of the Homes in Africa are for children, for the simple reason that the elderly are well looked after in African society, unlike in Europe, whereas the children are at the bottom of the ladder of priorities when it comes to disability. It is sad to see how grandparents are treated in Europe, where they are put away in homes and very often forgotten, sometimes left to die. It is shameful, and could never happen in Africa.

Leonard met and subsequently married Sue Ryder, later to become Lady Ryder of Warsaw. Sue worked as an underground nurse during World War II, and travelled extensively in Poland, visiting prisons and helping the war wounded. She started the Ryder Homes, now known all over the world, numbering about eighty in total. There are four Ryder Homes for elderly people in Ireland. Sue proved to be a wonderful partner for Leonard, with both complementing each other's work for the poor and underprivileged, for the homeless and the handicapped. Both the Ryder and Cheshire Homes are expanding all the time, as the need for such care increases.

Leonard Cheshire's great friend, the secretary general of the overseas branch of the Cheshire Foundation, Ron Travers, travelled all over the world with him, carried his bags and looked after him. Ron had a lively sense of humour, and always kept our spirits up.

Leonard's personal secretary was Joan Masters, who stood by him in all situations. She worked very closely with him during the Biafran war, in his efforts to mediate peace between the warring sides.

Lynette Learoyd was Ron's overseas secretary, and a great friend of mine, who helped me a lot in Africa. Denise Tabernacle also did amazing work in the foundations for new Cheshire Homes for the handicapped in Africa. The teamwork was good, co-operation was always forthcoming, the spirit was enthusiastic and the result was very satisfactory and satisfying. God was with us all the way.

I travelled with Leonard Cheshire quite a lot in Africa. We went to Zambia for a Cheshire Homes regional conference, to Zimbabwe to see the Homes in Baines Avenue, Harari and Westwood, to Botswana to open the Cheshire Home in Gaberone in the presence of President Maseru, to Lesotho to visit the Home in Maseru, to Swaziland to see the Home for Disabled Adults, and to Addis Ababa for another regional conference of Cheshire Home. Peter Rowley, Chairman of the Overseas Homes, and his wife were usually in attendance at the conferences, making valuable contributions to the discussions. Henry Marking was another frequent attender, delivering sparks of good humour at will, spontaneously dispensing his largesse to all.

The International Committee did not always agree with Cheshire and he was often out on a limb in his efforts to help people in distress. But Leonard would always find a way out of his dilemma. When the committee refused to accept his efforts to take on heavy medical cases, he turned to his wife, Sue Ryder, for help.

Sue Ryder had devoted herself to the stateless and disabled survivors of the Nazi concentration camps and already had numbers of supporters up and down the country. At the beginning of the war, while she was yet only sixteen she had managed to join Special Forces, the organisation responsible for sending agents in and out of occupied Europe. She was seconded to the Polish section and there she learnt at first hand the full horrors of the Nazi occupation, a knowledge which has always remained with her and still drives her unceasingly in her determination to help those who suffered under a tyranny unparalleled in history.

The story of her work and the Forgotten Allies Trust, as her organisation is called, is a book in itself. Ryder drove the length and breadth of Germany, visiting the camps, the hospitals and the prisons, bringing a personal service which, even if it was not large in relation to the problem, restored hope and self-respect to more people than will ever be known. Undaunted by the opposition which she met in England, and supported by loyal helpers, she laid the foundations for what was to become a unique organisation.

It was not surprising then, that when Leonard Cheshire needed a partner to help him set up his International Centre, he should turn to Sue Ryder. The Centre was intended not only to take the emergency and difficult cases that the local homes could not and would not accept, but to counteract what seemed to him the shortcomings of his own foundation. The two organisations could, he felt, by some form of collaboration, help one another to strengthen and grow. Sue's was a personal work which did not easily lend itself to delegation or administration. It had the spirit, but not a strong organisational framework. The Cheshire Foundation had, on the other hand, its trustees, its committees, its rules of procedure but was for that very reason in danger of losing its spirit.

At the very moment when Cheshire was settling down to his task of founding the International Centre, Sue Ryder was setting out on one of her most arduous and adventurous missions – to see if anything could be done for the survivors of Nazism in Poland itself. In those days entry into any of the Eastern European countries was difficult in the extreme, yet she travelled alone, without any kind of official backing or introductions or contacts. In the ten days she spent in Poland she visited about ten hospitals and saw something of the immense needs of the sick in a country where 1,800 hospitals had been systematically destroyed during the war. She persuaded the Deputy of Health to convene a conference of doctors and other officials to discuss the problems. The conference, after a difficult start, ended by deciding that any help she could get would be welcome, and invited her to return as soon as possible to draw up a formal agreement and so put her plan onto a firm and proper footing. Thus was opened another road on the Ryder and Cheshire common goal of extending their work to different countries of the world. In the light of this, the International Centre clearly took on an altogether new significance.

The impact of this on the International Committees was unsettling. They had just got over the shock of Leonard's first overseas trip. Yet whatever doubts the Trustees had about this new development, Cheshire had none. His plan was to team up with Sue Ryder, somehow or another. She would concentrate on Eastern Europe and Russia and he would concentrate on China and the Far East. Together they could plan the International Centres, unhampered by trusts and committees.

To some of us, inevitably, the whole concept of a world-wide movement seemed like a utopian dream. But in the next few years Leonard and Sue were to put their combined efforts into taking the first steps to turn a dream into a reality.

CHAPTER 6

PEACE INITIATIVES

In 1969 I became involved in peace-making and, at a meeting with Colonel Ojukwu and Bishop Whelan, it was decided that I should travel to London to make some peace initiatives. Colonel Ojukwu believed that London held the key to peace.

I arrived in London on 30 June 1969, and arranged for my brother Mike to come from Ireland. I then asked Leonard Cheshire to make contact with the Foreign Office. A meeting was arranged with Maurice Foley, the Under-secretary of State, Lord Hunt, Norman Tebitt, and one or two others. We hoped that a delegation would travel to Biafra at the invitation of Colonel Ojukwu. At the beginning of the meeting Maurice Foley spoke about the necessity of getting food into Biafra. I intervened, saying that the Ibos were not interested in food from Great Britain, but in peace. The Biafrans in fact had asked why the British should want to feed the Ibos, while they were only interested in shooting them. The Ibos were very conscious of the fact that Britain was supplying arms to Nigeria. I explained that Colonel Ojukwu had asked that our discussion should concentrate on peace.

I insisted that the Biafrans were interested in peace, and I believed that the key was in the hands of the British. The discussion then turned to the possibility of sending a British Peace Delegation to Biafra. Colonel Ojukwu had already said he would accept Lord Goodman as negotiator, along with one other. We spent five hours in the Foreign Office debating the issues, and it was finally agreed that Maurice Foley would set up the delegation. The proposal would be submitted to the Cabinet office for approval and we would be kept informed of the developing situation.

I offered my services to go ahead of the delegation back to Biafra so as to make all necessary arrangements for their mission. It was important that it should succeed.

We visited Cardinal Heenan on the same occasion. He assured us that the Prime Minister, Harold Wilson, was most anxious to end the war. The cardinal offered to support our relief operation and our efforts to get the delegation off the ground. He wrote to Wilson immediately, seeking a meeting with him, but was unsuccessful. Two days later the papers carried a lead story on Cardinal Heenan, in which he said: 'We are ashamed of our Government. '

I went to Ireland to be on standby until the Foreign Office would call me. I waited and waited but I was never called. When I eventually made contact with them to find out what the situation was, they said that although the delegation has been set up, it was not travelling to Biafra – the deal was off for the present.

On 14 September 1969 we met Sir Louis Mbanefo, the chief Biafran peace negotiator, in London. He was to see Maurice Foley in the Foreign Office the following day. Sir Louis was not optimistic about the outcome of the meeting.

You can imagine my disappointment at the breakdown of negotiations. The British had alternative plans, and Harold Wilson was to make a trip to Lagos shortly afterwards.

Leonard Cheshire worked very hard for peace. He had several meetings with Sir Louis Mbanefo. He was also in touch with Colonel Ojukwu's roving ambassador and arms negotiator in Europe. It would appear that Cheshire was deceived by a Biafran in whom he placed great trust, and whom he thought had the ear of Colonel Ojukwu. This roving ambassador failed to turn up for a vital meeting when the prospects of peace were very high. It must be said that Colonel Ojukwu was loyal to the end and sent several positive messages to Leonard Cheshire from time to time. Leonard was very disappointed to be let down, his efforts wasted.

The American government was also working towards a peaceful settlement. I had met Ambassador Clyde Ferguson, Ambassador to Biafra, and Arthur Gene Dewey on a mission of peace in Biafra. I became a close friend of Gene Dewey, a deeply Christian man who was greatly concerned about the civil war. They both invited me to Washington and promised us maximum cooperation in making contact with government officials and other influential people in the United States.

Mike and I accepted the invitation to America to bring about peace between the warring sides. We had contacts at various levels and argued strenuously in favour of our intervention.

We travelled to New York and had lunch in the Catholic Relief Services with Bishop Swanstrom, Ed Kinney, Rocco Sacci and Father Dermot Doran. Our discussion ranged over the whole spectrum of relief efforts, especially with regard to the US Government and Africa Concern. They questioned us on our visit to Washington, its purpose, etc. When we made it clear that it was at the invitation of Ambassador Ferguson, their minds were set at rest. Ed Kinney pledged his cooperation with Africa Concern and emphasised that Libreville was becoming more and more important to the whole relief effort.

In a radio interview that night, we broadcast a final appeal for a superhuman effort by the Americans both for relief and peace. Tom Davis of Twin Circle, who was on the panel, went much farther than we did and suggested that the US send an armada with relief supplies, backed by all the publicity and personalities that could be summoned, and sweep aside all the diplomatic difficulties in order to achieve a breakthrough. Our comment was: 'We are pleading for a starving people – as long as they are fed, we are not concerned about how you accomplish it.'

The Vatican was very concerned about the Biafran war and sent a papal delegation to Nigeria and Biafra to act as intermediaries for peace. Those chosen included Mgr George Roschau, director of Secours Catholique, Paris, and an Irishman, Bishop Dominic Conway of Elphin. To avoid diplomatic complications, the delegation was officially to visit the bishops of the whole territory. They were, of course, received by General Gowan in Lagos and Colonel Ojukwu in Biafra. They went first to Lagos and toured the war areas, which took them to the Niger, from where they could look into Biafra, which Bishop Conway referred to as the 'Promised Land'.

The trip to the Biafran side was organised by Fr Tony Byrne CSSp and the delegation was accompanied by Fr Dermot Doran CSSp, who planned the route inside Biafra. The Pope's representatives received a very warm welcome everywhere in Biafra. In Onitsha they were received by Bishop Charles Heery, and in Owerri they were met by Bishop Joseph Whelan. Crowds lined the road everywhere they went.

The Vatican delegation expressed the concern of the Holy Father, Pope Paul VI, for the people, and they pledged to continue the humanitarian relief work, through Caritas Internationalis. They also pleaded for peace.

CHAPTER 7

THE BATTLE FOR SURVIVAL

The outbreak of the war in June 1967 was a new experience for the missionaries, and we saw starvation for the first time. We had to change our roles to meet the emergency. Many of the missionaries distinguished themselves in their new challenges. The Ibos were surrounded by federal troops and a complete blockade cut off all food supplies from outside.

Father Tony Byrne organised the massive relief programme, which he managed from the Portuguese island of São Tomé. He flew thousands of tons of relief supplies into Biafra at night-time, and he risked his life on many occasions. He became known as the Green Pimpernel. He was ably assisted by Father Tom Cunningham, and they worked closely with Mgr Carlo Bayer, the director of Caritas Internationalis in Rome. They used Enugu and Port Harcourt airports until these were captured, but they were eventually forced to use Uli Airport which was an improvised airstrip on a widened road. One night they succeeded in landing forty-two planes of high-protein food.

Bishop Joseph Whelan, Bishop of Owerri, was in charge of supplies and responsible for their distribution throughout the country. The supplies were off-loaded in Uli, loaded onto trucks and dispatched to Ihioma, where Father Michael Courtney arranged the sub-distribution to the missionaries all over the stricken area. Father Michael did an excellent job in building new warehouses and organising truckloads to go to all corners of Biafra. He was assisted by Noel Gavan, who worked tirelessly for the relief programme.

The missionaries at the airport had the toughest job of all – the off-loading of the planes was very dangerous, as the bombers of the federal government were trying to strike the airport to put it out of action. Father Des McGlade was hit by shrapnel and still has some embedded fragments to remind him of that time. Other priests to serve in the airport were Jack Finucane, John Doyle and Billy Butler.

Over twenty pilots were killed trying to land in the darkness.

They were Canadians, Danish and others who risked their lives night after night in their efforts to bring supplies to the starving Biafrans. The dead pilots were buried near the Catholic Church in Uli, not far from the dangerous airstrip.

I will never forget the air raids, which used to come like a flash out of the blue. The roar of the engines was frightening and deafening – Ilyushan jet fighters from Russia. If you were travelling on the road you jumped from the car and threw yourself flat on the ground, in a ditch if possible, to avoid flying shrapnel. Then you waited, listened and prayed. You heard one explosion after another, and saw the smoke rising from houses or factories. Then there was silence and the sky was clear again.

Then there were the post-mortems – there were usually a lot of casualties. We missionaries would go to places that were hit by bombs to offer our help. It was very important to be with the frightened people at that time, and we were well aware of how much it meant to them. We shared the dangers with them, and they knew we were one with them in their losses and grief. It was an important pastoral role, in addition to giving absolution to those dead or being carried away. The poor people picked up the bodies and loaded them onto trucks – sometimes they could not identify the bodies. Umuahia was a frequent target for the fighter jets as it was the seat of the Biafran government for most of the war after the collapse of Enugu. I remember on one particular occasion going through the streets in the aftermath of a bombing and watching a cart being loaded with broken bodies. As the cart was being driven away, someone shouted 'Wait, Wait', and he rushed forward with an arm which had been blown off. I stood numbed by the horror of it all, helpless without something to do, someone to help, someone to console, or just a silent prayer to say for the poor innocent victims of a futile war.

> Lord, make me an instrument of Your peace,
> Where there is hatred let me sow love,
> Where there is injury, pardon,
> Where there is darkness, light,
> Where there is despair hope.

Spadeville was started by Father P. J. O'Connor, Father John

Daly and Brother Gus O'Keeffe with some volunteers. Their aim was to produce more crops, and to explore the possibilities of growing new crops such as rice in the overcrowded remaining territory of diminishing Biafra.

Father Donal O'Sullivan, our religious superior, used to visit all the missionaries once a month in every kind of weather. He would bring an update on the front, the relief programme and any items of news that trickled in from Ireland. It was a joy to see him coming for the night. He was always encouraging and hopeful. Donal lived and worked in great danger, but was always cheerful.

Father Dermot Doran did extraordinary things to assist the missionaries. He was the first to show his face after the outbreak of the war. We had been cut off by the blockade from June until December 1967. Dermot arrived in Okpala one morning with bundles of letters for Christmas, having travelled on an arms plane from Lisbon. He would cheer us up with his witty stories and thrilling escapades. He worked for Catholic Relief Services of the USA, which sent massive humanitarian assistance to Biafra. Dermot had little thought for himself and his safety – he was the first link the missionaries had with the outside world. He had had good practice of getting out of tight corners as a student in Kimmage under Father Mike Doheny. Dermot had no time for grand theories about logistics – he would role up his sleeves and get on with the work.

Father Fintan Kilbride and Sister Michael Joseph of the John of God Sisters landed in Port Harcourt out of the blue with a planeload of medicines. The plane crash-landed and caught fire, but the passengers escaped. They risked their lives trying to salvage the much-needed medical supplies.

Father Dick Kissane had the narrowest of escapes when his plane burst into flames on landing in Uli. The crew moved down the plane and opened the side door. They showed Dick how to swing himself on a rope to the tarmac, away from the flames. He followed them, but landed awkwardly on the runway. He ran for his life across the melting tarmac and got away safely. He was lucky to live to tell the tale. Fred Forsyth was on the spot, and turned the episode into a comedy with his poem 'The Ballad of Dick Kissane':

The aircraft coming from the Isle,
Was packed with stockfish pile on pile,
And sitting back in lordly style,
Was Dick Kissane.

A DC6 from São Tomé
Flying relief by night and day,
Well, flying in darkness anyway,
With Dick Kissane.

They landed fine on Uli strip
With ne'er a lurch and ne'er a slip,
'That was an uneventful trip,'
Said Dick Kissane.

But hark, what hovers in the sky,
A vandal bomber flying in the sky,
The pilot has his beady eye
On Dick Kissane.

The bombs came whistling one, two, three,
Fast down upon the argosy,
'Where did I put my rosary?'
Thought Dick Kissane.

No time for prayer – the ship's on fire,
Turned into a funeral pyre,
'This is the end – I shall expire,'
Cried Dick Kissane.

The Lord above spoke loud and clear,
We have no room for you up here,
We're fully booked so come next year
Dick Kissane.

The Lord had spoke, so Dick obeyed,
And staggering to the door he swayed,
A Marist Brother with him stayed,
'Up to you, Kissane.'

The door was wide, the drop was long,
And Dick Kissane not feeling strong.
It's now or never, move along,
Dick Kissane.

Then engineer, he threw a wire,
'Jump,' he cried, or face the fire,
'Into thy hands, O Lord, O Sire,'
Prayed Dick Kissane.

First went the doughty engineer,
And Brother Walter followed clear,
But fell in manner very queer,
'Neath Dick Kissane.

The flames reached out, our Dick to smother,
He thought of Kerry, thought 'O Mother.'
'I cannot jump upon a Brother.'
Good Dick Kissane.

The fire came round in burning walls,
You cannot go to Heaven's Halls,
So hold your breath and mind your calls,
Bold Dick Kissane.

He jumped at last some fifteen feet,
And landed on his rev'rend seat,
The tar was burning from the heat,
Bravo, Kissane.

Our Dick got up and stumbled clear,
Into the Biafran bush quite near,
He'd hurt his arm and burnt his rear,
Poor Dick Kissane.

The plane was burned to ashes red,
The vandal left to go to bed,
He'd done his job, but failed instead,
To kill Kissane.

The pilot, mate and engineer,
Were safe, though death had been so near,
The Brother in a sweat of fear,
But not Kissane.

This man who would not yield to fear,
They carried him like conquering Nero,
The Fathers cried, 'you are our hero,
Dick Kissane.'

He'd lost the fish, and oatmeal too.
His specs, his passport, luggage new,
Had all gone up into the blue,
Bankrupt Kissane.

'But still', he thought, 'I am alive,
I've shown them how one must survive.'
The losses all we'll soon forgive,
To Brave Kissane.

Father Mike Doheny had a close call one night when his Danish pilot Gunar Ostagaard tried to land in Uli airport. They made three attempts before landing safely on the makeshift runway, hidden in the tropical forest. The pilots had only thirty seconds of runway lighting to land the plane and then had to taxi down the runway on their own lights, which had to be switched off on stopping.

Father Mike Cunniffe and Father Milo Smithwick did extraordinary hard work in the Ezinehitte area. Milo kept the confrères happy with his witty anecdotes and hair-raising adventures. He has a vivid imagination and was given to humorous exaggeration. He supplied much-needed comic relief.

The Holy Rosary Sisters did heroic work in hospitals and feeding centres. I used to bring journalists to Nguru to see the thousands at the feeding programme each morning. It was run by Sisters Columba and Conrad. Sister Helen King and Sister Dr Calasantius Tyndal did marvellous work in Emekuku Hospital.

Father Joe McHugh was very active in the Enugu front, visiting the troops before they went into battle and bringing relief supplies to the civilian population.

Father Frank Mullan, a Vincentian, had come to Owerri diocese a few years previously, and was there for the war. He was imprisoned with the other missionaries and, of course, expelled.

The Kennedy family gave invaluable service by establishing the relief organisation, Concern. John Kennedy and his wife Kay organised the relief operation from Ireland, while Raymond Kennedy organised the airlift from Libreville into Biafra in the beginning. Later, Father Gus Finucane took over the operation from there.

I must also mention a charismatic Jew called Abe Nathan, who organised a shipment of food from New York. He then arranged for the airlift of these supplies in São Tomé with Father Tony Byrne. On arrival in Biafra, he divided the cargo into three, one portion for Dr Middlecoop of the World Council of Churches, one for the government and one portion for me. He was a peace-maker, and on one occasion flew in his own plane to Cairo from Jerusalem in an effort to reconcile the ongoing conflict between Jews and Arabs in its early stages. Cairo Airport was closed to Israeli aircraft at the time, so he risked his life in his effort to establish the peace process.

There was great co-operation between the International Donor organisations. Caritas Internationalis played a very significant role, as did Misereor (Germany) and Missio (Germany). Swiss Caritas were very generous with supplies, and they also established a communications network linking Biafra with Europe. CAFOD in London was also very active, under the direction of Noel Charles. The Canadians did a great deal both in sending supplies and in supplying pilots for the airlift into Biafra.

Even war has a lighter side
A sense of humour is a valuable asset in wartime, to keep your heart up and to get you over difficulties. The Holy Spirit can also help, by providing inspiration to say the right thing in times of frustration. I will give you a few examples of how these two combined to help us through our difficulties.

'Caritas' was a good name in the Biafran context because of the massive airlifts of food and medical supplies which that organisation provided. One evening, while making my way home, exhausted after passing about twenty-five check-points, answering so many questions and enduring so many searches, I was in no mood for yet another check-point when I was brought to a sudden halt once again. A Biafran soldier put his gun through the window of my car and asked the five standard and compulsory questions:

'Who are you?'
'I am Father Caritas.'

'Who is with you?'
'It is Sister Caritas.'

'Where are you coming from?'
'I am coming from Caritas.'

'Where are you going to?'
'I am going to Caritas.'

'What are you doing?'
'I am bringing Caritas.'

The soldier lifted the barrier and shouted – 'Carry on, Caritas.'

On another occasion I was rushing to Uli airport with my brother Mike and Father Tom Clynes to catch a plane. The plane would bring them to São Tomé, to catch a flight to Europe. It was important that they catch this European flight that night, or they would have to wait a week for the next one.

We had to pass through five check-points near the airport, and we had to drive with side lights only. This very strict ruling was to minimise the danger of attracting the 'intruder bomber', whose purpose was to hit the airstrip and knock it out of commission. It was essential to pass through the check-points quickly. When a soldier jumped out from the bush in camouflage, I decided to forestall him by asking him questions.

'Where is Marcellinus, I want him quickly?' I shouted. The Ibo soldier did not like to admit that he did not know Marcellinus, so he said, 'He is not here tonight.'

I thanked him profusely and drove off to the next check-point, where I asked the same question. And so on for the whole five check-points, which we passed through in double quick-time. Tom Clynes wanted to know who this Marcellinus was and why I wanted him. I admitted Marcellinus was a name I picked out of my head, a name that is quite common in Nigeria.

We had radioed São Tomé with a message that the plane should wait for two Church dignitaries who were slightly delayed, but who had to get to Europe that night. The pilot reluctantly delayed the departure.

On arrival in Kimmage Manor, Mike and Tom Clynes were walking down the corridor when they were met by the superior, Father Farrell Sheridan, who welcomed them back and then introduced an African priest: 'Meet Father Marcellinus from Biafra.' Mike and Tom burst out laughing. 'We're so happy to meet you, Marcellinus. We searched for you in Biafra and we had to come to Kimmage to find you.'

A sense of humour goes hand-in-hand with the grace of God in overcoming difficulties, and should not be overlooked.

CHAPTER 8

AFRICAN SOCIETY AND THE CHURCH

It is difficult to penetrate the African mind, to find out what makes an African 'tick' – for a missionary, it is the work of a lifetime.

Africans are very family-oriented, with the man as the superior being. The oldest merit the greatest respect, children are severely controlled and disciplined, and there are numerous taboos, both medical and social. Africans place the same value on efficiency as Europeans do. Kindness is infinitely better. For an African to say that a missionary is a kind person means that he or she has time for everyone, and, indeed, what could be more Christlike? Christ had time for everyone, even on the road to Calvary. Africans also value education and the greatest penance they could be given is to keep them from their studies. On the debit side, they will never admit that they are wrong. If they fail an examination, they will say that the examiner did not understand them. When working with African seminarians I would plead with them to tell the truth and to admit they were wrong, but it was very difficult for them.

The administration of justice in many parts of Africa is primitive, and thieves would often be punished by cutting off one or both hands, or one or both feet depending on the gravity of the theft. They might in some areas be treated to a drink of liquid concrete, which would solidify inside and kill them. Crowds would come from miles away to witness a good execution, an event that would be dragged out for hours. But then there were similar executions at Tyburn, and during the French Revolution, and even today in Bosnia.

African marriages are generally arranged between parents, a dowry being paid by the groom according to the relative charms, abilities or education of the future bride. Women are regarded as child-bearers, carriers of wood and water. Men socialise with men, and barely speak to their wives. Likewise, the women socialise with each other, and social events are frequent and well-structured.

My cook, Everist, lost his first wife and one day I asked him if he had ever thought of getting married again. He replied, 'All right, Father, if you say so.' I explained that it did not depend on me but was only a suggestion. He said he would consider my suggestion. A few days later he asked me if he could go home for the day to arrange his marriage. He returned in the evening and told me everything was fixed. I asked him how things had gone for him. He said that in the morning his parents had brought him to see a girl, but he did not want her because 'she was ugly'. I asked him to explain what he meant by this. He said, 'She was too short and her face was no good. But towards evening they brought me to another girl and now everything is fixed.'

I questioned him about what standard of education the girl had and he said 'Standard five'. He himself had standard six – it was important that his wife should not be as highly qualified, because this would give her greater authority in deciding family matters. I suggested that I should pay his salary in advance so that they could get married soon. All was accomplished in one day, according to their native law and custom. They got married and brought up a very happy family.

Religion is very important to the African people. Even the pagans are surrounded by juju practices and customs. The people build their own churches – the women carry sand and water on their heads, the children also participate, and even if it takes years to build a church, it is completed by the people themselves. The churches are theirs, built by their sweat and blood, and during the war they were very conscious of this and protected them.

African children are generally not weaned until the age of two years. One parish priest solved the problem of noisy children in his church by asking mothers not to breast-feed until the Gospel, so that there would be silence in the church at least for the Gospel and sermon. It worked.

The Catholic Church spread very rapidly through Nigeria, especially in Iboland. Today it has its own bishops and priests, and the seminaries are full of students. The sisters too have proliferated at a wonderful rate and are spreading into other African countries, bringing Christ to many lands. Their sufferings, especially in the Biafran war, purified them and made them stronger Christians. And suffer they did. The war brought immense starvation, great privation and unbelievable hardship. It opened my eyes to realities of hunger and destitution which are difficult for Europeans to understand.

On one occasion when I travelled out of Biafra the contradictions between that world and most parts of Europe were brought home to me. I landed in Zurich in winter. The streets were being sprinkled with salt to melt the snow, whereas in Biafra a cup of salt would have cost as much as £3. This is just a small example of the wastage in European countries, which would feed thousands in Africa or India. We in the West complain so much about small things. Our shops are full not merely with the basic foods, but with so many varieties of the same commodity – we can pick and choose to meet every taste.

Another contrast struck me when I reached Ireland. I offered my services in the local church to the parish priest, who asked me to say the Sunday Mass while he would preach. His sermon that Sunday morning consisted of a complaint about the untidy condition of the town, the litter in the streets after the Saturday night activities and the disgrace it was at a time when the town was to be inspected for the Tidy Towns Competition. As I tried to listen I was haunted by the images of starvation in Biafra, the children dying in great numbers and the flood of refugees on the roads escaping from the war fronts. The priorities were poles apart. Yet he was a very good priest, doing a lot for his local community. How could he speak on starvation, when he had never been in that situation? My sermon, I assure you, would have been quite different.

When we went to Nigeria it was a British colony, and I must admit that we missionaries were tainted with colonialism. Our attitudes betrayed us on occasion. In Okpala Seminary we had a band which was trained to play Irish marching tunes, like 'O'Donnell Abu', 'Tara's Halls' etc. Why did we not play African music, with drums and African instruments?

We also condemned their juju, instead of trying to Christianise it and baptise it. We ignored inculturation for the most part, and we were very wrong to do so. We even built Irish-style churches in a climate which called for greater ventilation and an African design. We did not master the Ibo language, which should have been a primary prerequisite for all missionaries. We were perhaps somewhat hard too on the African clergy. We could have received them more quickly into our missions as brothers. There were even some incidents of open hostility, fostering animosity on occasion, though this was very rare. Power was often associated with the White man. We also had access to money, which naturally led to jealousy. One Sister in Ethiopia said to me: 'Why do you want to put up such fine buildings? Is it to show us up?'

The Irish missionaries had all the top jobs, while the local clergy felt they should have had more access to prestigious positions. The Irish were holding on too long, while the local clergy wanted to take over too quickly. There were difficult teething problems for all. The war solved it when the Irish missionaries were expelled and the Nigerian clergy took over everything, and did so very successfully.

The work of Providence

Before the war I inherited the responsibility of completing the roof of the church in Okpala seminary. The steel roof had been sent out from Ireland, but was lying on the ground in bits and pieces. I was searching for a way to get this roof up onto the wall plates – about thirty feet high – a formidable task. I went to Aba, a neighbouring town about eighteen miles away, in search of help. I visited the church there, hoping to find a solution. I knelt in front of the altar and prayed for assistance – 'Lord, it is your church. Please help me to put the roof on.'

As I drove down the street I saw a man descending from a high mast outside the post office. I decided to ask his advice about the roof of the church. He was Welsh, very friendly, and listened to my problem. He said that he had just finished the job at the post office and would be moving to another job after the weekend, but he would come and see the church for himself.

It was Friday evening when he inspected the church. He said he would send his equipment – a winch, basically – and some men to put the roof on. By Sunday evening the steel frame was on the church at a cost of £10 – a gift for the local workers. It was a direct answer to my prayer.

How Providence works – God directed me into the church in Aba to say a prayer and I saw the man coming down from the mast. If I had been a few seconds later I would have missed him. He had finished his work with the post office that very day.

The Okpala church was designed by Niall Meagher, an Irish architect. Niall introduced a new architecture into Nigeria, which took account of the climate and the culture of the people. He realised that with the tropical climate he could dispense with walls and instead insert wrought-iron grilles between the pillars. He designed a sloping roof, with a veranda all around the church to protect it from the burning sun and the torrential tropical rain. He planned a sloping floor from the centre outwards, so that if rain penetrated the grilles, which occasionally happened during a tropical tornado, the water would flow out naturally. It was a very unusual, practical and artistic design, which was completely different from the missionary's amateurish approach. Niall contrasted the situation in Nigeria with that in Ireland. He said: 'In Nigeria the missionaries build without any plans, all the time, whereas in Ireland we are planning all the time and build nothing.' How true. We used to build our churches on the Irish model. They were carbon copies of the Irish churches, with the result that they were hot and stuffy. Niall did an excellent thing, not only for Okpala, but for Nigeria. Pierce McKenna did similar work in the Calabar diocese, revolutionising the architecture of that missionary area.

I never cease to thank God for my Biafran experience. After our expulsion the Holy Ghost Fathers spread into new and varied vineyards. I went to Swansea to study in preparation for going back to Africa to meet the needs of the people. The course was a great blessing – a time to rethink, reflect and prepare myself for another new approach to a different apostolate. It opened up a new literature for me, and was an ideal way to rest and rehabilitate myself, and prepare for the future. The loss of our mission and the separation from a people we had loved was very painful – we gradually realised that we could never return to Nigeria on a permanent basis. But there were many other places where we could work, and I found myself volunteering for Ethiopia.

CHAPTER 9

THE LAST DAYS OF BIAFRA

The Ibos were wonderful people, full of initiative; but with a capacity for self-deception they could live in hope bordering on fantasy, especially in a crisis. They could live in a world of make-believe. They never believed they could be beaten in the war.

Uli airport was a case in point. It was an extension of an already straight road, built to replace the Enugu airport. Mentally the Ibos never admitted that Enugu and Port Harcourt airports had been captured. When Father Alo Dempsey landed at Uli airport, they stamped his passport with an Enugu stamp. When Alo was leaving, he went to Uli airport and said to the commander, George Akabogu: 'I came into Biafra by Enugu, but I would like to leave by Port Harcourt.' George said there was no problem, and he used the Port Harcourt stamp instead of the Enugu one. So Alo landed in Enugu on arrival and left from Port Harcourt, both from the same airstrip in Uli. This gift of fanciful thinking helped their morale during the war.

The greatest victory of the Biafran ground forces was the total destruction of the Abagana military convoy making its way from Enugu to Onitsha. It was a carefully planned attack which prepared the way for the total destruction and capture of a major city, to end the bloody two-and-half-year-old war.

The federal army of Nigeria was full of confidence – nothing would stop it – so they thought. Their blockade was very effective. What effect could a few tons of weapons have against such a mighty military force on the federal side?

The Biafran army was tired and showing signs of exhaustion bordering on surrender and their arsenal was diminishing rapidly. As the convoy reached Abagana, the Biafran soldiers were almost in despair. It was a convoy of between sixty and a hundred of the most sophisticated weaponry of the Nigerian army. They fired the only shell in their arsenal which, fortunately for them, hit an oil tanker, blowing it into smithereens. This explosion set off a chain reaction of fires and more explosions. Confusion ensued, and in the chaos that followed the federal forces panicked. Some tried to turn around to retreat, but their tanks either overturned or blew up in the air. The few who survived fled in disarray. It was a total loss, not merely of military hardware, but of the morale of the federal troops. It was a resounding victory for the Biafrans.

The Biafrans looked on their victory as an act of God, divine retribution. For them it was a miraculous release and an indication from God that their war was justified and that ultimate victory was theirs. They said God was truly on their side and they could not be beaten. We know what happened subsequently. They were defeated and forced to surrender on 8 January 1970, thus bringing the horrible conflict to an end.

However, the Biafrans accepted defeat like the brave soldiers they were, and soon forgave and forgot the atrocities on both sides. They taught us the salutary lesson of reconciliation by continuing their lives in harmony and peace. It was an example for the entire world.

Bob Eberhart CSSp, accompanied by Fr Tom Clynes of the American Province (East), chose to spend Christmas 1969 with the confrères in Biafra. The following is an extract from his journal:

24 December
I celebrated Mass after one of the parish priests who was getting an early start to a very busy day. They had to visit their twenty-eight feeding centres and afterwards face the exhausting prospect of long and tiring hours in the confessional – it was Christmas Eve. These twenty-eight feeding centres were dispensing two meals and milk three times a week to sixteen thousand people. A nearby mission took up the task on the other days. The curtain was beginning to lift on these mercy operations. I was in for more staggering figures in the ensuing days.

We reached Ihiala in time for the evening meal, which was more like a coffee break for the parish fathers, since the confession lines were still long and promised to go on far into the evening. It was Christmas Eve, all right. I was scheduled to sing the 7 o'clock High Mass in church the following morning.

25 December
Christmas Day dawned sunny but sticky. High Mass began at 7.30

a.m. because of the vast numbers for communion at the 6 o'clock Mass. There was an experience in store for me – preaching in English while each sentence was translated into Ibo.

I could say how happy I was to spend Christmas Day with them. The words 'Merry Christmas' would stick in my throat. I spoke of the hope that is born every day with a person's re-awakening and reminded them that Christ's coming to earth symbolised that hope. Many of the upturned, intent faces seemed to tell me that hope was beginning to dim. It was a difficult sermon, even with time in between interpretations to get my next sentence together. I ran the hope theme into the ground. It has always been a favourite with me. One of the few quotations I can remember is Scott's: 'Despair is never quite so deep in sinking as in seeming, Despair is hope just rocked to sleep for better chance of dreaming.' During the day I visited some of the feeding centres and tried my hand at dishing out the fare. The patience and discipline among the 400 or 500 people at each of the centres was surprising. I spent the remainder of the day visiting various projects, among them an orphanage that was soon to be completed and taken over by native Nigerian nuns.

* * * * *

These lines are being penned exactly four days after our arrest by the Federal Nigerian troops at Awa-Amama in Orlu Division. Looking back on those weeks, weeks of movement under armed escort, of waiting, of trial and imprisonment, it is difficult to sort out one's impressions of the last days of Biafra. For us in the House of Theology in Owa-Amama the end of term brought activity of a different kind: we moved into parishes where help was needed. In my case, I did supply work in a parish without a priest for the period of the vacation. Father Gerry Creedon divided his time between the seminary, where feeding centres were still functioning under the care of the Holy Ghost Scholastics, and his old mission of Issu, which was being cared for by Father Gerry Gogan.

One's general impression of Christmas was one of ceaseless activity, supervising the feeding centres, maintaining the supply of medicines and listening endlessly to individual needs and problems. At the same time, the pastoral work of the parish continued smoothly – due in large measure to the wonderful staff-work of the catechist – against a background of increasing misery and disillusionment.

For Spiritans working in the parishes, generally in twos but often alone, the Christmas celebration held in a central station or mission was great for morale. Despite the personality problems one expects in any group, their wartime experience had forged a bond of confidence and sympathy which made life much more than merely bearable: this experience was to prove valuable later on when the first groups were rounded up and brought to Port Harcourt.

The week that was

We had a get-together in Okpala on 4 January 1970, in spite of the fact that the federal forces were within two miles of us in Owerrinta. They had come there suddenly on 16 December 1969 and had been stopped at the bridge over the Imo river just one mile from the seminary. Everyone had fled in panic – civilians, seminarians, six hundred sick children and patients from the sick bay in St Finbar's school. Father Broderick and myself had moved into a small, private, native hut, away from the empty seminary, about a mile away from immediate danger. All our work was destroyed in half an hour. An Africa Concern team was to arrive that very day, but we had to divert them to Ezenehitte for the time being.

About 7.00 p.m. seventeen people arrived, including Bishop Whelan, Fathers George Lahiffe, Dennis Foley, Stephen D'arcy, Dermot Kavanagh, Matty Murphy, Frank Caffrey, Eamon McMahon, Tony Kelly, and our foreign visitors Bob Eberhart (Rome) and Mike Doheny (Dublin), Seán Broderick and myself. Little did we realise that this would be our last night in Okpala and our last week in our mission in Nigeria.

Monday, 5 January
Fathers Tom Clynes and Bob Eberhart left Biafra for Libreville with Mick. Father Broderick fed his five thousand children as usual in the various feeding-centres.

Tuesday, 6 January

Nothing exceptional. A gathering of Fathers in Mbutu-Okohia similar to that in Okpala. Plenty of hope and good cheer in spite of the proximity of the Federal troops.

Wednesday, 7 January

A day to remember. I was returning from the airport after seeing my brother off with Fathers Clynes and Eberhart when I got the news that Okpala was evacuating. I rushed down but could not get past Mbutu-Okohia. Father Broderick had been rushing to and fro all day on his own. An attack had started in Alulu about ten miles to the south. The mortaring was heavy and all the determination of the Biafrans could not withstand it. The Nigerians under the Black Scorpion broke through. At 1.00 p.m. they were at Obokwe, and at 3.00 p.m. they reached the tarred road. At 5.00 p.m. they were in Uwuru – an advance of sixteen miles in one day. The jets passed over our heads twenty-five times, rocketing and strafing. We spent the night evacuating Mbutu-Okohia with Des O'Sullivan and Earl Roe. All relief material went to Umohiagu. The roads were black with people – invalids hobbling along on crutches, patients carrying drips on their shoulders; children crying, trying to keep pace with their parents; many looking for lost relatives. Suffering on every face, despair in many hearts, death around the corner for some.

Thursday, 8 January

The Federal forces moved in two directions:
    a) Through Mbaise, via Aboh and Amumara.
    b) Towards Owerri. At 8.00 p.m. shells were falling both in Owerri township and Egbu.

Seán and myself had moved to Atta. The Fathers evacuated Owerri and also Emmerienwe and Obube. I got clearance in Owerri for some of the Africa Concern team to leave – Rita Gahan and Margaret O'Connor. Margaret had been working in the Ivory Coast for Africa Concern and had come to Okpala on 15 December 1969, where they were within two miles of the front lines. Rita had joined her in Ezenehitte when the sick bay was transferred there.

Friday, 9 January, 7.00 a.m.

With Father Broderick I tried to get into Ezenehitte to see the Africa Concern team and Sisters, not knowing they had already left. We ran into a shower of bullets from the Nigerian Army. We had to turn. We were lucky to escape alive. It was the worst experience of the whole war. It was the closest I ever came to my own death. We were right on the firing line. Many good people must have been praying for us. The driver swept the car around. He could not make it in one sweep. He had to reverse. They were agonising moments. We crouched down in the car. I don't know how we escaped. We made for Amaimo. All Mbaise people were on the roads moving into Ikeduru. It was impossible to drive a car. They were a frightened, terrified, hungry, naked, courageous lot. It was a horrible sight; a depressing thought to realise that hundreds of thousands of these people would be sleeping under trees, trying to keep alive just a little longer.

We met Father Frawley in Amaimo. He appointed me to Libreville to help the Africa Concern team there and ordered me to leave as soon as possible. Bishop Whelan arrived later, having completed a tour of Orlu, and he endorsed Father Frawley's decision. I should try to initiate a massive airlift from outside Biafra. I spent part of the night in Amaimo and left with Father Vincent McDonald for the Uli airstrip about midnight. We did not know what to expect. Would we reach the airstrip? Would we get a flight? We knew the Nigerian army was making very fast inroads into the Biafran enclave. The circle was closing in around us. We had no exit permits, an essential requirement for leaving the country. Father John Doyle, an experienced airport priest, was consulted.

'You must travel on a Red Cross plane, as a Red Cross worker', he advised. 'So get over there and take over that last plane. Use vile language by way of identity with a French Red Cross relief worker, and show no weakness.'

I whipped off my cassock and fortunately I had a pair of very short briefs on me, much like what the French workers wore.

John Doyle's good advice was strictly adhered to. My language was occasionally questionable. Vinnie and I literally took over the plane. Our authority was never questioned. I shouted orders in all directions, to get the plane unloaded, which happened, as never before, in double-quick time. The crew of the plane were, no doubt, very pleased with my fast performance. I was amazed at how everyone responded to my commands – perhaps it was because everyone was nervous and presumed I was in charge.

Shells were actually falling around the airstrip, making the atmosphere very tense. I ordered the pilot to close the door and at about 2.00 a.m. the plane took off. We landed in Libreville at about 4.30 and Father Aengus Finucane was on the tarmac to meet us. He knew the ropes in Libreville and managed a visa for us, somehow.

Saturday, 10 January
We spent most of it in bed. I awaited news from the night's flight. The Africa Concern plane took off as usual, but returned at midnight, without landing, with the news that two Government planes had landed and had taken out the Red Cross and Biafran personnel. Colonel Ojukwu was among the passengers. He left at the request of his cabinet, without any luggage. Two planes, C97s, flew in at considerable risk and took out relief workers. The runway had been hit by a bomb and shortened. Reports said that Federal forces were within two miles of it and shelling it.

Captain Johnson flew in especially from São Tomé to help evacuate. He brought no cargo. A number of French Red Cross personnel were left behind and two hundred Biafran children due for evacuation were abandoned on the airstrip.

Sunday, 11 January
I left for London to see what could be done to mount a massive airlift, now that the war was virtually over.

Monday, 12 January
On Monday morning I saw Cardinal John Heenan who said I was not fit to be seen in public in such shabby clothes. He lent me some of his own and sent an urgent personal letter to the Prime Minister, asking him to see me. A reply soon came to say that the PM's private secretary would meet me with members of the Foreign Office on Tuesday at 12 noon. I realised that this was a brush-off, but attended the meeting on Tuesday. At 3.00 p.m. on the same day an emergency meeting was convened by the Prime Minister.

We tried every means possible to get an invitation, but failed. Noel Charles of CAFOD was furious to be excluded.

Father Mick had joined me from Ireland, and had decided that we were going to the meeting in 10 Downing Street, no invitation notwithstanding. We arrived there before a barrage of cameras and press. Mike told me to pose deliberately for the cameras, and speak briefly to the BBC, in the hope of getting an interview to explain the dreadful plight of the Biafrans. We walked into 10 Downing Street as if invited, but we were stopped inside the door. Wilson's private secretary met us, explaining that as CAFOD we were not invited – it was only the Big Five – namely Christian Aid, British Red Cross, Save the Children, OXFAM and War on Want.

Mike spoke up, asking a very awkward question. Was it because we were Catholics that we were being excluded? After all, we had helped in a substantial way in the relief of the civilian population in Biafra. It was an awkward question because the British would not wish to appear to be discriminating against anyone. The private secretary went upstairs to consult with the Prime Minister. He came back with the answer that it was just for the Big Five. Mike had another trick up his sleeve. He asked, 'What are we to tell the journalists and the BBC waiting outside the door for interviews? We have promised to give them the latest information from Biafra since we have just arrived from there, and to tell them of the findings of the meeting here in No. 10.' The secretary had to consult once again with the Prime Minister. He returned, again with a negative answer, saying that we could not attend the meeting, but that the Prime Minister would meet us after the meeting.

We were shown into a parlour to wait. What a ridiculous situation. We were sitting in a room next to where this important meeting was being held, and were not allowed to attend it, even though we had a full, up-to-date report ready, even in writing.

The secretary came back to us to tell us that the Prime Minister had been called away unexpectedly, but we should see Cardinal Heenan who would be having a meeting with him later.

'Does that mean that we too will be meeting the Prime Minister?' we asked. He replied that we should speak with the cardinal.

Was this not another brush-off?

We returned to Cardinal Heenan to be told that he was invited to meet the Prime Minister at 7.30 p.m. We should come along and the Cardinal would request a meeting for us. What a lot of bureaucracy, while people were dying of starvation in Nigeria.

We were eventually allowed into the presence of Harold Wilson and spent about three-quarters of an hour explaining the sad situation. Now that Nigeria had won the war with the help of Britain, the British Government should control the use of arms given to the Nigerian army, and prevent the genocide of the Biafran people.

We proposed the following:

1. It is absolutely necessary to provide instant relief to Biafra. There should be a twenty-four-hour airlift of supplies to all possible airstrips inside the stricken enclave.

2. Relief supplies should be flown in from all existing suitable air bases, such as São Tomé, Libreville, Coutenou, and San Isabel.

3. All existing relief agencies should be allowed to continue the work. The missionaries knew the people and the language and had established a very effective and efficient relief programme.

4. Food should be channelled through all existing airstrips in Biafra, not merely through Lagos, but through Uli, Enugu, Port Harcourt, and Calabar.

5. Ships should leave as soon as possible for Port Harcourt, Coutenou, San Isabel, São Tomé and Libreville to supplement the supplies.

6. The food should be handed over to the relief agencies – Joint Church Aid, Red Cross and Africa Concern – who were still operating in Biafra.

7. Eighty Irish priests and twenty Irish nuns were still working for Caritas under Bishop J. B. Whelan. The relief programme should not be handed over to the Nigerian army. At least ninety-five per cent of the food sent to Biafra was reaching the people through these well-established agencies. While Nigeria was in control of the airports, it should not control the relief operation.

8. A strong force consisting of several hundred observers from neutral countries should be flown in at once and

scattered throughout the country to prevent atrocities. Already we had received reports from Ngwa that five hundred men had been shot after the take-over. These numbers came from people who crossed the lines. They are unconfirmed.

9. I suggested also that the Churches should play an active part in the observer force by sending representatives — otherwise reprisals would be inevitable.

10. The Biafrans are terrified of atrocities and reprisals. They base their reasons on recent history.

The Prime Minister listened carefully to our presentation, but we feel that little if anything was done. We had at least tried. We began to see the rough side of politics, which left us very disillusioned and frustrated. There are always vested interests which are beyond our understanding.

One good thing about our intervention at 10 Downing Street was that CAFOD were no longer excluded from emergency meetings, which had, up to then, been reserved for the Big Five.

What a week this was – from Biafra to Libreville, to London, with America, and perhaps Canada, ahead of us.

The fate of the missionaries

The story of what happened to the missionaries following the collapse of Biafra is told in the following excerpt from the diary of SMW:

Monday, 12 January 1970
The news is confirmed that Owerri is overrun by the advancing Federal troops. For the Fathers their decision has already been taken – to remain in their mission-stations, and when the time comes, to identify themselves as missionaries. The last plane left on Saturday and those from the various relief agencies who did not wish to stay in Biafra at the end, have gone.

4.30 p.m. A small group of Federal soldiers entered the grounds of Ihioma mission and advanced up the avenue, without any undue display of force. The Fathers, dressed in white cassocks, and the others living in the mission came forward to meet them, hands held high over their heads. The officer in charge greeted the missionaries politely and discussed the situation with them. One of the Fathers was allowed to accompany the soldiers to the Holy Rosary convent nearby. The troops were well-disciplined and helped to restore order and suppress looting, which had already begun. The officer in charge was billeted in Ihioma mission house and it is from here that contact was made with Mr Eke, the Minister of Information, who brought the news that Colonel Effiong had surrendered.

Tuesday, 13 January
High-ranking officers of the Biafran army assemble in the mission compound and from there proceed to Owerri to meet the Federal High Command. For the next two days, Tuesday and Wednesday, the Fathers live with the Federal army, whom they found, on the whole, well-behaved.

Wednesday, 14 January
In the evening we were told that all the 'Caritas personnel' would be assembled and brought to Port Harcourt the next day.

Thursday, 15 January, 9.30 a.m.
The missionaries, driving their own cars, were brought in convoy to Owerri, where their passports were taken and examined for about two hours. Afterwards the convoy proceeded to Aba, where we passed the night – some accommodated in the C.O.'s house, others in their cars. We discovered that another group from Owa-Amama had been detained here in Aba for the past four or five days.

Friday, 16 January
The convoy continued its journey to Port Harcourt. Here the missionaries were searched and brought to the Cedar Palace Hotel, where the living conditions were good. We were asked to make statements admitting illegal entry and mentioning our connection with Caritas Internationalis. Some made statements, others did not. For a week we remained under house arrest. Movement was very limited as our cars were taken away. However, we received welcome visits from Archbishop Aggey, Father Rod Crowley CM, Father McGuinness SMA, and an Irish Embassy secretary, Mr O'Toole. Every effort was being made to secure our release, but

there was no way of knowing what the authorities intended. Bishop Whelan, who at this time was free to move around Owerri, was called. We learned that another group of missionaries was being detained in the Officers' Mess in Port Harcourt.

Monday, 26 January
We were told to be ready for an interview at 8.00 p.m. This was to take place in Port Harcourt Prison, where we were brought. We spend the night in the prison warden's club, a building belonging to the prison, but not inside the prison walls. Two of the Marist Brothers established contact with Mr J. Small of the Irish Embassy, which had not been informed of the proceedings.

Tuesday, 27 January
At 10.00 a.m. we were whisked by jeep to the magistrate's court and in the interval between descending from the jeep and entering the courtroom, we were handed a charge sheet, thus learning for the first time that we were to stand trial. The charges against us were: a) illegal entry, and b) unlawful employment.

The proceedings began at once. The Sisters and Brothers were taken first and ordered to pay a fine. Then came the Fathers' turn. When the first Father had taken his stand in the dock, the prosecuting counsel made the charges, and added the insinuation about 'so-called missionaries' who gave military and other help to the rebel regime. At this there were loud protests in the courtroom, and the magistrate adjourned the court. On resumption those responsible apologised – the magistrate seemed to take a serious view of this contempt of court. Now he proceeded to hand down a sentence of six months' hard labour to the defendants on each count. Almost all the missionaries, fearing to provoke the authorities, pleaded 'guilty' and admitted that there were no extenuating circumstances. However, four were not sentenced to prison for reasons that were not always consistent – length of service in the country; service in the 'Rivers' area of which the capital is Port Harcourt; recent entry into the country etc. But the validity of these same reasons was not admitted in the case of others who were in the same situation but sentenced none the less.

The business of the court ended at 4.00 p.m. and twenty-one of us were conveyed to prison in a Black Maria to serve the sentence. Along with us was a Holy Rosary Sister who had pleaded not guilty and was remanded in custody. Another Sister elected to stay with her in the prison. The following day the Sister was fined and discharged.

The twenty-one men were put into a small hut which was designed for two prisoners. Conditions were fairly bad; there were some beds but no mattresses or bedclothes. The situation improved shortly. A second hut was provided, so we split into two groups of ten; one of the Brothers had paid a fine and was discharged, leaving us twenty in all. So, twenty of us lived in two huts, which would normally accommodate four people.

The superintendant of the prison reminded us constantly that we were convicted criminals, not prisoners of war, but, at the same time he did what he could to make our stay less unpleasant. He allowed us to eat European food, cooked at the hotel for us by the Sisters, and in fact some of us ate better in the prison than we had for a long time. Again, those who had been fined and discharged were allowed to visit us and bring mattresses, medicines and other necessities.

We very soon settled into a regular pattern, partly imposed by the prison regime and partly by ourselves. At 8.00 p.m. we were locked into our little huts, at first in the dark, but eventually we got electric light and could use the time profitably. At 6.30 a.m. the doors of the huts were unlocked and we could spend the day in an enclosed 'compound' of about one acre in which our huts stood. For our morning ablutions we had one tap and three buckets. Then there was concelebrated Mass in the open air. Fortunately it was the dry season. We had one Mass box and the local Yoruba clergy provided us with hosts and wine. Apart from the chief celebrant we celebrated in our white soutanes. After breakfast there was a period for lectures and discussion on scripture and liturgy, etc. We were a varied group. The pastoral clergy were glad to be able to avail of the services of the seminary professors to bring them up to date, while the seminary professors were very interested in the practical pastoral applications which the active missionaries could contribute. Then there was reading, talking and pastimes of various kinds. For a while there was even a football, which had been kicked over the wall, but eventually it was punctured.

It is worthy of note that on 2 February, one of the seminary professors delived a paper on Father Francis Libermann. He spoke on 'abnegation' and 'missionary adaptation'. Was there ever a more moving tribute to our founder? It was he who started it all; it was because of him that we had come to Africa and were now in prison. But like the Apostles we could only 'rejoice that we were counted worthy to suffer in the name of Jesus' (Acts 5:41).

In this way a week went by. We were visited by the magistrate who had condemned us, by the Attorney General, the Commissioner of Police, etc. We also received a visit from Bishop Whelan but were distressed to learn that he, too, along with a group from Owerri, was now in detention in Port Harcourt, as we had been before our trial. And yet, Father Frawley and the group in Enugu were allowed to move around freely and do their mission work. In fact they had been issued with passes, but only of short duration, a month or two months.

It would appear that the difference in the treatment of missionaries was due to the policies pursued by different military commanders. South of Uli airstrip the country was occupied by the Third Marine Division, whose Commanding Officer was very much opposed to Caritas Internationalis and the activities of the missionaries. The area in the North was under the command of the First Division.

The commander judged it useful that the missionaries should remain to help with the relief operations – at least till they could be replaced.

Tuesday, 3 February

An unexpected visit from the Prison Superintendant at 11.30 a.m. We were given three minutes to collect our 'luggage', and instructed to leave behind whatever might be of use to other European prisoners (Bishop Whelan and the other Fathers perhaps). We were taken by army lorries to the Cedar Palace Hotel to collect our belongings and here we were joined by those who had been fined instead of being sent to prison. By 1.30 p.m. we were on our way to Lagos. At the airstrip in Lagos there was quite a welcoming party – apart from our military escort. The Apostolic Delegate was there along with his secretary; Archbishop Aggey, Mgr Fitzgibbon and several Fathers from the Lagos area. The Irish Ambassador was also there and diplomatic representatives from the

American and British Embassies. Security was tight and the press were excluded, but when we had been brought to the Airport Hotel we could meet our distinguished visitors who had been joined by Archbishop Arinze of Onitsha, Bishop Murray from Makurdi, and Father Obioku. We learned that we were to be expelled from the country, but it was not clear if this was officially and legally 'deportation'. The following morning we concelebrated Mass with Bishop Murray. At 10.30 the first group left for Geneva and the rest about one hour later.

In all, twenty-three Fathers were expelled, of whom seventeen were in prison. Another group of twenty-nine, among whom was Bishop Whelan, was awaiting trial in Port Harcourt. There were still two groups left at their work. One was in Orlu where there were extensive relief works, in particular a specialised paediatric hospital recently built by German Caritas and caring for eight hundred children. Further north around Enugu, Father Frawley and his group appeared to have full freedom of movement still.

And the future? For the present we do not know. We are all anxious to return to work among our well-beloved people for whom we have already done so much. We hope that before long, the powers that be will come to realise that all we ever intended or did was for the good of our flock, our fellow human beings. Since our expulsion was not officially deportation (our passports had not been endorsed) it appeared that the legal obstacles to our return were not unsurmountable. In any case we are pledged to work for the spread of God's Kingdom on earth and for the service of our neighbour – if not in Nigeria, then elsewhere. There are very many places in the world where the harvest is so great and the labourers are so few.

Colonel Ojukwu, Head of State in Biafra, returned to Nigeria after the war and stood for election as president of the country. Had he been in Europe he would surely have faced a firing squad. We sometimes write off Africans as savages, brigands, barbarians and blood-thirsty guerrillas. Perhaps we should think again.

Ojukwu went a step further. He had valuable property in Lagos which had been confiscated by the Federal government. He tried to reclaim it but the government refused to hand it back to him. So he sat on the steps of his house, and his wife started cooking his meals on the streets of Lagos. The Ibos rallied round him, and then the press picked up the story. Eventually the international press became interested, and the Federal government were forced to relent. Could this have happened anywhere else but in Nigeria?

Fred Forsyth has the greatest respect for Ojukwu and described him as a potential leader of Africa, who understood his profession as an army commander, was popular with soldiers and civilians alike, and showed great promise as a head of state had he won the war. Forsyth saw him as a man of integrity and unusual courage, with an attractive charm that could convince the hardest scoundrel to play his part in peace or war. The international press looked on Ojukwu as a carbon copy of Adolf Hitler, but Forsyth would compare him with Charles de Gaulle. He claimed he was a man apart, an unusual mix, a rare bird:

> The elements were so mixed in him that nature could stand up to all the world and say 'This is a man'.

Some outstanding people of the war years

Princess Cécile de Bourbon Parme was a person of great stature, who worked so hard for the starving people, especially the children. She simply rolled up her sleeves and fed countless people. After the war she gave evidence in the State Department in Washington, along with Dr Davida Coady, Father Mike Doheny and myself. Princess Cécile was very committed to human rights.

Among the local clergy, one stood out as exceptional. He was Godfrey Okoya, Bishop of Port Harcourt. He was a great support to the missionaries, and defended them on every occasion. Once, when a missionary was badly treated at a road block, the bishop called the officer in charge and made him kneel down and apologise for the way his staff had treated the missionary. Bishop Godfrey had close links with the government and sought peace at every available opportunity.

Sister Helen King from Spiddal, County Galway, was a remarkable Holy Rosary Sister and Matron of Emekuku Hospital. She was assisted by some fine Irish nurses, among whom was Rosaleen Caron. Sister Helen was tough as nails but kindness itself, a born organiser and totally dedicated to her work. She was forced out of Emekuku Hospital during the war but she set up a field-hospital in Amaimo, and continued the medical work there, assisted by Sister Mona Tyndal, a very efficient and gentle doctor.

Johnny Haines was a volunteer teacher in Okpala Seminary, a great footballer and skilled teacher. It was recommended to him that he should leave as soon as possible after the outbreak of hostilities. Being English, he was likely to have security problems in Biafra, as the British government was supplying arms to the Federal government. The only way out of Biafra at that time was to cross the Niger River by canoe, travel by taxi to Lagos, and then on to London by air. However, the first part of this journey could be tricky. I set out with Johnny to Onitsha, from where we boarded a canoe to cross the Niger to Asaba, where there was a very strict security check-point. I must have said my prayers during the crossing. As we queued up for the check-point I wondered what I should say, but Providence was on my side once again. Before the security man could utter a word, I asked, 'Where can a European go to the toilet here?' The security guard was taken by surprise at this question, and being proud, as are all Ibos, he was not prepared to admit that he didn't know where there was such a facility. He calmly pointed in the direction of some buildings, and said something like, 'Go over there.' Fortunately the buildings were on the far side of the check-point. I told Johnny to follow me, and so we passed through without any security check. Johnny took a taxi to Lagos and got home safely.

Lord Carrington came out to Biafra towards the end of the war. He was a very skilful negotiator, and had proved himself such in the Lancaster House Agreement which ended the fifteen-year civil war in Rhodesia, making peace between Ian Smith, Robert Mugabe and Joshua Nkomo in 1980. He spent some time with me and we had lunch in Okpala. He wanted to hear more about the war, the civilian situation, and was looking for possible solutions for peace.

Father Johnny Kearns, a diocesan priest from Ossory, had spent several years in Calabar, and he came out to Biafra towards the end of the war to show his concern and solidarity with the missionaries. He was very popular, well known for his great generosity and good humour. He played bridge with Bishop Whelan, Father Mike Doheny and others. He was arrested by the Nigerian soldiers after the surrender and put in prison with Bishop Whelan and many Holy Ghost missionaries.

Other visitors to the missionaries in Port Harcourt Prison

included Gene Dewey, from the State Department in Washington, who showed the solidarity of the people of the United States. Gene even brought food to the missionaries.

When the imprisoned missionaries were formally expelled, they were flown to Lagos and from there to Rome, where they were received by His Holiness Pope Paul VI. On their return to Dublin the missionaries received a tumultuous welcome at the airport and later in Ely Hall. Bishop Joseph Whelan was given the Freedom of the City of Limerick.

The Irish people appreciated the stance taken by the missionaries during the war. The fact that they stayed with the Ibo people throughout the cruel and gruesome war was acknowledged as courageous and the correct thing to do. The Irish people had supported the relief efforts with great determination and generosity. They had identified with the sufferings of the war victims on both sides of the divide. The Irish government too was proud of the missionaries. The Irish Embassy personnel did much to support them in prison and worked for their release.

From a human point of view, it seemed like a rather sad and inglorious end to a great missionary era, but in reality it was all providential. Our removal allowed, even forced, the local clergy to take responsibility for the Catholic Church in their country, and they did so with unqualified success. Today Nigeria is one of the most active and progressive places for the Church, with many local bishops in newly formed dioceses. The seminaries are full, and ordinations to the priesthood are perhaps the most numerous in the world. The Lord works in mysterious ways.

CHAPTER 10

CHESHIRE'S FINAL BID FOR PEACE

The last episode in this story is both sad and dramatic. Again Cheshire showed his lack of interest in anything but the real problem – the suffering of the people of Nigeria, especially the children. It was this single-minded and passionate pursuit of his objective which resulted in the refusal of the Federal government to allow him back into Nigeria. Without full knowledge of what had gone before, it might have been excusable to take him for a partisan supporter of the defeated Ibos. In the light of what had actually happened during the preceding eighteen months, such a conclusion should have been out of the question. Unfortunately, his press conference in the Cheshire Headquarters on the afternoon of 14 January 1970, given as it was with the briefest of notice, and minutes before he set off with Sue Ryder on a lone bid to get into Uli airstrip, inevitably produced reports in the world press which looked like defiance of the sovereignty of the Nigerian government.

On the morning of 14 January the national press, understandably, was full of the Biafran surrender. Cheshire was about to set off that afternoon from Heathrow Airport for Paris, with the intention of reaching either São Tomé or Libreville, from where he planned to commandeer an aircraft, load it with food and medical supplies, which he knew were lying in these two places in quantity, and fly it himself into Uli airstrip. He would organise an airlift and arrange to distribute these supplies in former Biafra. Sue Ryder was going with him. Many people in the Cheshire Foundation believed that for Cheshire and Ryder to go into Nigeria by the back door, through the captured airstrip, symbol of Ibo rebellion, via the French African country which had been supplying Biafra with arms, was unsafe and unwise. They would almost surely be shot summarily if there were any Nigerians on the strip, and it was certain that there would be. If they landed safely they would be taken prisoner, and subjected to discomfort and possibly worse. Some suggested that Cheshire should go first to Lagos with the approval of the Nigerian government and clear his position, making everything legal. He would also meet his friend, Sir Louis Mbanefo, and Brigadeer Effiong in Lagos. Cheshire's reaction was: 'Thanks for the advice. But I'm afraid we've got to go through with it.'

Leonard Cheshire and Sue Ryder reached Paris at 5.30 p.m. where they had a tight connection to catch the long-distance Air France flight to Gabon. As they came down the aircraft steps, a British Embassy car drew up at the bottom. The air attaché got out and handed Cheshire a message which had just come from the Foreign Office, saying that the British government would be embarrassed if he and Ryder continued their journey to West Africa. There were only four minutes in which to make a decision. Reluctantly they agreed to drive to the British Embassy in Paris for a talk with Ambassador Christopher Soames. So there was nothing for it but to spend the night in Paris.

The couple were given a room in the Embassy. It so happened that Mrs Soames was active in trying to get a Cheshire Home going in France. While they were having supper in their room, Christopher Soames left a dinner party to come and talk to them. He apparently suggested that Cheshire should try to get a visa for Lagos from the Nigerian ambassador in Paris.

Cheshire decided to accept Soames' advice. He phoned the Nigerian ambassador the next morning and asked if it would be in order for him and his wife to fly to Lagos without a visa. The ambassador was extremely co-operative, knowing who he was and about his work in Nigeria. He said they could safely go to Lagos without a visa. He would telex the Federal government. But to make doubly sure he would order his Consular Department to issue a visa at once, and would try to see that he got it before taking off. Cheshire asked that the visa be dropped at the Air France office in Paris. They were due to take off shortly before lunch.

At this stage another actor appeared out of the blue on this dramatic stage. Michael Pallisser, a senior official of the Foreign Office, flew in from London in a great hurry with a verbal message from the foreign secretary. The British government would be embarrassed if the Cheshires continued their journey, even if it were to Lagos, and even if they should receive a visa from the Nigerian authorities. Evidently it was a difficult interview and there was not much time to catch the plane. Cheshire thought for a minute. Then he put forward a suggestion. 'Let's leave it to the Nigerians. If they issue a visa we will go. Is that fair?'

Pallisser had no option but to agree. Then Cheshire rang the Air France office. Had the visa arrived? Yes, it had. So Pallisser went back to London, and Air Commodore Hoad, the air attaché, drove the Cheshires at breakneck speed to Le Bourget. They made it to the aircraft, and the Air France manager drove up the tarmac with the two visas in his hand as the aircraft was taking off. There was, of course, the back-up in the shape of the Nigerian ambassador's telex to Lagos.

When they reached Lagos the inevitable had happened. The interviews with the British and international press as well as the TV coverage at Cheshire Homes HQ on the previous afternoon had all been reported to and monitored by Lagos. One British national paper had as its banner headlines:

'Cheshire defies the Nigerian Government.'

When the aircraft landed in Lagos they were refused permission to leave the plane. Cheshire managed to smuggle a note to the chief justice, Sir Adetokumbo Ademola, by the hand of an Air France employee who came to the aircraft while it was being fuelled. Then they took off for the last sector of the flight to Duala, capital of the Cameroons. At this rather Graham Green-like destination they were relieved of their passports by the immigration authorities. They tried to find a hotel, but the absence of passports made a room for the night impossible. Thanks to the American consul, who heard of their plight, they were able to sleep in a bed.

Next morning the aircraft turned around. They were handed their passports. First stop on the return flight to Paris was Lagos. Here they hoped that Sir Ademola would have been able to straighten things out. There was also the Nigerian ambassador in Paris and his telex. All that had happened was that the Air France employee who had taken the smuggled note to the Nigerian chief justice was able to smuggle back the reply, which read:

'If you had been able to give me some reasonable notice of your plans, I might have been able to persuade General Gowan to let you land. But the lack of notice and the damaging publicity has made it impossible.'

Chief Justice Adetokumbo Ademola

What a tragic end to a dramatic attempt by Leonard Cheshire to bring peace to Nigeria and to assist the starving people on both sides of the conflict. Through sheer courage and persistence he almost succeeded in doing the impossible. He had spared no effort, had travelled thousands of miles, spent thousands of pounds, met hundreds of people of every rank, and suffered many sleepless nights in his futile efforts to alleviate the sufferings of others.

My guess is that Leonard did far more good than he will ever be given credit for. His final trip to Lagos may have saved thousands of lives. He caused embarrassment to the Nigerian government and made them aware that they must not neglect the Ibos, or attempt to impose a genocide on them, which could easily have happened. It made the Federal government so sensative to criticism that their troops in the captured enclave of former Biafra were very well-behaved. At the same time Pope Paul VI called on the Nigerian government to avoid genocide, which made them angry, but aware that the world was looking on. Cheshire's love of the people on both sides could never be questioned. He was fearless in the face of the greatest danger.

CHAPTER 11

THE AFTERMATH OF WAR

Father Mike and myself visited Washington on 21 January 1970 and we were invited by Senator Edward Kennedy to give evidence about the latest situation in Biafra. The meeting took place in the New Senate Office Building at 2.10 p.m., with Senator Kennedy in the chair. Present were Senators Kennedy and Goodall, Dale de Haan, David Newsom, assistant secretary of state for African Affairs, Clyde Ferguson, special co-ordinator of relief victims of the Nigerian Civil War – and four witnesses on the Biafran situation – Princess Cécile de Bourbon, Dr Davida Coady, Father Mike Doheny and myself.

Dr Coady was the first to speak. She said that the condition of the people when she left on 11 January was extremely critical. It was far worse than when Senator Goodall was there in February. She proposed sending in fifteen thousand tons of food as a top priority. The distribution, she said, would be very difficult, as the weakest and the sick would be at the end of the line.

I was asked to make my report. I spoke about my background as a missionary, my involvement with the relief programme and about the numbers in my parish. There were twenty-two thousand in my parish, along with sixteen thousand refugees, making a total of thirty-six thousand. Six hundred of those were in a very sick condition. I was feeding five thousand children every morning and bringing subsistence rations to 950 destitute families. I had 350 orphans on my hands. Luckily, I had a good team of volunteer workers. I had asked Doctor Karl Western to make a medical survey of the people in my parish. He reported:

> Your ordinary people, the people you are not bringing any food to, who are walking around the roads, who are carrying on their work, I surveyed those people for you, and 62.3 % of your parishioners to whom you are giving no relief are suffering from famine oedema.

I continued that after the incidents of 7 January, when the

Federal forces over ran my parish, thirty-six thousand people were driven out onto the roads in a period of three hours. On 10 January the relief operation had been totally suspended. Therefore there was no relief; the people were out on the roads, living under the trees, with no food and very little clothing.

So, I proposed a few things. Firstly, there should be a massive airlift of food and medicines, not just to Port Harcourt, not just to Enugu, but to the enclave, Uli airstrip. I emphasised that while I considered the civil war a tragedy, I considered the present situaton a greater tragedy. The food was there but was not getting in, despite the fact that we were supposed to have peace-time regulations now. Only a twenty-four-hour, non-stop airlift from all existing airstrips outside, could possibly save the present situation.

Secondly, there should be independent observers to supervise everything, for the protection and security of the people. I pointed out that it was in the best interest of the Nigerians to have observers in former Biafra.

Father Mike was the next to speak. He pleaded with Senator Kennedy to ensure that the missionaries would be left to continue the work that they had started, built up, and perfected during the course of the war. They are the people the Biafrans trust, he said, and they had worked out a very efficient and highly organised system by which food arrived in Biafra and within twenty-four hours was in the mouths of the people in the most remote parts of the country. He emphasised that there were about a hundred missionaries, both priests and sisters, who were in danger of being removed from the scene, and that they were the only people who could ensure that the food would get in in an orderly fashion, and be distributed to the best advantage.

'Now I had a message this morning,' continued Mike, 'as we were in contact with Dublin, that twenty of our missionaries are in Port Harcourt and may be transferred to Lagos and expelled from the country. This would be a disaster as there is no use getting food and medicine in there unless there are people who know how to distribute it, who have the confidence of the local people. Missionaries are not involved in politics or military matters. Their concern is solely for the people. Whatever can be done to keep the missionaries on the spot should be done.'

Princess Cécile made some really powerful statements. Amongst them were the following:

> I have worked in the feeding centres ... I have seen children who could not eat any more, I have seen children who could not cry any more. I think they will cry a long time in our conscience...
>
> When we were evacuating children I remember one little girl. We were on the airstrip in Uli on the runway and she died under the wing of the plane. We could have saved her. Please, I ask you and I ask the Government of America and all the Governments of the United Nations, don't let any more children die under the wing of the plane... 'Too late' is a terrible phrase when you speak about human life, especially when it could have been avoided.
>
> The help from America has been marvellous. The people have great faith in you and you have saved many lives...
>
> Our Pope has been falsely criticised for not speaking out in defence of the Jews in World War II, and now our Pope is criticised because he expresses his fears...

She was referring to Pope Paul VI, who spoke out by appealing to the Nigerians not to inflict genocide on the Ibos after the surrender to the Federal troops. This angered the Nigerians, but I believe the Pope saved many lives and prevented a lot of suffering for the defeated Biafrans.

Senator Edward Kennedy was very pleased with the evidence submitted, and invited us to a very enjoyable lunch in the Senate House with his wife Joan. When saying goodbye to us the Senator said he would see us when he came to Ireland, where he had been invited to give a lecture in Trinity College. We took it that this was a polite way of saying goodbye, and that we would not see him in Ireland, but in fact we did meet him when he came in person to Kimmage Manor to ask about the situation in Biafra. Several other missionaries had returned after being in prison and were able to update him. He spent about an hour discussing the situation.

We have great admiration for Senator Kennedy for his interest in Biafra, as it had nothing to offer to a politician by way of votes. It was a dead country, and others would be quick to forget it and dissociate themselves from it. Father Mike met him on many more occasions later. During the Pakistan crisis in 1971/72 they met in Salt Lake Refugee Camp, outside Calcutta, where there were about eight million displaced people.

I met Senator Kennedy in Ethiopia during the famine and had breakfast with him and his son and daughter. He had a genuine interest in the poor and oppressed. Unfortunately he fell on difficult days later on, but I still respect him as a genuine person with a good heart.

The great diaspora

Leaving Biafra with no hope of returning was a very painful experience for me. I had been there for sixteen years and had grown close to the people, especially during the conflict. I had suffered in exile with them and shared their fate. I was haunted by the starvation endured by so many women and children. I felt like a rat leaving a sinking ship, yet I knew that I could do more from outside than from inside the country.

According to reliable statistics, at the end of the war there were 103 missionaries left inside Biafra, 102 of whom were Catholic, mostly Holy Ghost Fathers and Holy Rosary Sisters. There was one Irish Protestant missionary there also, a Mr Burke from Galway. That sharing of life and danger with the Ibos was the ultimate proof of our love for them. Personally I waited in hope of returning, but as time went by it became evident that the Nigerian government would do everything themselves from now on. Soon we began to adjust to the fact that there were many other missions of the Lord in which we could make an equally valid contribution. It was not the end of the world. After some reflection we realised that the needs of the Church were even greater elsewhere, and we should be flexible enough to undertake new challenges in God's vast Kingdom.

The Irish Province had a problem, with three hundred missionaries looking for new apostolates all at once. The provincial was sick, and he advised them to seek a temporary ministry in Ireland or America until they were contacted again for new work. Many went to the United States and Canada but were never recalled. There had been no experience of such a phenomenon in the congregation, and the province did not know how to deal with it. Most of us were upset and in need of counselling, which was not available. Many went on courses, as I did, which was a great help in the rehabilitation process, and a rest from the disaster and the mission. It was a great scattering, as some made their way to other missions in Kenya, Malawi, Zambia and elsewhere. Many new ventures were undertaken by Father Christy O'Brien, who became provincial superior.

Psychologically it was a very difficult time. We needed help to overcome the terrible trauma we had been through, but the help was not there. We needed someone to listen to us, to have the patience to help us get the war experience out of our systems. People did not understand us, and we only succeeded in antagonising our own confrères by talking incessantly about Biafra, about the war and about the great mission in Nigeria.

Eventually we recovered and new missions opened in Australia, in Papua New Guinea, in Pakistan and Zambia. A South American mission had been opened by Father John Jordan, and some ex-Biafrans went there, including Fathers Berney Murphy, Larry Doyle and others. A very small number left the priesthood, at a time when many were leaving.

People have asked me if I ever doubted my faith when I saw the suffering in Biafra. When we look to the Gospel we see the life of Jesus Christ, with its culmination on Calvary, on a cross. Suffering is a great mystery, which we have to accept in our lives.

The Biafran war opened our eyes and our hearts to the realities of poverty, starvation and suffering. It helped us to develop our talents – we learned to survive in such a disaster; to practise ingenuity and to develop a capacity to cope with major disaster situations; to develop the skill of organisation with patience and prudence, with strength and strategy, with kindness and perseverance. The missionaries often surprised themselves by what they could do when their backs were up against the wall.

A welcome break

The war over, a rest was called for, a change of occupation, a rehabilitation programme if possible. I was lucky. I signed on for a development course in Swansea University in Wales. I named Leonard Cheshire and Winston Churchill as my referees. I was chosen to be one of six students from all over the world and I started the course in October 1970. I based myself in the Catholic Church in Clydach, outside Swansea, where I offered my services to the parish priest, Father Michael Donovan, a kindly Limerick priest who did more for me than he realised, after the trauma of the war.

It was a wonderful year – for reflection, for catching up with some reading, for normal life, for looking back, for planning the future, and for putting up my feet.

The course too was wonderful – 'Community development and Social Administration'. I began to discover the value of development through the community. One of our professors was an expert on community and on the non-directive approach to development. By motivating people to do the work themselves rather than doing it for them, you enable them to learn to be the leaders of their own people. You work with small groups rather than with big ones. You do social analysis of the neighbourhoods, and steer the inhabitants into developing their own talents and inherent skills for the benefit of the entire community.

It was an exciting time in the Catholic Church, just after the Second Vatican Council, with plenty of changes taking place. The Church was now putting an emphasis on development, on justice and brotherly and sisterly love. Pope Paul VI produced the famous encyclical *Populorum progressio* – the development of peoples. He said development was another name for peace, and brought development onto the centre stage of Catholic thinking. He brought to the fore the holistic approach to human development. The pastor must involve himself in all aspects of people's welfare, with much emphasis on the poor, the outcasts and the oppressed. I was gradually linking up my development course with the modern teaching of the Church, which was now giving greater authority to the laity, establishing parochial councils which would take over more responsibility for religious affairs, and which would participate more in decision-making in the community. A revolution was taking place in the Church and in the community, with great potential. The wind of change was blowing. It was a truly exciting time in which to live. A later development of these changes was the creation of 'small Christian communities', which began to flourish in Africa, in the young churches.

I did my thesis on the subject of conflict and found it fascinating. I came to the conclusion that conflict is a very healthy and positive concept in any community. In fact, I suggested that if it does not exist it should be created. Of course I refer to creative conflict and positive criticism, leading to democratic decisions, resulting from active dialogue. A community without dialogue is virtually dead.

Leadership is absolutely necessary in an active community, to direct discussions, to stimulate interest, to instil motivation, and to carry out agreed plans. Some communities have natural leaders who, with some basic training, can do great work.

Youth leaders are invaluable in the development of the talents and skills of our young people in all fields, including the social and religious. Young people have a great deal to offer. They are generous and enthusiastic, as is shown by the thousands who volunteer their services in the most difficult and remote corners of the earth, serving the poor and the needy. I meet them in Calcutta, in refugee camps in Africa, and in our own streets in Ireland. We can all learn from them. The modern missionary in not necessarily dressed up in a religious habit, and is often not noticed in the slums of our cities, serving the poor and the oppressed. These young men and women deserve great praise.

Mother Teresa has put hundreds, even thousands, of young volunteers through her hands. She registers them in Calcutta, which entitles them to stay as long as they like in India, where the usual visa lasts only three months. She loves them and they love her, and no doubt learn from her.

Many will tell you that their time with Mother Teresa is the highlight of their lives. I have seen them at Mass at 6.30 a.m. in the motherhouse of the Missionaries of Charity in Lower Circular Road, Calcutta. Many have rediscovered their faith in the slums of Calcutta, or nursing a dying person in Kaligat Temple, run by Mother Teresa's Sisters, rather than listening to a sermon in church, however eloquent. The grace of God comes in mysterious and unexpected ways. Young people are not slow to see that religion is not just words and pious platitudes, but rather genuine action in helping a neighbour in need. St James put it bluntly:

> What does it profit, my brethren, if a man says he has faith but has not works? Can his faith save him? If a brother or sister is ill clad and in lack of daily food and one of you says to them 'Go in peace, be warmed and filled', without giving them the things needed for the body what does it profit? So faith by itself, if it has no works, is dead ... Show me your faith apart from your works and I, by my works, will show you my faith.
>
> *James 2:15-18*

I sometimes attend a youth Mass in St Kevin's, the crypt of the Pro-Cathedral in Dublin, at 8.00 on a Saturday night, where 200 to 300 young people form the congregation. It was started a good number of years ago by Father Martin Clarke, then diocesan youth leader in the city. The Mass is a very moving experience, the liturgy being arranged by the young people themselves. It is a folk Mass, with guitars and beautiful singing. It begins with five to ten minutes of meditation, with the congregation sitting mostly on the floor. The service lasts about one hour and fifteen minutes, sometimes more, with nobody in a hurry. It is a Taizé-type service, with Father Martin celebrating the Mass on a low table near the floor, and encouraging full participation of the congregation. A cup of tea is available afterwards, which gives an opportunity for people to talk and exchange views. Father Martin is very welcoming, and he is available after Mass for a chat or for confession. Many have rediscovered their faith here, others have returned to the sacraments after leaving the traditional Mass on Sundays. Many find Jesus Christ in one another.

Father Martin also leads retreats for the young in Glendalough, County Wicklow, in St Kevin's Retreat Centre, and he conducts pilgrimages inside and outside the country. I was introduced to St Kevin's Community by Patricia Bourke, who is deeply involved in youth work among the poor in Dublin. She also spent some time in Calcutta, working with Mother Teresa for the lepers and the children in her homes for the dying. Patricia loved it all. She is just one of many young people, full of drive and generosity, searching secretly for God in the poor and the forgotten. Patricia told me about some of her work. She visits elderly people living alone, often in untidy and poor conditions. She chats with them, asks if they need something, gets whatever it may be, and leaves it at that. She does not clean the house if she isn't asked to, for fear of destroying the friendship. She sees the person rather than the broken furniture or the untidy house. We can learn from Patricia. We can hurt people and wound their pride by fussing about. Mother Teresa often speaks of the poor in the West who experience loneliness and isolation. It is more difficult to cure than the poverty of the developing world. Human contact, with love and kindness, is superior to all the grandeur of this world.

CHAPTER 12

FAMINE IN ETHIOPIA

I spent an invaluable year at Swansea University. My brother Mike had settled in Calcutta and was working with the five million East Bengali refugees in Salt Lake camp, while their country fought for its independence. Mike was happy there in the midst of that enormous disaster. After independence was granted to Bangladesh, he moved with the refugees into Dacca, as a worker with Concern.

In January 1972 I was assigned to Ethiopia, one of the poorest countries in the world. It had a per capita income of $150 per annum, as compared with about $20,000 per annum in the US. Nevertheless, we are speaking of a country that is rich in ancient history, with origins possibly older than Egypt's and biblical references to it as far back as 1000 BC.

As Abyssinia, it came to prominence in the West in 1936, when, under Italian occupation, it had a few years of chequered history. It was taken over by the British in 1941, and eventually united – a euphemistic expression in this instance – in 1962 with Eritrea under Emperor Haile Selassie I, King of Kings and Lion of Judah. It came to the attention of the world in 1970-72 after two years of horrendous drought and inter-tribal war, which led to a most critical situation.

Ethiopia is a vast country, more than fifteen times the size of Ireland and consisting mainly of a high plateau with precipitous edges. There is a great rift valley holding a chain of lakes, famous hot springs and plentiful supplies of mineral water. In places the mountains yield to desert, and although there are three river basins, the most famous being the source of the Blue Nile, only this latter reaches the sea.

Climatically it is a country of anomalies. Although situated in the tropics Addis Ababa is over eight thousand feet above sea level, and the climate is cool and bracing, whereas the valleys are intolerably hot and malaria-ridden. Over the years 1972-74 the rainfall had been almost nil, causing terrible drought.

Europeans of the Middle Ages regarded Ethiopia as a land of mystery, and it has remained so up to recent years. Many a young reader viewed it with wild surmise on reading the story of Prester John, or speculated on the romance between King Solomon and the Queen of Sheba. And what young student has not pondered on the fate of Sen, Cham and Japhet as they left Noah's Ark? I marvelled too, in 1972, at the mixture of ethnic groups parading before me.

Ethnologists believe that the early inhabitants of Ethiopia were descended from two sons of Noah, and from these again were descended the Amharas and the Hamites. The official language is Amharic, with English, Italian and French also in use. Early Egyptian writings show that there was trade between Ethiopia and Egypt as far back as 3000-4000 BC, and it is equally certain that there was considerable contact between Jews and Ethiopians. Who could have believed the Israeli airlift of the Falashas, the Ethiopian Jews, who had preserved their cultural and religious inheritance throughout the centuries?

The influence of Judaism is still seen in Ethiopian church architecture. There is the innermost sanctuary for the Ark, to which only priests and deacons are admitted. There is segregation of men and women, and there is the same emphasis on music as when David danced before the Ark.

Mohammed was born in 570 AD and during his lifetime the Islamic religion spread from Mecca across the Red Sea. Though subsequently Christians and Moslems have lived together in peace and freedom of worship there have been many dark periods. The armies of Islam overran Egypt in 640 AD and though the Coptic Church was there, they managed to survive. For a thousand years the Coptic Church existed in isolation.

The historian Rufinus tells us of the beginnings of Christianity in Ethiopia. Two sailors in the Roman merchant fleet, Frumentius and Aedisius, were abducted and taken to the court of King Ella at Axum. As Christians they became very influential and began to form small prayer communes. When King Ella died, his heir, Ezara, became a Christian (probably in 323 AD) and Christianity permeated every facet of life. Even the coins were minted with the Sign of the Cross. Eventually Frumentius and Aedisius were ordained bishops and they are still revered by the Ethiopian Orthodox Church.

There were difficulties, of course, between Rome and the

Ethiopian Christian Church because it was so closely identified with the Egyptian Coptic Church. The chief bone of contention was the dual nature of Christ. However, the contribution of the Ethiopian Christians to the religious and cultural heritage of the world is becoming increasingly known and appreciated.

Fasts and feasts

Fasts and feasts both feature prominently in the Ethiopian Church calendar. I have had the experience of travelling through the country during Lent and being unable to get meat in a Christian area. We had to drive on into a Muslim town. On the other hand, feasts are celebrated on a colossal scale. Mescal (which means Cross) has been celebrated for 1,900 years in Ethiopia and commemorates the finding of the true Cross by the Empress Helena, mother of Constantine the Great. In Ethiopia it is celebrated in September, thus incorporating the ancient pagan festival of the Spring Rites.

In Addis Ababa on Mescal Eve, 26 September, there is a huge procession of priests, students, brass bands and armed forces carrying flaming torches, and floats with huge lighted crosses. Thousands gather, singing 'O, My flower Meskal has dawned', and a giant fire burns all night. The next day is a public holiday and strangers are invited into every house to partake of Tella and local beer.

Timket, the Epiphany, is the greatest festival and goes on for three days. It is preceded by dramatic and colourful processions. A night of prayer and fasting follows, culminating the next day in the commemoration of Christ's baptism in the Jordan, and, finally, on the third day, the Feast of St Michael the Archangel, Ethiopia's most popular saint, is celebrated. Special food is prepared, gifts are given to the children. If new clothes are not available, old ones are laundered to a dazzling white. There are many customs – the Old Testament tablets, symbolising the Ark of the Covenant, and the two tablets of Mount Sinai, are blessed and reconsecrated. All this is accompanied by great ceremonial processions, ringing of bells, blowing of trumpets and burning of incense.

Lalibella is the ideal spot to experience the true spirit of Ethiopian Christianity, the best time being the eve of any of the great feasts. A few steps down from ground level takes one into the rock-hewn church, and another world. The ceremonial has not changed for a thousand years. The light is dim, and one hears first the drum, the trumpet and the jingling of brass bells. The air is heavy with incense, but eventually the priest can be discerned, richly-clad in ancient vestments. The people, in lines, slowly gyrate to the rhythm of the music, so slowly that the movement is almost inperceptible. This continues during the night, and the isolation from the world and the experience of something so spiritual, so traditional, has a purifying effect on the observer.

It is not only such festivals which set the Ethiopians apart from the Western world, but the fact that they have adhered to the ancient calendar of Pharaonic Egypt. When Pope Gregory reformed the Julian calendar in 1582, giving us the form we now follow, the Ethiopians continued as before. They have twelve months of thirty days and one month of five days or six in a leap year. Their famous tourist slogan runs 'Come to Ethiopia for thirteen months of sunshine'. I have been able to celebrate two Christmas Days, two Easters and two Pentecosts.

The arrival of missionaries

When famine hit Ethiopia in 1972/3 there was a great convergence of missionaries to assist the country in the disaster. These included the Holy Ghost Fathers, the Franciscan Missionaries for Africa from Dundalk, the Good Shepherd Sisters, the Holy Rosary Sisters, Concern from Ireland, and, much later, Goal.

In 1972 a group of Holy Ghost Fathers was appointed to Ethiopia, to the province of Goma Goffa. Father Harry Mullan was accompanied by Brother Gus O'Keeffe. Later Father Gannon, a very experienced missionary, went there from Kenya. They began by assessing the situation of the Roman Catholic Church and the Ethiopian Orthodox Church, and, in a spirit of ecumenism, they started to build up a close relationship with this ancient Christian tradition. The Orthodox were not in communion with Rome, but there had been no formal separation or accusation of heresy.

The Holy Ghost Fathers began to work very closely with the Orthodox personnel, using the same structures, assisting them even in the training of their clergy, thus helping to revitalise the Christian communities. Our missionaries put their resources at the service of the entire local community in order to create a better way of life, socially, morally and spiritually. One such mission I witnessed was for mother-and-child care in Chencha under the direction of Father Owen Lambert. Chencha is situated at an altitude of nine to ten thousand feet above sea level. The terrifying approach was like the ascent to Croagh Patrick. The people were small farmers with an average of two acres of land, and those who were landless had to depend on crafts such as weaving, ironwork, woodcarving and leatherwork. The mission fosters three main programmes: Community Development, Health and Social Welfare, and Ecumenism. Father Lambert has spearheaded the improvement of relationships with the Orthodox Church by the creation of a seminary for their clergy. Father Emmanuel Fritz, a Spiritan from the French Province, speaks the local language fluently, and is very close to the Orthodox way of thinking and, consequently, to the Orthodox Church. Fathers Martin Kelly, Pawdy Kelly and Brian O'Toole arrived later, but all shared the same vision of working with the Orthodox Church rather than building the Roman Catholic Church. The ultimate aim was unity.

Father Brian O'Toole has done remarkable work with the Hammer tribe in a remote area about 155 miles south of Gomma Goffa, near the Kenyan border. He has become totally integrated in the tribe, speaks their language fluently and has produced its first grammar and dictionary. He is a wonderful missionary who identifies completely with the people.

Father Owen Lambert has forged a link between Ireland and Ethiopia, through an organisation he set up in Hacketstown, County Carlow, called 'Self Help'. The organisation, well known among the farming community of Ireland, promotes self-help by the Ethiopians as a means of improving their situation. The farmers have been supporting a 'Grow Fund' for the planting of trees and general agricultural development in Ethiopia, including the very successful growing of potatoes.

The communist takeover

The 1962 Unification of Abyssinia and Eritrea under the leadership of Haile Selassie had never been a happy one and, as in all countries where there is a vast gap between the 'haves' and the 'have nots', the country was ripe for communism. I had a chance to study communism for eight years in Ethiopia. It started almost simultaneously with the famine, which aggravated the escalating tension in the country. It started in a small way – a strike by the taxi drivers. The emperor ordered the military to crush the strike, but for the first time in history they refused. A body of people was becoming disenchanted with the emperor. The communists took courage and worked closely with the military to overthrow the emperor.

Eventually the military took over, and Amman Amdom from Eritrea took control. There was an opportunity for uniting the country under him. However, the radicals were not happy with him and one evening his house was surrounded and he was asked to surrender. He refused and was killed in the ensuing battle. Fifty-nine others, including ministers and educated people, who were considered dangerous to the government, were shot and buried in a mass grave.

Communism is designed to have a strong public appeal for the lower and middle classes, who are led to believe that the future holds more for them than the past. The people were told that the vast wealth of the emperor would be turned over to the masses. The carrot was swallowed by most of them, and they willingly cooperated with the new government. The old government was toppled, the rich were dispossessed, the educated were liquidated. The Churches were weakened by the confiscation of property, and Church attendance was discouraged by the slogan 'Religion is the opium of the people'. Communes were formed from neighbourhoods bundled together, each kebele or commune being set up to increase control over the entire people.

All houses were searched for arms and offensive weapons, and all rented houses were nationalised. At 6.45 one morning, about ten men knocked on our door saying they wanted to search the property. I invited them in, armed as they were, and asked them to search every corner of the house, room by room. I insisted that they open every drawer or box, and in this way I embarrassed them into leaving the house in a short time.

The land was nationalised and divided into communal farms. The kebeles were indoctrinated by force in the principles of communism. Meetings were called and the people were harangued and threatened for five hours at a time. During these lengthy sessions those attending were told that if any one of them had said or done anything against the government they should confess and they would be pardoned. The leader would present a list to the crowd and say that some of their names were on it, and if they did not confess they would be imprisoned.

The people's minds were in turmoil. Towards the end of the meeting a number of people would come forward and confess, then more would follow suit out of fear. At the end of the meeting those who confessed would be taken away for training in the doctrines of communism. In this way the officials were successful in dividing the people – father against son, mother against daughter, etc. Even in schools children would report other children if they said anything against the government – some as a vendetta, to settle old scores. This mental torture was a dreadful thing. It was called 'white terror'.

Disillusionment and frustration led to an underground movement being started, as the eyes of the peasants were opened to the gloomy reality of what was happening around them. This underground movement began in 1977 in Addis Ababa, but was quickly crushed by the 'Red Terror'.

'Red Terror' refers to a ruthless method of stopping all opposition in a very effective way. The government would collect twenty youths at random in the streets at sundown, take them to vantage points in the city, and shoot five at a time, leaving the bodies at roundabouts, on public squares, and in front of prominent buildings like the municipality or university. On their backs they would attach stickers with slogans like 'I deserved what I got for opposing the government'. The boys they killed in this way were innocent youngsters, mostly students going home from night school. Next morning the people would find the bodies on the streets. At about 10.00 a.m. the army would collect the bodies and dump them in the mortuaries of the hospitals. The parents would go from one hospital to another until they found their children. They would then have to pay to get the body back, and they were warned not to mourn them – their children were traitors. Mourning is sacred for the Ethiopians and the tradition is to wear black during the period of mourning. They defied the government by wearing black, and in fact it became so common that black was said to be the national colour. It was a shattering and frightening period for everyone.

Communism is based on fear, fraud and force, on deception, division and destruction. On the other hand, we cannot condone the evils of capitalism. What we need is a middle course where the rights of people are respected, where freedom of speech and religion is practised, and where people can live in peace and prosperity. The state is created for the people, but with communism, the people are for the state. 'Man is born free, but everywhere he is in chains.' Under communism, the press is strictly controlled, and journalists are screened and shadowed. Silence, secrecy and security are more important than frankness and openess.

The new head of state, Mengistu Haile Mariam, was an extreme autocrat, ruthless in his methods. Communism took a firm hold on the country. A Red Square was erected, much of the property of St Joseph's Catholic School being confiscated to extend it. Regular political rallies were held – the people were ordered to attend on pain of losing their rations in the kebeles.

Many shopkeepers were shot by over-zealous communists for hoarding food supplies. Property was confiscated by the government and the emperor was denounced for his great wealth. It is said the Mengistu Haile Mariam suffocated the emperor on his sick-bed. The princesses were put in prison.

It was a dreadful upheaval and the people were forced to accept a system which they hated. Atrocities were commonplace, as the population were cowed into submission. The Orthodox Church suffered greatly, and much of its property was confiscated. It is not known how many people were murdered. About two hundred thousand died of starvation in the two provinces of Wollo and Tigre.

The size of the army was increased dramatically and the commune system was used in the recruitment. Each kebele had to provide so many young men. Bribery was a common method of escaping recruitment, so the poorer people were badly hit.

Resettlement became a useful instrument for weakening the population. It divided tribes, spread suspicion and dissipated liberation movements. People were forced to move from one area to another under the pretext of unequal ratio of population, or from one marginalised agricultural area to another more fertile area. As a result, families were divided, old people abandoned, and orphans artificially created.

The settlements were state collective farms. Villagisation was another strategy of social control. Country people were forced to abandon their traditional homes and had to live together in villages, where they were promised good schools and medical facilities, together with better living conditions. This was meant to reduce the people's strength, independence and power of resistance, to uproot, control and scatter them.

The famine of 1972/3

Four hundred years ago the agricultural potential of the country was so vast that the people in the countryside openly boasted to travellers that even in years of poor harvests, they reaped sufficient food to last for three years. Nevertheless, Ethiopia suffered more than twenty-three major famines over the period of 260 years between 1540 and 1800. The greatest natural disaster in its history was the famine of 1888-92.

There was a serious student demonstration in Addis Ababa in Easter 1973, during which its leaders openly stated that the Government was trying to cover up not only the effects of the current drought and famine, but even the existence of any sort of famine in Wollo and Tigre, as well as in southern Shoa. It was obvious that the government would have to take more positive action than had heretofore been initiated. The Ministry of Social Welfare asked me what the Catholic Church could do for the stricken people of the provinces of Wollo and Tigre. This was the peculiar situation in which I found myself in 1972, when I was appointed to Ethiopia. I was first assigned to the Diocese of Jimma, under the able leadership of Mgr Herman Teuben, a Vincentian priest and vicar general of the diocese, an accomplished administrator. He was a powerful man, well versed in the culture and traditions of the country. He helped me to get established before I took on the Welfare Desk of the Ethiopian Catholic Secretariat. Mgr Herman was perhaps misunderstood, even by myself. He sometimes gave the appearance of being strict, but he was in reality kind and gentle. He refused to become a bishop, claiming that an Ethiopian should be consecrated to the position. He was a plain, blunt man who loved the people. I may have wronged him a number of times, but we remained good friends up to the time he left Ethiopia. I visited him several times in Holland, when he joined CEBEMO, where he was greatly respected for his in-depth knowledge of Ethiopia. He helped me to make contact with Dutch development agencies. He passed away to the Lord while still a young man. May he rest in peace.

In the Catholic Secretariat I took over the Welfare Desk from Brother Michael, a Christan Brother from the US. Abba Stephanus Tedla, a very clever, hard-working Ethiopian, became secretary general. He suffered from the chaos and confusion brought about by the communist takeover, but he kept a brave heart in the midst of the confusion. He was a good and very efficient leader, and we worked closely together.

Archbishop Paulus Tzadua succeeded Archbishop Asrat Marian as Archbishop of Addis Ababa. He was very clever, and had studied law in Rome. He was an able leader, kind and helpful to everyone. He too had seen the disintegration of his country under communist rule, and a dreadful drought which claimed the lives of millions over the years. He made great efforts to establish a local, native clergy, to replace the ever-diminishing missionaries. Mgr Paulus was a quiet man, who generally kept out of the limelight. I had occasional disagreements with him, but by and large we got on well. I found him very approachable and very helpful.

The coming of the Good Shepherd Sisters was an important event. A superior from Rome approached me to ask if there was need for her congregation in Ethiopia. I pointed out to her that there were an estimated eighty thousand street girls and prostitutes in the streets of Addis Ababa, and I begged her to send Sisters who specialised in this form of apostolate. Soon Sisters Margaret Doyle, Mary Ryan and Evelyn Fergus arrived with a few others and set up workshops for the street girls, teaching them sowing, needlework, carpet making, etc. Gradually they got many of them off the streets, where they did not want to be anyway. Ato Berhe Beyenne and I helped the Sisters to set up the programme.

The Franciscan Sisters for Africa came to Addis Ababa in 1973, by a strange intervention of God. A plane crashed in Addis Ababa, in which the superior general, Mother Benedict Cahill, died. Two Sisters travelled from Uganda to bring her remains back to Uganda. The Sisters saw Mother Benedict's death as a sign from God that they should help in the famine in Ethiopia. Sisters Eugene Connell and Jeanette Watters arrived soon afterwards, and I walked the

The family together – a rare occasion.
Front row: Mike, Jack, Des, Back row: Kevin, Maury, Tom, Joe.

Fr Kevin Doheny inspecting the identity tags on children in preparation for their departure for San Tome, during the Biafran war.

Seeing starvation in Biafra for the first time – 'it was shattering'.

A painting of Leonard Cheshire – completely true to life.
(Portrait by June Mendoza)

Fr Kevin with Lady Ryder of Warsaw

Biafran refugees, forced on to the roads, flee to safety from the fighting. (1968)

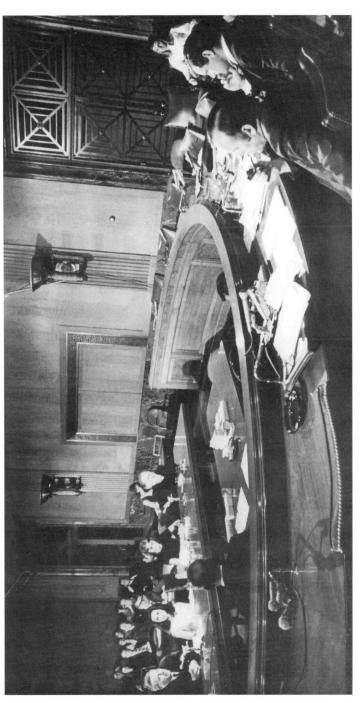

Giving evidence on the Biafran needs before the Senate Sub-committee on Refugees: In the foreground: Senators Goodall and Edward Kennedy. In the background: Fr Kevin Doheny; Princess Cécile de Bourbon Parme; Dr D. Coady; Fr Mike Doheny.

Leonard Cheshire speaking with Father Kevin outside the London H.Q. of the Cheshire Foundation, after a planning session on the Cheshire Homes of Africa.

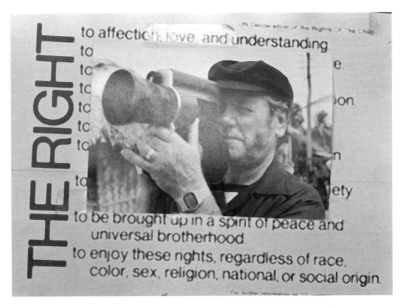

Father Mike Doheny, making a film on 'the rights of the child'.

Father Mike Doheny, in Salt Lake Refugee Camp, in Calcutta, India.

Mother Teresa, a woman for all times and seasons

Father Kevin and Mother Teresa reporting to Pope John Paul after returning from Iraq.

*Father Norman Fitzgerald, Executive Director, organises a
Plane Push for refugees.*

Mrs Imelda Connelly, Refugee Trust Chairperson, Kilkenny, receives the Bene Merenti Award from Bishop Laurence Forristal, on 3 November 1995.

Bishop John Magee, Bishop of Cloyne, confers on Mrs Josephine O'Connor,
Mitchelstown, Co. Cork, the highest Vatican Award, the Bene Merenti Award, for her
work with refugees and the poor since the Biafran War (1967-70).
The presentation took place in December 1995.

Refugee Trust Board members and some staff members with the President:
Front row from right:Fr K. Doheny; Miss B. McKenna; President Mary Robinson; Fr N. Fitzgerald; Hervé de Wergifosse. Back row: Mr J. Dooge;
Mrs. L. Stynes; Dr J. Barnes; Mrs. E. Pearce; Mr G. Dunnion; Mr J. Bradley.

Father Kevin with Gene Dewey in Washington.

Frederick Forsyth and Kevin Doheny in London.

Brother Thomas O' Grady with a displaced Bosnian boy.

Father Norman Fitzgerald CSSp, Executive Director of Refugee Trust.
As pastor of his refugee flock, saying Mass in a refugee camp in Rwanda.

Over-crowded church in Kigale after the civil war. (1994)

Mother Teresa speaking with Fr Kevin Doheny and John Whalley.

streets of Addis Ababa, looking for a house to rent for them. Sister Eugene was a doctor, Sister Jeanette a radiographer, and they took up work in a local hospital with Sister Nelezina, a laboratory technician. Later, other sisters, including Sisters Lena and Francis, went to Goma Goffa and worked with the Holy Ghost Fathers, teaching in the local school and doing medical work.

The Holy Rosary Sisters, led by Sister Helen King, who had done such great work in Biafra, also responded to the famine. Sister Helen took over the clinic in Metcha and was joined by Sister Marie Teehan. The mission was run by Father Matthew Von Enckevort, who built a beautiful church. Sister Margaret Ledwith used her influence to send many sisters to help. It was hard work, especially during the revolution and communist takeover, but the sisters were equal to the challenge.

Sister Mary Dixon was the first Irish Sister I met in St Mary's School for Girls in Addis Ababa when I landed there in January 1972. It was wonderful to meet such a helpful person, just as I was embarking on a strange and new mission. She later went to Makele, where she did heroic work with the displaced people in the Tigre Province.

CHAPTER 13

THE CHRISTIAN RELIEF AND DEVELOPMENT ASSOCIATION

The poverty of the people increased as we battled to help them. I was asked by two government officials, Ato Desta Girma and Ato Kassa Kebede, what the Catholic Church could do for the victims of the famine, which was raging in the Provinces of Wollo and Tigre. I assured them that the Catholic Church would play its part, and that I would immediately make an appeal for funds in Europe, but I insisted that all the Churches should be involved. I suggested they call a meeting of the Churches and discuss it openly. This had not occurred to them, as famine had not been mentioned up to this time, for political reasons. They asked me to call the meeting of the Churches and get them involved. I refused, and explained that if I, as a Catholic priest, called a meeting, no one would attend – the Churches were isolated from one another, each living in its own cocoon, not telling each other what they were doing. So I suggested that the Minister of Social Welfare, Ato Mulato Debebe, should call the meeting and the Churches would attend, out of politeness if for no other reason. I would help them and supply addresses.

The plan worked. The meeting was called for 14 May 1973 at 11.00 a.m. in the Minister's office. It was a memorable and historic meeting, the first of its kind in Ethiopia. It was not before its time. In fact, time was running out and fast. Our first meeting was chaired by the minister himself, and representatives of about twenty Churches were present. It was a delicate meeting.

The minister gave us a run-down on the cause, nature and extent of the famine and he asked the Churches to contribute to the relief of the affected population. The minister outlined for the first time the seriousness of the situation and the inability of the government to come to grips with the famine. An emergency Relief Committee was set up consisting of nine ministries with sub-committees, to control the distribution of food aid, to receive and coordinate donations, and to plan for the immediate future and for short- and long-term assistance.

I asked if the Churches could meet to discuss the situation

among themselves. It was a daring question in the context of Ethiopia at that time. The minister expected the Churches to make large financial contributions to the government, but that was not what I had in mind. After coming from Biafra I was very conscious of the famine and how the Churches working together could help to meet the needs of the people. The minister paused for a long time, but eventually agreed to my proposal.

The minister told the meeting that some 700,000 people were in dire distress, though a previous commission had put the figure at only 300,000. Immediate supplies of grain, powdered milk and baby food were required urgently. Cattle had been dying in their thousands. He said that he hoped to obtain 20,000 tons of food from USAID and asked the Churches to help.

Immediately after the meeting I asked the heads of the Churches to meet to discuss the emergency. They were on the point of dispersing. Reluctantly they agreed. I asked where we should meet. This was an important question, as there had been no contact between the Churches up to this point. One tall Ethiopian, Ato Berhe Beyenne, from the Church of Mekane Yesus (an Ethiopian equivalent of the Lutheran Church) spoke up, offering his board room for the meeting. Nobody reacted until I said I would be there. The Churches were not ready to meet one another. I suggested a meeting at 10.00 a.m. the following Saturday and it was reluctantly agreed to.

The second meeting, on 17 May 1973 in the LCMY boardroom, proved to be a success. We had made a major and historic breakthrough. The meeting was attended by about twelve Churches. I invited Ato Berhe Beyenne to take the Chair. He graciously accepted, and took out his big Arusha pipe and lit up. He opened the meeting with a prayer and said, 'We have gathered to discuss the famine, and we have one thing in common – only one.' There was a long pause as he puffed his pipe. He continued, 'All of you in this room are inhaling the smoke from my pipe. We have nothing else in common.' This comment relieved the tension in the room.

It was true. The Churches had nothing in common – they did not know each other or want to share and there was no trust beween them.

The meeting made a number of significant resolutions:

- To visit the famine area together to assess the situation and to make an evaluation of the extent of the disaster.
- To meet regularly on the first Monday of each month to discuss the situation, to share information and to start working together.
- To open a bank account and to appeal for assistance to our European counterparts. Berhe Beyenne and I pooled the money we had in our pockets to open the bank account after the meeting.
- To call our new organisation the 'Christian Relief Association', which was later changed to the Christian Relief and Development Association (CRDA).
- To avoid interference with anyone's religion or already existing projects, and to support all Churches or NGOs who were assisting the poor, especially in the famine areas.

One Church member read a prepared written statement saying that he wanted it to be clearly understood that his Church was not prepared to participate officially in the meeting, but if there was food or money to be distributed, his members would be prepared to assist.

In the event, the only Churches to visit the famine area were the Lutheran Church of Mekane Yesus and the Catholic Church. It was on this trip that I first met Brian Neldner of the Lutheran World Federation, based in Geneva. As we moved along through the villages we became close friends, and by the end of the trip we had shared all our information and plans for helping each other and working together for the good of the people. Sister Juta and I represented the Catholic Church on this memorable trip.

CRDA grew very slowly. Oxfam was the first to subscribe to it financially through the good offices of Toby Gooch, the East Africa field director, who gave £1000. CRDA grew from a felt need. It took the poor to bring us together, and to knock sense into us. For me, it was an outgrowth of the Biafran war. I would not have got the idea were it not for Biafra. CRDA eventually grew from half a dozen Churches to 105 Churches and NGOs in the space of the next twenty years. Brian Pearce, a Concern volunteer, became the first co-ordinator, and he and his deeply committed wife, Eilish, built it up gradually.

Brian was a born diplomat, a patient man who could get around any difficulty. He was succeeded by Brother Gus O'Keeffe, who has become a legend in the organisation, with a fleet of sixty trucks on the road bringing food to all the stricken parts of the country. He made CRDA into a huge efficient organisation – an unqualified ecumenical success. Brother Gus is accessible to everyone, of whatever religious or cultural grouping. His stamp is indelibly imprinted on CRDA. His opinion is universally accepted, and he is visited by politicians and directors of international bodies from all over the world. It could be said that Brother Gus *is* CRDA.

CRDA has a well-thought-out constitution which regulates its relations with the Ethiopian government and its member organisations. The organisation's smooth and effective running has won worldwide recognition.

The *Spiritan Newsletter* of February 1985 had this to say:

> In connection with the way CRDA works it may be worthwhile to mention how it deals with problems familiar to all aid agencies – administration expenses.
>
> This is funded partly by member organisations themselves and partly by international organisations. This means that when funds are forwarded to CRDA with the proviso that they be spent directly on alleviating hunger and not on administration, CRDA is in a position to give the necessary guarantees. It has a high reputation for efficiency, honesty and good management.

The Politics of Starvation, written in 1995 by Jack Shepherd, with an Afterword by Stephen J. Green, paid tribute to the Christian Relief Fund (CRF):

> As the peasants continued shuffling into the market towns, the Church and Mission agencies stepped up their feeding programmes. On May 19, 1973 twenty religious leaders – no one, however, joining them from the powerful Orthodox Church – met in Addis Ababa to discuss their particular contribution. They agreed to mount their own programmes, coordinated with the Government programme and supplementary to it. These

Protestant and Catholic Churchmen – Ethiopian and foreigners – set up the Christian Relief Fund (CRF) with an Irish priest, Father Kevin Doheny, as Chairman. This small group, working with various missionaries and volunteers, provided the first substantial aid to the famine victims. In the next seven months, these dedicated Churchmen would give more medical and food aid to starving and sick Ethiopians than all the international agencies and donor nations combined.

The Christian Relief Fund made contact with funding agencies overseas and started sending whatever aid it could to the provinces. The relief workers plunged in. CRF kept detailed minutes of its weekly meetings in Addis, in effect compiling a history of the famine. Reading these, especially 'Reports from the field', conveys the grim sense of spreading disaster. The first group of relief workers, for example, arriving at the market town of Kobbo, found thousands starving. There were no cooking utensils to feed the large numbers of people, so the workers cut water barrels in two, and the hungry held pieces of torn plastic sheeting in their hands to receive the hot food.

20 June 1973 – Report from the field
Merca: 30 kms south of Weldia. The situation is very serious. People were seen dying of starvation.
Sheket: It is very difficult to purchase foodstuffs in Asmara for Sheket. 200 quintels purchased by Seventh Day Adventists at 21 dollars per quintel, but the price is gradually rising up to 26 dollars per quintel in a short time...

25 June 1973 – Report from the field
Makele: Father Kevin Doheny reports that 800 famine victims are in camp in Makele and more arriving every day. They get two meals of injera and wat per day. Gross overcrowding... Many TB cases – Skin sores resultant from lack of water. All are malnourished... last week five children died... The overall picture is gloomy.

Father Kevin O'Mahony quips: 'Our immediate worry is not faith and revelation but faffa and water.'

Alamata had 8,000 refugees, and ten per day died of starvation. Sister Helen, working in Tigre, reports to CRF: 'The people will continue to come, some days up to 30 in number. Each new group seem to be more ragged, tired and sick than the former. There are more than 250 elderly women and children living out of doors.'

Father Doheny started packing the trunks of cars heading north from Addis, with drugs and medicines for the relief camps springing up along the Addis-Asmara highway.

This is how CRDA operated, collecting information about the famine from missionaries and relief workers all over Ethiopia. In this way they made a huge impact. Their information went to embassies, who promptly sent them to their governments, who quickly moved into the relief activities.

The Churches sent the minutes to their respective headquarters overseas, who came up with tremendous support. Camera crews arrived from Europe and the US and the news spread like wildfire. Mike Doheny was one of the first to bring films of the growing tragedy to London, which sparked off Band Aid and similar international movements to raise funds for the starving in Ethiopia.

The famine reached the city of Addis Ababa, where thousands had come from drought-stricken areas in search of food. One of the most famous journalists to visit the scene was Jonathan Dimbleby. When he arrived I told him where to go, who to meet, and how to get the story out to the world. He made his way to Dessie, the centre of the famine, and met my friends the Capuchin Fathers, who brought him into the camps and showed him the real suffering. He was apprehensive about getting his film out to London, as he feared it would be confiscated, so he sent his researcher, Peter Bluff, home with empty reels. When Peter got through, Jonathan left with the real film. He broke the news to the world and was responsible for an avalanche of assistance. When the Communist Revolutionary Council saw the film, they used it to discredit the emperor and the former capitalist government, blaming him for the famine. They mixed it into an Ethiopian film of the emperor, showing his lavish lifestyle, his banquets, and even his expensive dogs, some of which were buried in a special graveyard with headstones over them. Jonathan Dimbleby became a national hero.

Jonathan returned to Ethiopia some time later and witnessed the massacres in the streets, and some of the other ruthless methods of the communists. His second film showed a different picture, this time of atrocities against the civilian population. For this exposure he became a prohibited immigrant, and remained so for some years, although he was eventually allowed back. Jonathan was a genuinely professional journalist who revealed what he saw, regardless of the consequences.

Liam Nolan came out on behalf of Radio Éireann. I met him in Kobbo in Wollo Province, north of Dessie. He made a wonderful forty-five minute programme and collected a lot of money for the famine victims. Liam had a great feeling for the people which was reflected in his programme and his writing. He wrote a book about his experience called *The Forgotten Famine*.

The information on the famine emanated largely from CRDA. There were several reasons for CRDA's success in Ethiopia.

- CRDA started out of a disaster. It was born out of a desperate need. It takes disasters to unite us and to put sense into our heads. I had seen too much 'flag flying' in Biafra. Agencies had everything marked with their name and logo to impress the people whom they were feeding.
- CRDA was a natural growth from inside Ethiopia. It was not superimposed from outside.
- CRDA was led by enlightened local leaders. I give great credit to Berhe Beyenne, our first chairman. He had great natural qualities of leadership, with his dignified and impressive figure, his expert knowledge of the local situation, his knowledge of the Orthodox Church which he loved, his quick sense of humour, and his ability to control a meeting. Berhe Beyenne set a high tone. He laid down a very important principle from the beginning. 'Let theologians argue about the faith as much as they want in Geneva, Rome, London and wherever,' he said, 'and let us get on with the work of helping the poor.' We never mixed

practical Christianity with theology. If we had, we would have split CRDA.

- CRDA picked an excellent staff, led by Brian Pearce and provided by Raymond Kennedy of Concern. Brian was a man of infinite patience, cool as they make them, solid as the rock of Gibraltar, with previous experience in Ethiopia, in Tigre Province in fact, the centre of the drought and famine. Brian was an excellent and natural public relations officer, so necessary in dealing with the demands of government, while at the same time pleasing a committee of such divergent interests. His wife Eilish played a prominent role in building up this reputable organisation.

- CRDA had a wealth of experience of divergent disciplines. I had learnt a great deal in Biafra, while others had gained valuable experience elsewhere.

- CRDA was strongly supported from Europe, morally and financially, without interference. It was extremely useful for representatives of agencies to attend CRDA meetings, meet its leaders informally and get a good picture of the disasters from all over the country.

- The decision to meet the first Monday of each month was a great move. It meant that agencies from overseas could plan their visits to coincide with the meetings and local participants could combine their shopping expeditions to the capital with attendance at the meetings.

- CRDA accumulated a vast amount of 'on the spot' reports, giving the true picture of the famine. These reports were sent all over Europe and had an enormous impact. It gave a very high profile to CRDA, adding to its integrity, and credibility.

- CRDA meetings attracted government representatives, embassies, United Nations agencies such as ILO, and all the non-governmental agencies and Churches. All added a new enrichment and experience to the reports and findings. It was the only consistent reporting of the famine.

- CRDA quickly saw the gaps in the service to the poor and displaced and started to place teams in those gaps. There was no Church or agency in Kobbo, Wollo, and so the Catholic Church moved in with a team of Franciscans and some lay volunteers. They started a feeding programme for 120 children three times per day. Alitena in Tigre Province was particularly bad, and the Catholic Church strengthened its already existing team there.

CHAPTER 14

MOTHER TERESA COMES TO ETHIOPIA

While in Ethiopia I received a telegram from the regional director of Catholic Relief Services in Rome, Mgr Joseph Harnett, asking me to meet Mother Teresa one Saturday morning. She was not as well known then as she is today. I was at the airport when this tiny little woman arrived with a few cardboard cartons of medicines, accompanied by Sister Frederick. I brought them to the archbishop who received them most graciously.

When Mother Teresa told the archbishop she had come to respond to the famine, and wanted to bring her Sisters, he said she had come at the wrong time. Since her Sisters did not have any qualifications, she would have to see the emperor to get visas and work permits. This was impossible at the moment because the emperor was celebrating his eightieth birthday, and his forty-third year on the throne of Ethiopia. He was receiving two heads of state, Archbishop Makarios of Cyprus and President Senegar of Senegal.

Mother Teresa thanked the archbishop and went to the Nativity Convent where she was staying for the three days of her visit. I went to my office, and an unusual thing happened. Princess Seble Desta telephoned me for some information about the Cheshire Home in which she was involved. I took the opportunity to tell her about Mother Teresa. I sensed that she had not heard of her before. I said she would very much like to see the Princess, and also if possible her mother, Princess Tenanyework, who was the daughter of the Emperor.

Princess Seble Desta explained how they were all so busy, and it would be very difficult. On Saturday afternoon I was at my desk when the phone rang and it was Princess Seble Desta saying that Mother Teresa should come to see her on Sunday afternoon at 4.00. We went and met both Princess Seble Desta and Princess Tenanyework.

Mother Teresa explained the nature of her mission, which was of great interest to them. When she asked if she could see the Emperor, she was told it would be impossible in view of all the celebrations, and in fact the Emperor would not even be in Addis

Ababa on Monday. They suggested that she should write to him, explaining her ideas. The princesses invited Mother Teresa to say a prayer.

We returned to the convent and Mother Teresa wrote a simple letter to the Emperor explaining her anxiety to help in the famine. I returned to the palace to deliver the letter in person. Mother Teresa also sent the Emperor a copy of *Something Beautiful for God*, by Malcolm Muggeridge, an account of her work.

On Monday morning I received a call from Princess Seble Desta. She informed me that Mother Teresa could see the Emperor at 6.00 p.m. on Monday and we should be at her office at 5.00 p.m. where we would be provided with a car to bring us to the Jubilee Palace. When we arrived at the palace in a very large state car we were shown into a large parlour, where the ADC to the Emperor questioned us rather aggressively on what we were doing in Ethiopia. I told him that I was working with the handicapped in the Cheshire Homes. The Cheshire Foundation was well known in Ethiopia and the princesses were involved in it. It was therefore a good card to play.

He then asked Mother Teresa to explain her mission. She said she had heard of the famine and would like to help, and to bring in some Sisters to assist in the disaster. He continued his questioning. 'What will your Sisters do?' Mother Teresa, in her own gentle way, said 'They will bring loving tender care to the poorest of the poor.' He became more blunt with her, 'Do you preach the Gospel?' to which she replied, 'Our preaching is the service we give to the poorest of the poor'.

At 6.00 p.m. we were shown into the presence of the Emperor for a very short interview. The ADC had by this time changed his attitude and was very supportive of Mother Teresa's bringing her Sisters to work in the famine-stricken areas. The Emperor was most gracious and thanked her for her visit and offer of Sisters. She could bring them in as soon as possible.

Mother Teresa had converted the Emperor in the short time we were in the parlour. The ADC was worried that we as Catholics should come into Ethiopia to convert the Orthodox to Catholicism. The Government had invited the Canadian Jesuits to run the university many years beforehand, but they were obliged to wear secular dress and be called Mister, not Father.

On the way back to the convent Mother Teresa prayed and thanked God, and asked Sister Frederick to stay behind while she went on to Yemen the next day. She promised to send sisters in at once, and within two weeks the first sisters arrived, with Sister Regina as superior. Sister Frederick and I walked the streets of Addis Ababa looking for a house, and soon the work began. I realised what an extraordinary person Mother Teresa was, how powerful and yet so gentle.

The arrival of Mother Teresa in the midst of the famine and national celebrations, the unprecedented telephone call from Princess Seble Desta, the eventual face-to-face meeting with the Emperor, and the permission to start work – all in a matter of three days – can only be explained as a miracle.

Mother Teresa returned to Ethiopia many times – she brought joy and happiness every time. She came during the revolution when the Emperor had been killed and the princesses thrown into prison. On one of her visits Mother Teresa said to me that she should go to see the princesses because they had been so good to us. After all, it was through them that the Missionaries of Charity were allowed into the country. I said it would be very difficult, but I would try. I asked a friend of mine in the government, Ato Kassa Kebede, to see Mother Teresa, and told him what she wanted. He received her very cordially and she put her case. Ato Kassa said it would be extremely difficult to get into the high security prison, but he would see what he could do. He made an appointment for us with the chief of prisons. We met this big burly man at 9.00 the next morning. He listened to Mother Teresa's request. He said, 'Mother, you are asking the impossible.' Mother said simply that they had been kind to us and that she felt it was right to visit them. He replied, 'Of course it is the right thing to do. I was in prison for ten years myself.' He then picked up the phone and spoke in Amharic to someone for a short time. He replaced the phone, and paused for about ten seconds. Then he said, 'Mother, you have done the impossible, you may visit the princesses.' He was astonished that he had got the permission, but he was also delighted.

I asked him for a note, but he refused, saying that he would inform the prison authorities to expect us. I drove Mother Teresa and Sister Regina to the prison in my Volkswagen Beetle. We approached the supervisor, who was waiting at the gate for us. He asked if the car was mine and said to bring it in. There was no searching, no security interference. We walked down the incline to where the princesses were, and saw Princess Seble Desta as she came to the door. There were eight princesses inside a small room. Mother Teresa went around to each one individually, speaking a few words of encouragement. I followed her. Their conditions were miserable – they had mattresses beside each other on the floor, with just enough room to walk between them. The emotional outburst at seeing us was great – they cried openly. Princess Tenanyework, being the oldest, was the most pathetic of all – she was sitting on her mattress on the floor. The other seven were her grand-daughters and they were learning to cope. They were all dressed in black.

When Mother Teresa completed the rounds she asked me to say a short prayer. We left and did not speak for about fifteen minutes. We were shattered. We had seen these princesses in all their finery, with attendants serving them in the comfort of their palace. They were being dehumanised and degraded beyond belief. The poor have learned to live with poverty, but the poverty of the rich was something I never thought I would experience.

The princesses spent fifteen years in prison and were then released. They were separated from their children, which was a great suffering for them. When they got out, they wrote to Mother Teresa and myself to say how much they appreciated that visit.

I learned a great deal from Mother Teresa and was privileged to have worked so closely with her for more than twenty years. Her unbounded courage stops at nothing in her efforts to relieve human suffering.

She is a mother for all seasons, for all times and for all peoples. She is unique, simple, humble, brilliant, sincere and holy beyond words. She represents a contradiction of this world's values and traditions.

Mother Teresa moves fast, both geographically and spiritually, never satisfied with the present but rising to great heights, despite enormous obstacles and opposition. She has a special charism of communicating with everyone, irrespective of creed, nationality, colour, language or ethnic origin.

She will visit new countries to open fresh houses for the poor, but only after deliberating for a long time with God and Our

Blessed Lady – they tell her when she should go. She usually leaves very quickly, with about thirty or forty cardboard boxes of food and religious goods such as chalices, ciboriums, vestments, miraculous medals and other such items. When she went to Albania, where all the priests were in prison, she brought a supply of consecrated hosts so that she could receive Jesus every day while she was away.

She is unpredictable, as I learned one day when bringing her to the airport in Addis Ababa. We were half-way to the airport when she said she would postpone her trip. So I made a U-turn and returned to her convent. I then arranged with the airline to take her the next day instead. She went on to Dira Dawa, completed her trip, and then she wanted to return to Addis Ababa some days later. However there was no plane, but she prayed, and towards evening she heard a plane in the sky. She rushed to the airport and was able to get a lift on a private aircraft going back to the capital. Mother Teresa never gives up.

She is fearless, ready for any challenge. This is why she has approximately 540 communities of Sisters in 146 countries, in the most remote and difficult corners of the world, and is hoping to visit China soon to open another house there. She has met with many heads of state, from the Presidents of America to President Nyerere of Tanzania, and Mengistu Haile Mariam, to mention only a few. What Rudyard Kipling wrote is true of her:

> If you can talk with crowds and keep your virtue,
> And walk with Kings nor lose the common touch,
> If neither loving friends nor foes can touch you,
> And all men count on you, but none too much.

We could borrow a leaf from her book, and also from her prayer-book. What the psalmist says could be said of her:

> O Lord, you are my lamp,
> A light which lights my darkness,
> With you, I can break through any barrier,
> With my God, I can scale any wall.

There are no limits to Mother Teresa's horizons. She thinks and acts big. She will go to the top if necessary to get what she believes is right. She is so tiny, so frail and so small, and yet she is so powerful, so great, so full of love and compassion, that there are no limits to her vision and insights. She is totally oblivious of herself, never thinking of her own needs. The Sister Doctor has to remind her of her medicine – she thinks only of others. On one occasion I arrived in Calcutta very tired, and when Mother Teresa met me she asked a Sister to set up a bed for me in the sacristy, so that I could have a rest. She then made arrangements for me to stay with the local parish priest.

Mother Teresa has a wonderful sense of humour and wishes everyone to enjoy themselves. She is never pessimistic, discouraged or downhearted. She once saw me looking downcast as we were poring over a map of Ethiopia wondering where we should go next in the famine areas. She always chooses the worst places, where no other agency is working. 'Father Kevin, never, never get discouraged. Just do your best and that is all God wants from you,' she said. And again she would say, 'If there are a hundred people in great need and you can help one, then help that one and then you will see that you will be able to assist more than one, perhaps even ten, or twenty, or even the whole hundred, because this is not your work, it is God's work and he is using each one of us as his instruments for the accomplishment of his work.'

Mother Teresa will always say, 'Let God use your weakness.' She will never say, 'Let God use your strength', because of ourselves we don't have any strength. We cannot lift a finger, or speak a word without the power of God. Mother Teresa always 'acts justly, loves tenderly and walks in the footprints of Jesus Christ'.

Mother Teresa's work prospered in Ethiopia. Her Sisters picked the most needy areas, and now have houses in Addis Ababa, Dire Dawa, Jijiga, Makele, Axum and Jimma. When Mother Teresa visited Ethiopia she was provided with a helicopter to travel wherever she wanted to go. The communist leader, Mengistu Haile Mariam, told her on one occasion that he understood that India was her first home, but he would like Ethiopia to be her second. Her work was much appreciated by Church and state, and the new government was equally welcoming to her.

Work in the prisons
Mother Teresa was the person who introduced me to prison life for

the first time. I had always wanted to visit the prisons but had never had any success. Now the way was open and I had a chance to do something through CRDA. A further motivation for me was the fact that Berhe Beyenne was imprisoned for alleged involvement in an attempted coup. He was put on TV with a group of others, and they were publicly disgraced. He was in prison for several years, not knowing his fate. I lost contact with him until one morning he telephoned me out of the blue and asked to see me in his house. I went at once and found him in fairly good form – he was on parole, allowed out of prison for a few hours on certain days. He was lucky to be alive, given the ruthlessness of the regime.

As chairman of CRDA he was always deeply interested in the prisoners, and felt that the organisation should be doing more for them. He had now been active from the inside and suggested to the prison authorities that he knew people outside who could improve the living conditions of the prisoners. He asked for permission to contact some of them and to invite them to see the prison. He invited me to meet the senior prison staff. Together we met the supervisor of all the prisons in Ethiopia and made proposals to help the prisoners.

There were 25,000 prisoners in all, with 3,500 in Makanisa Prison in Addis Ababa. Here there was gross overcrowding and poor sanitation facilities. Our first project was to erect a washroom and toilet block. We also brought food and medical supplies for the prisoners.

Berhe Beyenne invited me to visit Wolisso Prison, about thirty miles outside Addis Ababa, where the prisoners were engaged in farming. I was pleasantly surprised to see the relaxed athmosphere on the farm. The prisoners worked quite well with the minimum of supervision. Thanks to Providence, we were able to fulfil our ambition to help them. Berhe Beyenne was the instument God used to reach them, and not without his own share of suffering and anxiety.

I was later saddened by the news that Berhe died rather suddenly. He was a great leader and a close friend. On one occasion when we were waiting for a meeting about the Good Shepherd Sisters' programme to assist street girls. I asked Berhe how much he had contributed to the recent government appeal, knowing that he had no great love for the new establishment. He said he gave 100

Birr (about $50 US). Then he turned to me and asked, 'What did you ever do for your government?' I said, 'I left my country for my country's good.' His reply came like a bullet from a gun: 'Could you help me do the same for my country?'

May his dear soul rest in peace.

A visit to a leper colony

I had read about Father Damian and his work for lepers in Molokai. His story would motivate a stone. Little did I think that the Lord would lead me to a leprosy settlement.

I had been in Ethiopia for only a week when a Dutch priest took me for a drive around Addis Ababa. We found ourselves in Alert (Africa Leprosy Research and Training), where the priest had done his course in leprosy control. Experts say there are about ten thousand lepers beyond recovery in Ethiopia, who are incapable of looking after themselves. People regard the disease as a revolting physical deformity, which carries a stigma and causes great isolation. It has terrifying implications for the children. The Alert Centre is about one mile outside Addis Ababa. At any given time there are thousands of leprosy patients gathered around its gates, unwilling to return home for fear of rejection. They now live in a shanty town of shacks, a ghetto of misery, overcrowded with out-patients receiving treatment from Alert.

We visited a few families, well known to my priest guide, and eventually we were invited to a meal with a very poor leprosy family. The husband was lying on a bed, with just stumps of feet and hands. The priest was very well received – he was educating two members of the family. The meal began with the washing of hands, as is done throughout Ethiopia – the food is eaten from a common dish, and taken with the hands. We had a beautiful meal of eggs and ingera, which is a brown, plastic-like pancake. Ingera is not particularly appetising but you acquire a taste for it. It was a fast day in the Orthodox Church. There are 250 fast days in the year, 180 of which are obligatory for all. The full fast must be observed by monks, nuns and priests. I have seen lay Ethiopians, who could ill afford to do so because of their health, refuse food in the famine areas because of the fast.

Sam, a young boy in the family, gave me my first lesson in Amharic. He spoke English quite well, even at the age of twelve.

You should have heard Sam laughing heartily at my pronounciation.

When I said I was from Ireland, Sam proudly showed his father our little island, whereupon the father replied 'chic-a-chic', which is the Amharic for a quarrel or a fight. He knew about the trouble in the north of Ireland from listening to the Amharic version of the BBC news. The only thing he seemed to know about Ireland was that it was a country of fighting and violence. I felt as if the ground would swallow me up. I was so ashamed. Here in the heart of Africa the Irish problem was being spoken of and discussed, with the slant of the BBC news. Here was I, a missionary, spreading the word of God, preaching a message of peace, while in my own country there was fighting, and people were killing one another. I left the house delighted with the warm reception, but saddened by the comments about our dear and cherished country.

CHAPTER 15

RELIEF EFFORTS CONTINUE

On my way back to Ethiopia in 1984 I stopped off in Rome as I usually do. This time I got a call from my sister Maura, a Sister of the Congregation of the Little Sisters of the Assumption. The congregation had just made a decision to respond in a very positive way to yet another famine raging in Ethiopia at that time. They wanted to assign three Sisters to the famine area, and asked me to investigate a suitable location. The place should be among the starving, and their aim was to set up a relief and medical programme in a remote place not covered by other religious congregations or relief agencies.

On arrival in Addis Ababa I telephoned my friend Father Kevin O'Mahony, a White Father lecturing in the diocesan seminary in Adigrat. Kevin spent all his free time in refugee camps, looking after displaced people. He was also an author of some distinction, a linguist who knew Amhara, Tigrigna and Guez. Kevin said he would consult with his bishop, Abunna Kidane, and call me back. When he rang me he was very definite about his request – the diocese would welcome three Sisters to do medical work in Edega Hamus, about nine miles from Adigrat, in a remote mountain area at the centre of the famine, where there was no existing relief team.

I relayed this news to the Little Sisters of the Assumption in Dubin. After a short interval, three Sisters arrived in Addis Ababa – Jacinta O'Sullivan and Marie McCaulley from Cork, and Teresa Maher from Tipperary. They had not worked in the Developing World before, and were thrown in at the deep end. They started from nothing, and gradually built up a huge programme. They were inundated with people suffering from acute starvation, kwashiorkor, and a multiplicity of diseases, some of which they had never encountered before. They could not refer patients to a doctor because there wasn't one in the area. They had to make their own medical decisions and treat the patients accordingly.

I went to visit them in Edega Hamus and saw the extent of their challenge. They would walk along by a queue of people and pick out the worst cases, which they would treat that day. Day in and day out they fought bravely against famine and disease, administering what medicines they had. They got help from Brother Gus O'Keeffe, co-ordinator of CRDA, from the diocese, from their bishop, Abunna Kidane, from Father Kevin O'Mahony, Father José Bandres, and others. It was tough going, but they took it on with a smile and made a fantastic job of it, in spite of their limited resources.

The team was replaced on a regular basis. Among the other Sisters who came there were Mary Malone and Anne Mary Bloeth from the US, and Attracta O'Reilly, Maureen Dunne, Brigid Fogarty, Carmel Hamill, Lucy Roache, Anne Kiernan and Bernadette Mangan from Ireland.

Their contract with the Diocese of Adigrat was for ten years. There are no words to express the appreciation of the local people and the diocese for their great contribution. A group of local Sisters took over from them when they finally left in September 1995.

The famine continued to rage throughout the country, and we tried to reach out to different provinces. I went on a trip to the Ogaden, a vast desert on the Somali border. The famine was very serious there, as we saw in Mishamo – a little village near the border.

It was here that I had a narrow escape. Leaving Mishamo, I asked the pilot of the Cesna plane where we would visit next. He said we had to go to Degabur to get fuel. He added that we had fuel for three-quarters of an hour, just enough to get to Degabur. I looked at my watch and took stock of the time. After three-quarters of an hour I looked again at my watch and we were still flying, and in fact the pilot had lost his way.

The pilot had no navigation instruments for directions and so was dependent on landmarks. How do you find landmarks in a vast desert where there is nothing but sand? An hour went by and still we were in the air. We landed after one-and-a-half hours, with the sweat of fear running down our faces. These are the hazards of our work, the risks we have to take. We were flying on a wing and a prayer, but God always looks after you.

On another occasion I was on my way from Addis Ababa to Asmara on a relief plane. I was sitting on a pile of food and I took a walk towards the cockpit. I saw clouds of smoke coming from somewhere. I was frightened and alerted the pilot to what was happening. He immediately drew his fingers down a string of buttons, putting out about twenty switches in one fell swoop. It solved the problem. We were flying over Axum, the centre of the Orthodox Church. It is said by the Ethiopians that if you are buried in Axum, you are sure of going straight to Heaven. Whatever the guarantees of Heaven were I certainly didn't want to die over Axum!

Air drops of food in Ethiopia

It was during the height of the famine in Northern Shoa, when the death rate, especially among the highland people, was very high, that I was invited to accompany the RAF on an airdrop of food supplies. On Sunday, 18 August 1985, we left Addis Ababa with Dr Eugene Connell, a Franciscan Sister from Dundalk. The episode brought home to us how modern technology could bring relief and save lives in remote places unreachable by any other means.

The target area, a hundred miles north of Addis Ababa, is one of great beauty, enclosed in the mountains but without roads. Getting there in a large Hercules aircraft demanded great skill and precision flying. The RAF have developed this to a fine art, making an average of four trips per day – a record of five on the day we travelled.

The pallets of food were prepared in Addis Ababa Airport, each containing a ton of supplies. They are specially secured so that the sacks break loose on impact with the ground, and scatter without breaking the bags. Even if they burst open, the grain is quickly salvaged by the people waiting below.

By 10.40 a.m. we were airborne and in thirty minutes we were over the dropping zone. This had been marked out by an advance team who had travelled there by helicopter. We flew at an altitude of 2,500 feet, affording us a magnificent view of the terrain – the mountain ranges and deep gorges, beautiful ravines and occasional waterfalls.

We saw picturesque little villages perched on the tops and the sides of mountains, whose inhabitants had suffered so much from the drought. Passing through low clouds at such an altitude was frightening, knowing we were surrounded by mountains, especially when visibility was poor, and sometimes we seemed to be totally lost. Coming near the target was even more frightening as we sometimes seemed to be going straight into the mountain, only to glide over the top at the very last moment.

The target was on a plateau and we zoomed in over the markers at a height of ten to twenty feet. The rear of the plane had been opened and the first four tons prepared for the drop. With perfect co-ordination between the cockpit and the rear, four British soldiers pushed the load on rollers through the gaping rear of the plane. Seconds later the sacks of food were dancing like snowballs on the field below.

As the plane rose into the sky, the men moved another four tons into position at the rear of the plane for the second drop. The men were strapped into mobile harnesses which allowed them free movement in safety.

It was an exciting, if dangerous experience for Sister Eugene and myself.

As the plane circled for the second drop, the sacks were collected by a group of local workers organised by the ground staff. The same exercise was repeated a second, third, and fourth time, delivering a total of sixteen tons of vital food to the area.

The round trip from Addis Ababa takes one-and-a-half hours and the plane is reloaded in seventeen minutes. This remarkable feat is a great example of people's genuine concern for those who are hungry and in desperate need.

To alleviate the suffering caused by famine is one of the great challenges of our time. Would that more people were aware of what can be achieved with good will and generosity. The joy of giving and of saving life cannot be surpassed.

Who to blame?

The question of who to blame for such suffering is always a pertinent one. During the horrific Ethiopian famine of 1984-86, a priest came out from America to view the situation. He found himself in Makele where hundreds of people were dying every day. He was horrified and became angry with God. He shouted out his anger. 'God, how did you allow this to happen? Why are there so many people dying? Why do you not stop it?' Then he realised what he had done – he had accused God and blamed him for the troubles. He realised his blasphemy and, after a short reflection, he heard God replying: 'Why did YOU allow this to happen?'

Yes, we like to blame God rather than ourselves for the evils in the world. Did God not give us a peaceful world to begin with? We must admit that we have made a poor job of it – through our greed and selfishness. We must accept the blame ourselves.

I was not long in Ethiopia before I realised the depths of poverty in the city of Addis Ababa, and not merely in the provinces of Wollo and Tigre where the famine was raging in 1973.

I was horrified to hear the story of a young married man with a wife and eight children who were starving to death. He belonged to an association called the Edder. According to the rules of this association, the members would contribute a small sum of money each month to a savings fund, as in a co-operative, in order to build up credit facilities for the rainy day when a member of the family would die. It was a very useful form of assistance, and very practical for people with a low income. This man, in his desperation, approached the organisation for his allowance, saying that since his children were hungry he would like to use the money to prevent death rather than get it when some of his family died. It seemed reasonable and logical. The officials did not agree, and said it was against the rules of their association, which, of course, it was. That night he went out and hanged himself from a tree in the neighbourhood so that his wife could claim the money to feed the family.

We might be inclined to condemn this poor man for his action – we would call it suicide, but I would leave that judgment to God. He died out of desperation in an act of love for his wife and family.

This story moved me, and I was trying to think how I could assist such cases in the future, when the idea came to me to form a branch of the Society of St Vincent de Paul. I called a meeting of Christians in Holy Saviour's Church in Addis Ababa, and from a small group, including members of the Congregation of the Daughters of Charity of St Vincent de Paul, we began our first Conference of St Vincent de Paul in 1975. It is still active in the capital today and has spread to another church on the Metcha Road.

The St Vincent de Paul Society in Ireland helped the organisation get off its feet, and Rome was very happy to see it functioning in Ethiopia. When Father de Reidmattin of Cor Unum visited Addis Ababa and asked the archbishop if he had a

Society of St Vincent active in his archdiocese, Archbishop Paulus Tsadua was proud to be able to say: 'Yes, our conference is doing well.'

CHAPTER 16

THE ZAMBIAN REFUGEE PROGRAMME

In 1978 I was invited by the Bishops' Conference of Zambia to go there to set up programmes for refugees. There were hundreds of thousands of refugees from the six neighbouring countries, Angola, Mozambique, Zaire, Namibia, South Africa, and a few from Tanzania. Zambia was generous in granting asylum to all refugees. I spent three weeks there making a survey of the numbers, the location and the conditions of the people who had been driven from their homelands. I also interviewed the heads of relief agencies working in the camps to see where the gaps might be and where we might most usefully get involved. I made a report which I circulated to all the bishops and to the major relief agencies in Europe. In it I made a list of emergency proposals. The first of these was to open an office in Lusaka, and to start ferrying food into the camps as soon as possible. The reaction of the bishops was one of relief that at last something concrete was being done, and so they were most supportive. The international donor agencies supported my proposals with finance and encouragement.

Maheba refugee settlement

I started with the Angolan refugees in Maheba, in the north-western province, where about thirty thousand had fled from the civil war in Angola.

I first visited Maheba settlement on a Sunday morning in 1979 with Father Joseph van Rickenbach, a Swiss La Salette priest who had been a missionary in Angola for thirty-four years. Father Joseph was getting old, but he was very active. He was also very clever, but quiet, and had his finger on the pulse of the people. He learned English quickly, and he loved the Angolan refugees.

The refugees had been there for ten to fifteen years. It was a very large settlement of rich agricultural land, uninhabited by the local farmers as it was infested with mosquitoes. The United Nations High Commission for Refugees (UNHCR) had divided the land into four-acre plots and built roads through the compound, each road being half a mile away from the next, numbered from 1 to 38. So it was fairly easy to get around this very large area, though the road surfaces were anything but good. We said four Masses that Sunday morning. About fifty per cent of the refugees were Catholic, but had been without the services of a priest for ten years and longer. However, they had constructed four churches on the settlement, and they used to gather on Sundays to pray together, sing hymns and socialise. The structure of the churches was very simple – just sticks for walls and a mat roof, but for the refugees these were sacred places. Understandably, some had fallen away from the practice of their religion.

Immediately after the Masses I talked with the refugees and asked them what their needs were. They said they were not beggars, but good farmers, and if given assistance they felt they could cope with the problems. They asked for agricultural tools, for seeds, for fertiliser. One elderly man stood up and said, 'We need a priest.' I asked him why he felt they needed a priest, who would look after him, where would he live, and how would he get around the vast settlement. The man gave me the sharpest sermon of my life in three words. He said, 'John 10:15', and sat down. I was unable to remember what the passage he was referring to was about. I shamefacedly asked him to quote it for me.

> I am the good shepherd. The good shepherd lays down his life for his sheep. He who is a hireling, and not a shepherd, whose own the sheep are not, sees the wolf coming and leaves the sheep and flees; and the wolf snatches them and scatters them.
> He flees because he is a hireling and cares nothing for the sheep. I am the good shepherd; I know my own and my own know me, as the Father knows me and I know the Father; and I lay down my life for my sheep.
>
> *John 10:11-15*

That old man certainly took the wind out of my sails. I explained to him that we had been negotiating with the government for permission for Joseph to live in the settlement. The government was delaying the matter, and they must be patient. A short time later Father Joseph got the permission and lived in the settlement in the midst of the people, sharing their hardships and troubles.

I reflected a great deal on what Peter had said. The presence of a priest was important to the people. Their spiritual lives were being neglected. In fact, the Church had abandoned these people, and yet they were loyal to the Church. The Church should have followed them into exile, to be with them in their darkest moments. I reflected on my Biafran experience, on how the people in exile valued the priest, how our presence among them meant more than the food we brought in to feed them. The Angolan refugees had a right to complain of being left to their own devices for more than ten years. Why had the Church let them down? Did it not care about people who were forced into exile? The priest who represents Christ must stay with his people no matter what the inconvenience, no matter how great the hardships. He should travel with them into exile, give them the privilege of Mass and the sacraments at a time when they need them most. The priest must be one with the people at all times.

In the Book of Ezekiel there is a beautiful passage on the Good Shepherd, which illustrates God's love and mercy in bringing back stray members of the fold:

> For thus says the Lord God: Behold, I, I myself will search for my sheep and will seek them out. As a shepherd seeks out his flock when some of his sheep have been scattered abroad, so I will seek out my sheep; and I will rescue them from all places where they have been scattered on a day of clouds and thick darkness. And I will bring them out from the peoples and gather them from the countries, and I will bring them into their own land; and I will feed them on the mountains of Israel by the fountains and in all the inhabited places of the country; there they shall lie down in good grazing land and on fat pasture they shall feed on the mountains of Israel. I myself will be the shepherd of my sheep and I will make them lie down, says the Lord God. I will seek the lost, and I will bind up the crippled, and I will strengthen the weak and the fat and the strong I will watch over; I will feed them in justice.
>
> *Ezekiel 34:11-16*

We have much to learn from the Africans – they have much

insight into the spiritual nature of things. We must be prepared not only to listen to them but to act upon what they say. I believe refugees are very close to God. Humankind, by and large, has abandoned them, and they readily turn their minds and hearts to God.

Father Joseph settled down in Maheba and was later joined by Father Martin Koolwyjk CSSp. Father Martin had been in Angola for over forty years when he was kidnapped by UNITA rebels. He spent three months in captivity, during which time he was taken about five hundred miles across the country. At times his captives were forced to carry him, sometimes in a bag on a makeshift stretcher. He liked to smoke and they used to cut a hole in the bag so that he could do so. His greatest hardship was that he could not speak during those three months. To do so would have resulted in a beating. He was eventually released to the Red Cross, flown to Johannesburg, and then back to the Netherlands. He was decorated by the Queen of the Netherlands for his bravery, but he could not wait to return to the missions. When asked if he would go to Zambia to minister to the Angolan refugees in Maheba, he readily agreed. He loved the refugees, and they loved him. His house was always surrounded by boys. Father Martin was a fisherman, and used to teach the children how to fish in the lake in which the great Zambezi river originates.

The Irish Sisters of Charity got involved in Maheba through Sister Mary Fallon, who told me she wanted to work with refugees. She was a teacher in a school in Kabwe, formerly Broken Hill, on the road to the settlement. I used to break my journey there for a rest and a cup of tea. Sister Mary came to see the refugees, and as a result a community of Sisters was established in the settlement on Road 18, beside the priests' house. The first Sister to be appointed there died shortly after her arrival. Later Father Des Arigho CSSp, formerly a missionary in Kenya, joined the priests, bringing their number up to three. The refugees were well cared for from a pastoral point of view.

The J. Z. Moyo Camp

Not far from the Angolan settlement, there was a camp of about nine thousand Rhodesian boys living under the trees in the forest. There was a similar number of girls in a camp near Lusaka. They were living in makeshift tents, in grossly overcrowded conditions. Their food was cooked in large cauldrons. They had nothing to do all day, so I decided to do something about it. I heard of a priest, Father Nigel Johnson, from Rhodesia, who had to leave that country because his life was in danger. He had been giving medicines and shelter to so-called guerrillas or freedom fighters. He had been a dentist before he became a Jesuit priest. I contacted him in London and asked him if he would work with refugees from Rhodesia, who were now living in Zambia. He readily agreed, and took up residence in the J. Z. Moyo Camp outside Solweze, in the north-western province of Zambia. He lived in the same tents as the boys and he ate the same food. I asked him to come out to Solweze for occasional rests, but he refused. When Nigel got sick I begged him to leave the camp for a while, but he said that when the boys got sick they had to get better in the camp, and so he should do the same.

I visited Nigel many times, though the boys did not know me. During one of my visits I sounded out the boys on their attitude to Nigel. I asked a group of them, 'What is this white man doing in the camp? Who is he?' They gave me a very sharp and definitive answer. They said, 'He is a good man – in fact he is one of us.'

It was a beautiful tribute to a man they appreciated very much. He would pray with them, read scripture with them and listen to them. He was their great pastor, their doctor and adviser. He was their post office, posting letters to their parents and getting back the replies. They loved him, as he loved them.

It reaffirmed my previous convictions about refugees – how important it is for the priest to be with them, to live with them, to share their sufferings and privations. After the example of Christ, Nigel became one of them. He identified with them personally, and knowing their language and culture was a great bonus. To be a refugee among the refugees is the ideal to be aimed at.

Other refugee settlements

In other parts of Zambia there were refugees from Zaire, from Namibia and from Mozambique. These latter settled in various parts of Zambia, some in Chipata, others nearer to Lusaka.

On one occasion the South Africans bombed a transit camp in Lusaka, mistaking it for a rebel camp. Fortunately no one was killed, but it sent a scare all over the country. At the time, I was on the way to the north-western province to make a film on refugees with my two brothers, Mike and Tom. Tom, a Marist Brother who had spent all his life since 1928 in the Far East (Sri Lanka, China and Hong Kong), wanted to visit Africa on his way home on leave. After the bomb attack, many security checks went up, and we suddenly realised we were getting into trouble with our camera equipment. Every white man became a South African suspect. At dusk we ran into real trouble when we were searched on the road near Solweze. Everything, including my address book, was checked. The address of someone in South Africa fell to the ground and we were arrested. We were driven under military escort to the police station in Solweze, where we were questioned. Mike and I were often in this kind of situation, and we invariably played different roles, in the hope that one of them would save us. So Mike became angry, saying he would report this incident to the president, Kenneth Kaunda, whom he had received in Ireland during the Zambian independence celebrations. He explained how we were helping the refugees. I took the opposite approach, and became placatory, saying it was a mistake that we had been arrested, that we were assisting the country. I then demanded that the bishop be informed of what had happened. So Bishop Potani was sent for. He was away in Rome, but his vicar general arrived at the police station. He immediately asked why we were being held, told them that Father Kevin was well known to him, and that in fact he was building a Cheshire Home in Solweze for disabled children. So our drama ended. Before leaving we asked for a letter to show at other security checkpoints on our way to make a film on refugees.

I eventually handed over the refugee programme to a Zambian, Crispian Mushoto, who had been recommended to me by Father Dick Cremins SJ, who was working in the welfare department of the Catholic Secretariat. I had arranged to bring a bishop into the camp in Maheba, and had informed all the bishops on a regular basis about what was happening and how the programmes were going. We had acquired a truck and we were hauling food from Malawi to the refugee settlements and camps, to supplement the work of UNHCR and the Lutheran World Federation.

The work went well in Maheba, and it still continues today, as no peace agreement has been signed between the Angolan government and UNITA. The rich agricultural settlement has made great progress, and sells its produce to towns within the copper belt. In fact, the Zambian farmers are envious of the Angolans because of their success. Maheba is an example of what can be done by refugees themselves when they are allowed to develop their full potential.

Father Nigel's report
Father Nigel Johnson spent about seven months in J. Z. Moyo Camp and I asked him to write a final report on the return of the refugees home to Zimbabwe. His reflections are very enlightening and significant, sometimes critical, deep and far-reaching.

J. Z. Moyo Refugee Camp – 22 August 1980
The eight thousand refugee boys at J. Z Moyo Camp near Solweze, left Rhodesia for a number of reasons. From conversations with them it appeared that some left after trouble at home or in school with the security forces. Some were looking for education which they were unable to get in Rhodesia. Some others were already in school but heard over the ZAPU (Zimbabwe African People's Union) radio broadcasts, that there were good schools waiting for them in Zambia. Others wanted to become freedom fighters. Another group left for no specific reason, it just appeared at the time that it was the thing to do. Most left home without telling their parents. They walked towards the border alone, or in small groups until they made contact with the ZIPRA freedom fighters, who looked after them. Some of the adults left to escape from the 'call-up'. Others were asked to leave by ZAPU, to do specific jobs in Zambia. Others left just to become freedom fighters, but were then asked to run the refugee camps.

The boys were originally based near Lusaka, but after the bombing of the guerrilla training camp they were moved to Solweze. This camp proved to be an unhealthy site, and it was moved to another site a few kilometres away. The boys' school camps were distinct from the guerrilla training camps.

The camp was entirely organised by ZAPU. They had established a primary school, secondary school, leatherwork, tailoring, metalwork and carpentry for the academic and skills education of the boys. There was a hospital, and three kitchens. The boys were organised into groups to collect firewood, dispose of refuse, construct roads, move provisions to the kitchens, spray the toilets and do agricultural work.

Help was provided by UNHCR and other agencies in the establishment and maintenance of water pumps, bore holes, electric generators. These agencies also provided the food, clothing, tents etc. The boys and staff used local materials to build shelters, school desks and benches, and small pieces of furniture such as stools, beds and tables.

The teachers organised the boys into football teams, choirs, drama and poetry groups. In many ways the situation was very like that of a rural mission in Africa, but very much larger and with no permanent buildings. The staff was outstandingly dedicated to the welfare of the boys and committed to the ideology of ZAPU. That ideology could be summed up as working for the liberation of Zimbabwe and the creation of a totally socialist society. The freedom fighters were fighting for liberation, while the boys were being prepared to create a new order in Zimbabwe. In that new order a socialist society was being created in the camp. It was an opportunity to try out their ideas, and put them into practice, now that they were free from the Rhodesian situation. No one at the camp received any salary.

The feelings of the refugees

In this little area of 'Free Zimbabwe' the refugees felt acutely sensitive to the fact that they were still dependent on outside aid for food, medicine, clothing etc. They accepted the reality of the situation that they could not produce these things for themselves, but for a group of people who were proud of having escaped from a society in which they had no control over their lives, unable to exercise their initiative and forced to be dependent on the Whites, who had the power and the money, it was important to maintain their independence. This is something that the outside aid agencies had no appreciation of and which was a source of great humiliation to the refugees.

A representative from an aid agency would arrive for a day to assess the needs of the camp for the next three months. He would discuss all the needs with the camp administrators, take notes and return to Lusaka. Telexes would be sent to the agency headquarters, and decisions taken about which things would be provided. Some time over the next three months, various items of the requested supplies would suddenly appear – the camp administrators had no idea what to expect, or when to expect it. The agency representative would arrive, expecting grateful thanks for what he had given to the camp, only to be greeted with the question, 'When will the new electric generator be coming? That's what we have really been waiting for, over the past three months.' And the reply, 'They decided in Europe ten weeks ago that you don't really need it', is accepted with expressionless resignation. When the agencies don't treat the camp administration seriously and say what they are going to provide and when, is it any wonder that the camp officials do not treat the agencies seriously and apply to many agencies for the same thing?

But this example illustrates a deeper point than this merely practical consideration. This whole type of procedure is humiliating because it is such a reflection of the paternalism from which the refugees have fled.

Many visitors from the various agencies are brought on tours of the camp and these are obviously essential if the agencies are to acquaint themselves with the situation in the camps. But feelings are very mixed in the camps about such visits. One white visitor from Zimbabwe was able to talk to them about what Zimbabwe was like at the time, and he praised them over and over again about what they had achieved in J. Z Moyo Camp – 'You must be very proud of your school and of the desks you have made.'

The reaction to him was very positive. He saw warm smiling faces and received many handshakes. Other visitors, especially if in large groups in a hurry to keep up with a schedule, with no knowledge of the home country and more interest in taking photographs of the worst sights and most ragged refugees, than seeking the achievements of the camp, find a different response. Their photographs show refugees with blank faces staring at the photographer. When published these photographs are interpreted as expressing the pathetic, listless helplessness of the refugee. In reality, however, they express the refugees' resentment of the callous photographer who has no real interest in them as persons.

I am not here making any attempt to give a balanced view of the work of the aid agencies (as is obvious from the above). I am trying to give some insight into the feelings of those who receive aid, so that in the future we may be more sensitive to those feelings.

These refugees are exiles from their homeland, living in a place with a different climate, geography and vegetation, culture and language. They long to go home, they sing about home, talk about home and dream about going home. They have not heard from relatives since they left. They have no idea about what has been happening at home. Was everything just the same as when they last saw it? Have whole cities been destroyed by the war? Maybe their parents, brothers or sisters are now all dead. The staff wonder what has happened to their wives and children in the years they have been away.

Until the ceasefire was well-established, security was tight; they never knew when the bombers would reappear on the horizon. No letters were allowed until after the elections. Only the most senior members of the camp administration were able to leave the camp. After the elections things improved a lot and choirs and teams would visit local Zambian schools. Then the desire to go home became even greater, as there seemed to be nothing to prevent them from going home now. But nothing seemed to be happening. No one seemed to want them to go home. No one knew anything; no one came to tell them what plans there were for their return. They heard over the radio news of the grants of money being promised for repatriation of the refugees, but nothing was changing; they were still left behind here in Zambia, while the broadcasts were full of news of what was happening in Salisbury. The camp was full of rumours.

The generally accepted explanation was that ZAPU had lost the election, and the ZANU government was not interested in them. The teachers were worried that all the money available for reconstruction would have been used up by the time they got home. There was no one to look after their families and make sure that they got their fair share in the reconstruction programme. They began to feel forgotten, unwanted and left behind.

Attitudes of aid agencies
The chief agency involved with J. Z. Moyo camp was UNHCR which operated through the World Lutheran Federation (WLF). UNHCR provided the finances, WLF provided personnel and most of the organisation in Zambia. The bulk of the food was provided by the World Food Programme (WFP). ICRC provided

some items (e.g. milk, soap, some of the medical supplies). The Swedish, Soviet and East German governments also gave aid, in the form of food, clothing and medicines. The Catholic Church in Zambia provided aid from the European Catholic agencies.

There was very little coordination or cooperation between the agencies at the Lusaka level. They could be divided into three groups: East European governments, UNHCR with WLF, and others. I have no idea how East European governments handled things since all I saw were the various items arriving from these countries. Until the last few months, UNHCR through WLF seemed to be very unwilling to coordinate activities through the other agencies. The other agencies seemed to be anxious to coordinate activities but found it difficult to know what was going on.

Part of the problem was that for so long, while the war was still on, the situation in Zambia had been so delicate. An example of this is the discussion in February about the shortage of food in the refugee camps. Figures were discussed concerning the amount of food supplied and the numbers of refugees in the camps, from which it was clear that sufficient food had been supplied. Nevertheless, although everyone acknowledged that the refugees were not receiving enough food, no one could acknowledge what they all knew – that a proportion of the food was being diverted to the freedom fighters' camps. The other agencies sought to remedy this situation by trying to find out what was lacking in the actual refugee camps and to fill in this gap. But this could only be done by going to the camps to assess the situation independently, and supplying the needs. The UNHCR, WLF and WFP were not able publicly to acknowledge the reality of the situation. This interpretation was later confirmed when the freedom fighters returned to Zimbabwe and the food situation improved dramatically. At the same time a lot of food and clothing started to arrive from the Soviet Union.

One small incident illustrates the point made in the previous section. This was the occasion of a fierce and resentful attack by one of the medical staff on a helper from one of the agencies who came regularly into the camp. This helper had a supply of medicines for the camp, which was being held back because she considered that they were being wasted (not that they were being used dangerously). The person in charge of the hospital was extremely angry that she had not discussed the matter with him, nor done anything to persuade the hospital authorities to remedy the situation. She had simply kept the medicine (antiseptic) in her house to limit the supply. She was thereby treating the hospital staff as the Whites in Rhodesia treated their servants – like children – and she got the appropriate reaction.

A further pitfall was the tendency not to see beyond the statistics on the desk. The refugee problem was approached simply in terms of mouths to be fed and kept alive until they could be transported from Solweze to Bulawayo, the final report written and the file closed. The larger the agency, the higher up in the administration the person concerned, and the less immediate the contact he or she had with the people living in the camp, the greater the tendency to approach the problem in this fashion.

Reflections from the experience of living in the camp
My reception was, from the beginning, politely welcoming. It was apppreciated that someone had come to help with the medical situation. But since nothing was known of me, the camp staff were reserved until they had time to assess me. On the other hand the boys were quick to come and talk with a new person, and were generally interested in a different face on the scene.

About two months after I arrived one member of staff whom I got to know said that, at first, he could not understand me. It was beyond his experience that a doctor from Europe should come and live like that in the camp, become a part of the camp and not expect special treatment (especially to sit on the ground and listen to the choirs, rather than expect a chair to be brought). He then discovered I was a missionary and that explained all. The greatest compliment I received was when this particular man described me to someone as being 'one of us' and when I was referred to as 'Comrade Johnson'. The fact that I knew Zimbabwe and had been involved in the liberation war and spoke some Shona were things to my credit (even though I knew Salisbury rather than Bulawayo, I'd been in a ZANU rather than a ZAPU area and I spoke Shona rather than Ndebele).

The fact that I was part of the camp, and that the Church in Solwezi town (eighteen miles away) had personnel and had aid facilities for refugees, and that they were in telex contact with the Catholic refugee office in Lusaka, proved to be an extremely successful arrangement. I was in constant touch with the needs of the camp, especially the sort of needs one does not think of from a distance and which no one thinks worth mentioning at official visitations. For small items locally available, a member of the camp administration would mention some need. I would give a note to be taken to the church in Solweze who would then supply the cash and the camp authorities would organise the purchase of the items, receipts and change being returned to the church. This was important because the items could be obtained immediately, the selection and buying having been carried out by the people responsible for running the camp.

With regard to my being a priest in the camp, it soon became quite clear that it was inconceivable to exercise anything of the traditional priestly ministry in terms of the Mass, sacraments etc. I celebrated Mass alone in my tent every night and even had a solitary Easter Vigil. But while a solitary Mass had previously seemed meaningless as a routine thing, here in the middle of the camp of nine thousand people it became full of the deepest meaning for me. My being here, sharing their life, somehow seemed to express the meaning of the Incarnation as lived out in a Christian's life – 'and he pitched his tent among us'.

I once asked why it was that there was no possibility of any external religion in the camp. I was given the reply: 'We were taught by the missionaries that you cannot hold the gun in one hand and the Bible in the other.'

This was told to me by a deeply Christian man and there were many like him, who were very confused at not being able to reconcile their Christianity with the obvious rightness of the liberation struggle. They had not rejected Christianity, but had put it in cold storage until the struggle was over. I think that my presence there said something about this problem, if only the vague statement that it is possible to be a Christian and be involved in the struggle, and that Christianity is concerned with the realities of life and not just the sacristy. It is unfortunate that it is all so late.

It is also unfortunate that through our ignorance, our lack of contact with the liberation movements, our susceptibility to

Rhodesian propaganda, our stereotyped concept of 'religious life', we abandoned these refugees once they had left Rhodesia and left them to sort out their problems alone. These refugees were like orphans, in need of as much love and affection as they could get, and immediately receptive to anyone who had a real interest in them for themselves. Love is something that Christians should be able to provide better than anyone else. What a need and an opportunity we missed here.

The future
A) REFUGEES IN ZIMBABWE
In these camps the refugees recreated a new way of life based on the principles of their socialism. Headmasters of English public schools are inclined to talk about the spirit and traditions of the school. But what they have is nothing in comparison to those who shared the work of building their own school, the suffering and starvation and the threat of bombing raids. It would be a tragedy if this were to be lost and wasted as Zimbabwe creates a new nation.

It will be very easy for us to see the returning refugees simply in terms of numbers to be fed until the harvest comes, or to ask ourselves how many of them can we push into a classroom without breaking the school administration. Or to hope against hope that they will simply disappear into the rural areas and be re-absorbed without causing us too many problems. All these attitudes are based on a negative assessment of the refugee as a poor unfortunate. The refugee is one who has experienced several years of living in the new order already, who was liberated long before those who stayed inside the country. The foundation for building the new Zimbabwe is to be found among the returning refugees.

B) REFUGEES ELSEWHERE
I would say that wherever there are refugees, the Church must be involved, and not simply from a distance. The Church is not just another international aid agency. It should be intimately involved in the suffering, Christians sharing the life of these people. If religious orders have any imagination, and are seeking to capture the spirit of their founders, we should find Brothers, Sisters and priests living in these camps. And if the local Church has any dynamism, we will find the local Christians willing to play their

part in helping the refugees they find on their doorstep. The refugees are foreigners, often resented by the mass of the local people at first, especially if they are an extra drain on already low food supplies and if they attract enemy bombers to the area. So the local Church is often reluctant to be seen apparently doing more for these foreigners than for the local people. With regard to possible future refugees from South Africa (or elsewhere) I think that this experience with the Zimbabwean refugees will be very valuable, because in both situations the refugees are highly politically and liberation orientated. The Church must establish a relationship with the liberation movements of South Africa (and elsewhere) so that it is able to make its own valuable contribution to the life of the refugee camps.

CHAPTER 17

MY WORK WITH THE CHESHIRE FOUNDATION

After the Biafran war I linked up with Leonard Cheshire, who asked me to assist him with the expansion of his Homes for disabled people in Africa. I could not refuse such a request and it fitted into my vision for my future work. When I was appointed to Ethiopia in 1972, I attended an International Conference of Cheshire Homes in Addis Ababa in 1972. Cheshire invited me to go anywhere of my choice in Africa to spread his work. When an opportunity arose I took off to visit Kenya, Tanzania and Zambia. I knew very little about the handicapped and what I know today is what Leonard Cheshire taught me.

Nairobi, Kenya

In 1974 I set out on my first safari for the Cheshire Foundation, starting in Nairobi, Kenya. I arrived at a critical time, when the committee members were meeting to close down the operation and disband the committee. Sir Francis Fressanges was in the chair, and other members in attendance included Dorothy Hughes, Sir Humphrey Slade, Gordon Bell, Alexander and Diana Stephenson. They had handed over the Cheshire Home in Nairobi to the government, having built it up to a point where they could no longer run it. They also handed over to the government the Home in Likoni, outside Mombasa.

I asked them not to disband, but to try again. Hughes and Sir Humphrey Slade backed me. We would continue to explore new possibilities. I was put in contact with the head of the Society of St Vincent de Paul, who had a property in Limuru, eighteen miles outside Nairobi. It was formerly a nursing home for Europeans, but was no longer in operation. It proved to be unsuitable for the Vincent de Paul because of its location and climate. The residents did not like it – they found it too far away from the city, where their friends were, and it was very wet, cold and foggy. We negotiated a deal and bought it as a new Cheshire Home in Kenya.

Limuru was ideal for people with disabilities. Sister Joan Doyle became the first sister in charge, providing a high quality of care. Later the Sisters of the Assumption, an indigenous congregation, took it over. It is now run by a local committee, a mix of Europeans and Africans. For occupational therapy the residents do handcrafts, which they sell locally. The sisters also run a nursery school for the local community, which helps to finance the home. Rehabilitation into society has been managed very successfully in Limuru.

There was a second Cheshire Home in Dagoretti, in the suburbs of Nairobi. This Home also had a separate unit, a workshop for making fishing flies. Dagoretti became a very important rehabilitation centre, and employed up to sixty adults. It had a large hall which was financed by the European Community. The motivating force behind this rehabilitation centre was Jeff, an Englishman with a great head for business.

Some years later we set up a third Home in Kariobangi with the help of the parish priest, Father Tom Maher. After a few years a sister of the Congregation of the Franciscan Missionaries for Africa, Sister Victoire, took over the running of the home. She did splendid work on the site and created a day-care facility for the poor of the neighbourhood.

Dodoma, Tanzania

My next port of call was Tanzania. Here I met President Julius Nyerere, who was keenly interested in Cheshire's work. He met Cheshire and plans were started for the first home in Dar es Salaam. Things move slowly in Tanzania, and it was eventually agreed to site the first Cheshire Home in the new capital, Dodoma. The government would put up the buildings, and the Cheshire Foundation would run the centre. It took more than ten years for the government to complete the buildings. Unlike our normal way of working, all the buildings were started at the same time and had to be totally finished before any children would be admitted. In the Cheshire Foundation we would generally plan such a venture in stages, and let it grow gradually, taking in children as the individual buildings were completed. A group of local sisters eventually took over the running of the centre. Viatores Christi sent volunteers to train the local sisters in the service of the children.

Lusaka, Zambia

After Tanzania I moved to Lusaka, the capital of Zambia. I arrived knowing nobody, as I had never been there before. I said to myself at the airport, 'Why have I come here? Where do I start? What shall I do?' Taking my courage in my hands I telephoned the archbishop's house. Archbishop Emmanuel Malingo told me to come to his office where he received me with open arms. After hearing of my intentions he put me in touch with Father Colm O'Riordan SJ, the head of the Catholic Secretariat, who was invaluable to me. Father Colm passed me on to an Italian Franciscan priest, Father Tessari, who was in charge of the Welfare Department of the Catholic Church. I was also recommended to see Father Paddy Walsh, the administrator at Roma Cathedral. Father Paddy invited me to preach in the Cathedral and this gave me the opportunity of speaking about the Cheshire Homes and of my hopes for establishing a home in Lusaka.

I appealed for volunteers to help start the first home in Zambia. A number of people expressed interest and approached me after Mass. As I walked around the back of the church greeting the people, a white woman came up to me, carrying a small baby. She told me she had appreciated my sermon, saying she was carrying a child who had club feet. She had two other children who were normal, but her husband was given to drink and had lost many jobs. He had left home and showed no interest in the family. However, from the moment this child was born he lavished great love on her and was transformed by her. He gave up the drink, was reunited with the family, took up a steady job and all was well once again. The woman commented, 'It took a disabled child to bring him back to his senses.' People with disabilities give us more than we can ever give them – this is a truth borne out by my own experience.

A committee was formed, with meetings held in Father Walsh's house in roma, Lusaka. Father Paddy knew anyone worth knowing. He was a personal friend of the president, Kenneth Kaunda, and used to travel to Salisbury in Southern Rhodesia to visit him in prison before Northern Rhodesia became the independent state of Zambia. He occasionally brought Kaunda's wife and members of his family to see him in prison. Father Paddy had access to the president and to many members of the Zambian government.

James Watson, a shrewd operator in the import business with a heart of gold, joined the committee and was a tremendous asset. He had a lot of valuable contacts. News spread that we were about to set up a Cheshire Home and were looking for a property. A businessman by the name of John Drysdale contacted us with a proposition. He had been chairman of St Joseph's Welfare Society for white boys in colonial times, but it was closed after independence. He could not sell it as it was given in trust, for charitable purposes. He offered it to us. We went to see it in Woodlands in Twin Palm Road. Although it was a small property it was in an ideal location and could be developed. Moreover, we got it for nothing. How providential – God was guiding me once again.

The home was empty except for the caretaker, Mrs Buckland, an elderly woman who loved cats. There were cats everwhere in the house. Europeans going on leave would ask Mrs Buckland to look after their cats while they were away – she had the care of about thirty cats in the home. Cats from the neighbourhood went there for meals!

James Watson became chairman of the Cheshire Home. He and his wife Ethel and daughter Jenny put a lot of work into the Home in the ensuing years.

I travelled to Ndola with Father Tessari to explore the possibilities in the Copperbelt, Zambia's smallest province. We met Bishop Nicholas of Ndola. Towards evening we wondered where we should stay overnight. Father Tessari suggested that we should go to the Franciscan mission in Ibenga. He had been posted there and had built a church there which he wished to show me. Next morning I said Mass for the Franciscan sisters beside the monastery. Over breakfast, the superior spoke about the needs of the sisters. One of their greatest problems was not having a base in the capital, Lusaka, where they had to go regularly. I asked them the nature of their work, and they said they cared for disabled people in the Copperbelt, in Ibenga and Luanshya and elsewhere. I proposed that if they would be interested in running a Cheshire Home for handicapped children, we would provide the base they needed in Lusaka. They were very interested but said they would have to consult with their Council members. Shortly afterwards they informed us that the Council had agreed, and had appointed Sister

Ilaria to undertake this work. Sister Ilaria was the ideal person for the job, and it was great to watch all the pieces fitting into place.

In three weeks I had a strong committee, an excellent chairman, a beautiful property and an ideal staff – having started from nothing just three weeks before. It was all thanks to the wonderful providence of God.

Back in Ethiopia I received the minutes of all the meetings and read about the growth of the home. Suddenly the minutes stopped coming. I wrote to Mrs Pierce, the secretary, asking for an explanation. She wrote back to me to say that they had been reading about Ethiopia and the terrible revolution there. They thought that I must be dead, and so they did not wish to waste postage stamps on me.

The minutes started coming again. Some of the stories they relayed were amusing. When Sister Ilaria went to visit the Home for the first time and saw all the cats in the kitchen, in the bedrooms, on the bed, everywhere, she just turned her car around and left, saying that she would not return until all the cats were put out. She reported her decision to James Watson, who could not understand what the fuss was about. 'What's wrong with a cat, sure everyone keeps a cat?' It took Sister Ilaria a few short moments to convince James that she would only return to the home when every cat had been taken away. She returned rather cautiously the next day to find that the coast was clear, the cats were gone, but the smell was still there. A lot of scrubbing had to be done and some burning of smelly cushions. Mrs Buckland was transferred to a very nice flat, and the cats were taken care of.

The Lusaka Home grew rapidly and became a model Cheshire Home for Africa. Sister Ilaria did a magnificent job with a staff of three sisters. Soon they had thirty disabled children receiving treatment and an education which would enable them to go to the local school when they left the Home. Great credit must go to the committee and to the Watson family in particular. James Watson was a great chairman for several years and gave wonderful leadership.

We often speak of great heroes, but seldom recognise the hidden heroes, like the children trying to get movement into their weak limbs, their persistent efforts to stand up in the struggle with polio or with limbs broken in accidents, etc. Let us not forget the real heroism in sisters who do their silent vigil over such little children for twenty-four hours of the day, and do it not grudgingly, but with joy and love, often in the midst of silent suffering. It is beautiful to see, even if we cannot match it.

I continued my work with the Cheshire Homes in Africa. Wherever I went I explored the needs of those with disabilities and the possibility of setting up homes. Our work prospered, thanks to God. From Lusaka the work spread, and Cheshire Homes were set up in Ndola, Chipata, Solweze and Mongu where they were run very successfully by religious sisters.

Harare, Zimbabwe

The Lusaka Home did much to publicise the work of the Cheshire Foundation throughout Southern Africa. I was asked to go to Zimbabwe after independence in 1980 to start a home there. There were many disabled people in Zimbabwe after the civil war, which had lasted fifteen years. I met some great people in Harare, among them Dr Pam Ryan, who showed great interest but did not believe that it would be possible to start a Cheshire Home in Zimbabwe. I suggested to Dr Ryan that she book a ticket to Lusaka and inspect the Home there. She did so and arrived in Lusaka one Friday evening. I brought her to the Home in Twin Palm Road, in Woodlands, and invited her to stay there over the weekend, rather than in a hotel. She was naturally apprehensive about staying in a home with thirty disabled children, but she accepted my invitation. She was not sorry.

I met her at a committee meeting on Monday afternoon, and got her reaction. She could scarcely believe what she had seen. She summarised her findings. 'You have achieved three remarkable things – the Home has discipline, it has cleanliness and it has happiness.'

It was, in fact, an accurate description of a Cheshire Home. She even saw the scout troop in action. The Lusaka Home is a place of great happiness – a rehabilitation centre for children, with a school to prepare them for integration into the normal school system. The sisters under the direction of Sister Ilaria had done a remarkable job. Dr Ryan was converted and could not wait to get back to Harare to start the work.

Dr Ryan gathered a committee around her, including people

like Tony Upfill Brown, John Graham and Mrs Carey, and began looking for premises. They were willed a very large house at 85 Baines Avenue, Harare.

Their first target group was disabled adults – a very needy group with many disabilities resulting from the war. The Home took in African and European residents, and the committee was also mixed. Working with mixed committees was delicate in the beginning. The bitter war of independence had left its scars. I insisted on picking an African for the chair. Meetings were difficult and I would invariably be approached afterwards by the Europeans, who complained about the Africans, and vice versa.

At one of our first meetings a White man questioned the wisdom of starting such a home, because he said that those who donate to such causes were leaving the country. After that meeting a number of African members complained bitterly – they were insulted by this comment and they insisted that they would support the Home just as well as the Whites.

A short time later a second property was acquired from the Marist Brothers in Westwood, on the outskirts of Harare, into which they received disabled children. The Westwood Home was run by a congregation of local sisters, the LCBLs. The children are very happy there and they attend the local school each day.

Sudan

In 1974 I went to Khartoum in Sudan to explore the prospects of starting a home there. I called to the British Embassy to discuss the matter, and was very fortunate to meet Ambassador Gordon Etherington Smith, who immediately took up the challenge. He invited some influential Sudanese to the embassy, and in fact made the embassy the regular meeting-place for the newly formed committee. We even used the embassy post-box for correspondence. The Home in Khartoum grew very quickly, and so I went to Juba to start another Home there. Denise Tabernacle followed me, and gradually the Juba Home got off the ground. Denise was a marvellous person, who worked extensively throughout Africa, following in my footsteps, putting the nuts and bolts together. She worked in many of the Homes throughout the continent. She loved the work. She too felt that it gives us back more than we could ever give it. It is a two-way traffic.

Gabarone, Botswana

I also travelled to Botswana, where I met a disabled man, Barry Eustace, who did a trans-Africa walk for those with physical and mental handicaps. Barry had lost the use of one of his legs, so he walked with crutches. The Cheshire Foundation in London provided him with two back-up vehicles. He started the walk on the borders of Uganda and Kenya, and walked to Nairobi and Mombasa. He travelled to Dar es Salaam, to Dodoma, and on to Zambia, via the Copperbelt, to Lusaka. He met heads of state, received much media publicity and proceeded to Botswana via Harare. The walk was a great success, highlighting what people with disabilities can do if they have the will-power, and creating a greater awareness of their plight.

We started a new Home in a beautiful building on the outskirts of Gabarone and Barry took over its chairmanship. It was officially opened by the President, Dr Masiri, with Leonard Cheshire present for the occasion.

Anamalenge, Namibia

Bishop Haushiku from Namibia saw the Ndola Home when he was visiting Zambia, and was so impressed that he wrote to me to invite me to Namibia to establish the same kind of Home there.

I travelled to Namibia before its independence and formed a committee in Windhoek chaired by a local businessman, Samuel Solomon. The bishop offered me a school in Anamalenge in the north of the country, which was empty because of the war. I went there with Solomon and found it to be an ideal location. The OMI Fathers were the missionaries there, most of them being from Germany. They became involved in the first Cheshire Home in Namibia. I arranged for some local sisters to go to Lusaka for training, and they eventually took over the running of the Home.

On one of my visits to the Home, I was introduced to the children, amongst whom was one boy whose arm had been blown off. He had been playing when he noticed a small round object on the ground. It was a hand grenade. He picked it up, taking it to be a ball, but it blew up in his hand. The explosion blew off his left arm, and burnt his side. He was brought into the Cheshire Home for treatment but his arm was beyond repair. He was a happy child, but of course he would never be the same again.

As I spoke with the sisters they told me about a Catholic church about ten miles away that had been destroyed by bombs. I asked the sisters if I could visit the bombed church and they brought me there. I was horrified to see the destruction before me. The roof was blown off and the walls were cracked beyond repair, though the tabernacle was intact. As I meditated on this horrible destruction I saw a simple wooden crucifix on the wall. The figure of Christ was severely damaged – the left arm was gone, and the legs were blown away from below the knees. It reminded me of the boy in the Cheshire Home. 'Was Christ identifying himself with the disabled? Was he giving us a message?' I asked myself.

Then I remembered a church that was destroyed during World War II in Bavaria in Germany. There too the crucifix had been damaged, but the priest had not repaired it, or thrown it away. Instead, he had put it in a place of honour in the new church and inserted an inscription underneath the broken figure of Christ, which read 'I have no hands but yours'.

That, I felt, was the message for us. Christ no longer walks our earth, he no longer preaches the word, but he has passed on this work to us, all of us – 'Go teach all nations…'. He no longer cures disabled people, but we are asked to do it. We are Christ's messengers, his ambassadors, his representatives. We are the feet of Christ to go his way, we are his hands to do his work, we are his voice to preach his word, we are his heart to love all people. We are 'Alter Christus'. This is the privilege he has conferred on us all. The work we do is not our work, it is Christ working through us, all of us – not just priests but everyone.

Lesotho, South Africa

I also visited Lesotho, an enclave, or homeland, of South Africa. I made contact with some people who formed a committee under the chairmanship of Bishop Paul Khaorai of Leribe Diocese. The committee emerged as a result of a film that I showed in the capital city of Maseru. Some government officials, including Mrs Mokhobo from the Ministry of Interior, were present for the film show. I gave a short talk on the needs of the disabled and the possibility of starting a Cheshire Home in Lesotho. I invited people to become involved.

The king was informed of the show by Mrs Mokhobo, and he

asked to see the film. So I was invited to the palace to show the film to King Moshoeshoe II and the queen. The king showed great interest in the proposed Cheshire Home, and when it was ready to be built, he personally laid the foundation stone. Father Joseph Le Clerc, the parish priest, found a suitable site in his parish. Dr D. Lebona was also a very valuable committee member. Sister Virginia Ginet from the Catholic Secretariat in Maseru gave invaluable advice and financial assistance.

A local community of sisters took charge of the running of the Home, which was built in a new housing estate just outside Maseru. The children attend the local school.

Swaziland, South Africa
Swaziland is a small homeland similar to Lesotho, also ruled by a king. I travelled there also to open a Cheshire Home. I preached in the cathedral in Manzini one Sunday morning and explained my mission. I invited people to come forward to help in the formation of a Cheshire Home. Mrs King, wife of the airport manager, approached me after Mass and offered her services. We built an active committee around her. Father James Sommers, a Salesian priest, was the Caritas representative, and was invaluable in the work of organising the Home. Mrs Cora van Ersel was also very dynamic on the committee, and had the strong support of Bishop Nlovu. A site was picked in the industrial estate, not far from Manzini. The target group was disabled adults. I left responsibility for setting up the Home with the committee but I took charge of gathering funds from European agencies to assist them in the beginning. Each Home should aim at self-reliance as soon as possible.

It takes time, especially in Africa, to get a project off the ground, but there is a great spirit of community there. The extended family system is very strong and people are very conscious of the needs of the community.

Cheshire Homes in South Africa
From Swaziland I was invited to Transvaal in South Africa by Father Charles Kupelweiser, based in Carolina, who was deeply involved in welfare schemes for the poor. He was responsible for the building of a home for disabled elderly people. He established a Cheshire Home within his parish, at no expense to the Foundation.

Cheshire had started other Homes in South Africa, in Durban, Johannesburg, Capetown, Port Elizabeth and elsewhere. There are now about ten Homes in South Africa.

I went to the Johannesburg Home during one of my visits. It is run by lay people and the residents are White. One German resident to whom I spoke had been a building contractor before being seriously injured in a fall from the top of a five-storey building. He was now in a wheelchair, but continued to do drawings and other such jobs for builders. His wife and children had abandoned him after the accident, and he was struggling to cope with life, but he was happy at his drawing-board. He was not merely physically wounded, but socially handicapped as well. He was very happy in the Cheshire Home where he was loved and well cared for. He said to me, 'The Cheshire Home has given me great security, and restored my dignity.'

In 1973 there were eighteen Homes in the African continent, and by 1990 there were fifty – a growth of more than one per year.

Christ has no body now but yours,
No hands, no feet on earth but yours,
Yours are the eyes,
Through which He looks compassion on this world.

Yours are the feet,
With which He walks to do good.
Yours are the hands,
With which He blesses all the world.

Yours are the hands,
Yours are the feet,
Yours are the eyes,
You are His body.

The Overseas Disabled Association
The Overseas Disabled Association came into being as a response to the United Nations declaration of the Year of the Disabled in 1982. I started the Association to create a greater awareness of the needs of disabled people, and to touch the lives of so many disabled people, especially in the Developing World. I felt that not enough emphasis

was being given to the many people in the world with handicaps. An estimated ten per cent of the world's people have some form of disability. In the Developing World such disabilities are due to disease of one kind or another, whereas in developed countries many disabilities are caused by industrial accidents.

I discovered that funding agencies were not very receptive to requests from people with disabilities. Agencies are generally divided into three categories, concentrating on development, emergency relief and pastoral needs. Development agencies tend to say that people with disabilities are not within their terms of reference, that they are subjects not of development but rather of emergency. If I pick a disabled child up from the street and give him or her physical, educational and vocational rehabilitation, surely this is development of the best kind – development of the human person. Emergency aid agencies are inclined to say that people with disabilities are not emergencies. On the contrary, they *are* emergency cases, for if a child is not operated on immediately, then it may be too late and the disability may become crystalised. With many disabilities, if treated at once, a child could lead a normal life. A child with a club foot is an emergency because if the correction is not made at once it will become permanent. The problem can be rectified, even without surgery, at an early stage. Likewise, the pastoral agencies say that people with disabilities are not their responsibility, they are not connected with Church activities. Why then did Jesus spend so much time with these people during his lifetime? Should not Christian agencies be supporting them, as Jesus did, by way of example for us all?

The organisation was launched in Liberty Hall by Jim Sherwin of RTE. Speakers included Bishop Joseph Whelan CSSp, Bishop of Owerri, Nigeria, John Pittock, and myself.

John Pittock became our first chairman, and Saundra Munn our national secretary. Our board members include Lady Valerie Goulding, Father Aidan Lehane CSSp, Maurice Kenny, Sean Ó Síocháin, Dr Victoria Coffey, Dr Gregg and Mona Costello. We have very active branches in Kilkenny, Carlow, Dundalk and Cork. Through the activities of these branches we have been able to reach out to many disabled people in Africa and the Middle East. The organisation works closely with the Cheshire Foundation and responds to requests, mostly from Developing World countries.

CHAPTER 18

MIKE DOHENY AND FIRODA FILMS

Father Mike was always interested in photography. He inherited the interest from our father and Uncle Bill. During the Biafran war he realised, possibly for the first time, the importance and power of pictures as a medium for bringing home to people the tragedies of the Developing World. He had acquired a small eight-millimetre movie camera with which he took some shots of various aspects of the war. On returning to London he showed snippets of the film to the BBC, who used some of his footage on *News at Ten*. It was then that Mike began to appreciate the great power of the visual image – he had been to places where no other camera had been before, in some of the most remote disaster areas. He had rare pictures of unusual scenes and interesting people. His photography would add immensely to his gift for writing. He was greatly encouraged by an Englishman, Paul Gane, who would edit the films he brought back from Africa. Mike learned a lot from Paul, who made the occasional trip with him into Africa. Mike used to say, 'I never went to school, but met the teachers on their way home.' Paul Gane was one of his best and favourite teachers, while there were others such as Paul Harrison, Carte Blanche Studios, and Allen Hart of *Panorama*.

Mike became the 'voice of the poor' and concentrated his efforts on bringing the story of the Developing World back home to the West. He filmed extensively for Concern. Eventually Mike set up his own film company, Firoda Communications, which received charitable status. Among the Firoda Films were:

> *Build me a World*. This film was made to highlight the International Year of the Child (1959). It focuses on children's rights and needs in India, Bangladesh, Singapore and Hong Kong, and was narrated by Glenda Jackson. Children's rights include the right to affection, love and understanding, to adequate nutrition and medical care. Love and affection were found in abundance even in the poorest countries, but the problem of abuse of child labour was rampant. Though many

of the conclusions of the film are shattering, it does not leave us without hope. The film has a been described as 'a little masterpiece in its own right'.

Forgotten Children of the Forest. A film about 9,000 refugee boys from Rhodesia living in the forest in Zambia. It was filmed on 12 May 1980, the day that Rhodesia became independent and was renamed Zimbabwe. So in spite of the great frustrations there is also music and song, feasting and dancing, sport and play. It was narrated by Jonathan Dimbleby and includes interviews with Father Nigel Johnson SJ who was living with the boys in the camp. The film focuses on the efforts of some of the beneficiaries including Bishop Potani who joins the celebrations.

Any More for Crutches? This film was made in 1982 to commemorate the International Year of the Disabled. It was shot mostly in the model Cheshire Home in Lusaka, Zambia, and in Ibenga. It was narrated by Jan Leeming, a BBC newscaster.

Seven More for Crutches. This is a film about refugees with disabilities shot in 1982 in Mishamo refugee Camp in Tanzania, where there were about 30-40,000 Burundese refugees. Mike chose seven people and told their stories in detail. It was narrated by Frederick Forsyth.

Where are all the Crutches Gone? This was filmed in 1980 in Tanzania, Kenya and Uganda, and emphasises the positive things being done to integrate people with disabilities into society. Mike filmed a school of blind children in Sototi in Uganda, out in the field, picking ground nuts. The children later played beautiful music, with drums and flutes. In Nyabondo, in Kenya, adults were filmed making dresses and handcrafts under the direction of Sister Damian of the Franciscan Sisters for Africa, an Irish nun from Dundalk. In Lumuru, in the Cheshire Home, a teacher was teaching normal children physical education and was even directing operations in the field from her wheelchair. The narration was by Frederick Forsyth.

Go Ye Afar. This is the story of the Holy Ghost Fathers working in The Gambia. It provides insights into the history, culture and traditional customs of the people in The Gambia, and the approach of the missionaries to the development of its people, most of whom are Muslims. It shows Bishop Michael Cleary CSSp and his co-missionaries Fr Joe Gough CSSp, Father J. Sharpe CSSp and others in their varied activities, including fishing, farming and education. They also run long-term programmes in health and nutrition. The Gambia was known as the White Man's Grave and with good reason. The life expectancy of the first missionaries in the country was five years. In 1905 a diminutive Holy Ghost priest, Father John Meehan CSSp, arrived there from Donegal, and he changed the course of its history. He died at eighty-one having survived forty-nine years in The Gambia. Missionaries have made an outstanding contribution to education in The Gambia and have built up remarkable relations with the Muslims, who form the majority of the population.

Seven Hills to Climb. In this film, a pilgrimage of disabled people from Cheshire Homes all over the world are gathered in Rome for an International Conference, and they have a special audience with Pope John Paul II. Leonard Cheshire and Lady Ryder were also present to mark the golden anniversary of their wedding, and were very well received by the Holy Father. The pilgrimage was expertly organised by Ron Travers, the International Director of Cheshire Homes. Mike endeavoured to show the joys and sorrows, the struggles and difficulties, the personal battles for normality, and the heroic courage of disabled people to be accepted into normal life. The film was narrated by Paul Harrison.

Upon this Rock. Filmed in 1981 on the borders of Zambia and Zaire, it illustrates the pastoral care of 10,000 refugees, mostly from Angola. Father Joseph Van Rickenbach, the pastor, spent over thirty years as a missionary in Angola. He was kind and gentle with the refugees, speaking their language and knowing their culture and traditions. He was assisted by Father Martin Koolwyck CSSp. An Irish volunteer from Dublin, Tom Kavanagh, is seen assisting the handicapped people in the camp.

Father Mike's Concern. This film was shot in California in 1986. It is a sermon preached by Fr Mike, illustrated with flashbacks to the poor in refugee camps in the Developing World. It is a very powerful appeal to get involved with the poor on this planet – a strong message of love.

Meet Me in Khartoum. This film looks at Concern volunteers in action.

Morning has Broken. Programmes of self-help in Tanzania are sharply contrasted with the desolate scenes of famine in Ethiopia. Drought had continued in Ethiopia for two years, affecting 500,000 people. The film was narrated by Pat Kenny of RTE who stressed that 'no misfortune is so great that with human will-power, we cannot overcome it'. The title of the film is taken from Cat Stevens' song 'Morning has Broken', and because of the singer's long association with Concern, he allowed Father Mike to use his song.

Babel Yemen – Gateway to a Nation. This film gives an insight into a people whose culture has survived unchanged for almost two thousand years. Father Mike filmed this in 1976. It is a twenty-eight minute production on one of the poorest countries of the world, where the people live in desert conditions. Father Jimmy O'Toole CSSp worked and died there, in the front line of the struggle against poverty. It is narrated by Trevor Howard.

The Tide is Turning. The tide often turns in Bangladesh, a country which suffers a great deal from huge floods, which leave many dead and many more homeless. It is a country that is grossly over-populated, with almost a hundred million living in poor, overcrowded conditions. Mike filmed a lot in Bangladesh, and every Christmas he would do the Concern fast in O'Connell Street, Dublin, and then go to Bangladesh as Santa Claus for Christmas, loaded down with gifts for the volunteers from their parents and families. Mike loved it all and the beautiful people of East Bengal. *The Tide Is Turning* was made in 1978, and the commentary was by Andy O'Mahony. It was sponsored by the Department of Foreign Affairs.

Karamoja Calls. Karamoja is in the north of Uganda, a vast desert, inhabited largely by nomadic tribes. They suffer from many droughts when the rains fail, which is often. This film looks at the difficult work of Concern volunteers in that poverty-stricken part of Africa.

Bridge of Survival. Father Mike visited Wollaita Sodo in Southern Ethiopia with Paul Harrison in the summer of 1984. There they saw the beginning of what was to become one of the worst famines of the century. The film shows the efforts of Concern volunteers as they deal with the problems of famine and starvation.

When the Crying Stops. Mike made this film in Ethiopia. It shows Irish volunteers bringing relief to the starving in Korem and Ibnat, in spite of the kidnapping of Tarina Kelly and Anne McLaughlin. This very moving film shows people in great hardship, having walked for miles in search of food and medicine. An estimated three million people were at risk in four provinces, thousands of them children.

One Day in Calcutta. This is, perhaps, Mike's best production. It was made in 1984. Father Martin Tierney, then director of Veritas, bought the rights to it and it is now on sale in Veritas bookshops as is *Any More for Crutches?* Father Martin said it was the best film on the work of Mother Teresa that he had seen.

The following is Mike's determined description of the making of *One Day in Calcutta:*

One Day in Calcutta

How to describe early morning Calcutta? I attempted it when I first saw it in 1971 and I know I failed lamentably. Here I am again in 1984 – this time in an attempt to capture what I might call 'the world of Mother Teresa' and I feel utterly daunted by the task. However, we must begin – and where better than where it all began – beside the Temple in Kalighat. Now, Kali, they tell us, is the Goddess of Destruction, and where could it be more fitting to build a world of survival, of peace and relative contentment?

Kevin and myself left our base in Sudder Street shortly after 6.00 a.m. The sun was just peeping above the rooftops as we faced eastwards down Royd Street. In Chowringee Lane there were sleeping bodies on the sidewalk and one family had just risen, thrown aside their flimsy coverings and were huddled, shivering, around an open fire. Here was good footage indeed, but that was not our aim this morning. There were thousands like them all over central Calcutta and, however interesting from a filming point of view, we had to pass them by. Our sights were set further afield. It is difficult to explain the fascination of Nirmal Hriday. It calls you back. I have heard this said many times before by people who were prepared to journey from the ends of the earth just to be there. I recall one lady who told me many years ago that she just wanted to be present in that setting. She did not even feel the need to do anything – just the commune with whatever spirit hovered over that (to her) enchanted spot. And yet it is Nirmal Hriday – Home of the Dying. Not a very alluring title.

We got there before 7.00 a.m. and, as the staff were busy with their morning chores, we went straight up onto the flat roof to see what we could find to convey something of early morning Calcutta. And we got more than we anticipated. The rising sun had just fought its way through the morning mist and emerged triumphant between the twin domes of the Kali Temple. We had to hurry, but we did capture what will, hopefully, be a memorable opening shot. When we turned our attention to the streets we got much more. Right below us and only twenty feet away was the open roof of a bus on which the passengers had made their bed for the night. They had evidently just wakened and were coming to terms with the need to be washed and dressed against a new day. It compensated for what we had missed in the streets. Further afield, on and along the crowded lanes there were already bustling crowds. Some were bent on prayer and hastened to the temple with votive offerings; the air was heavy with incense and the fragrance of flowers. Other more mundane things were in progress – the barbers were doing a brisk business on the sidewalks close to the water spouts while washing activities were in full swing. We had a clear view of the open-air stoves where instant hot food was turned out to the motley crowds of passers-by. In the background and partly shaded by a gaunt and lonely tree was a rubbish dump. In the thin morning light I could see a woman and her children already foraging for anything they might find – food, possibly.

Everywhere there were crowds, crowds, crowds. I said to myself: 'Here is Calcutta in miniature.' Yes it was all there; not only the beggars; not only the naked, the lame, the blind, those broken in body who tended to gravitate towards the Home for the Dying, but also the well-to-do. The Goddess Kali seemed to attract them all. Some of them seemed to be marching in procession, and I guessed they may have come from afar. I have often thought that there is no more becoming apparel than a sari worn by an Indian. I had a grandstand view. The men too, in their well-cut kurtas and flamboyant headgear added colour to the scene. Yes, it was all there – the contrast that was Calcutta; and if the film does eventually hit the screen, it must be all about contrast. Otherwise it tells nothing of what I saw or felt as I stood between the Temple of Kali and the Home for the Dying.

I recalled what Rudyard Kipling wrote about Calcutta:

> Chance directed, Chance erected, laid and built on the silt,
> Palace, Byre, Hovel, Poverty and Pride, side by side,
> And above that packed and pestilential town, Death looks down.

Poverty and Pride, Yes – but Death no longer looks down unchallenged.

8.00 a.m.

As we pass from the crowded streets into the semi-darkness of the Home for the Dying the first thing that catches the eye is a notice which says 'WELCOME TO MOTHER'S FIRST LOVE'.

Desmond Doig, in his book *Mother Teresa,* describes the scene:

> A board at the entrance carries the name Nirmal Hriday,
> the Place of the Pure Heart. There are no doors – it is
> always open. One enters directly into a reception area of
> sorts which is part of a men's ward and is, more often than
> not, occupied by patients. The first impression, as one's
> eye grows accustomed to the gloom, is the tiers of closely
> packed litters, a colourless, slow moving of people and a
> nameless smell that antiseptic cannot overpower. Then
> individuals take shape – gauntly emerging from the
> anonymity of the hopelessly ill, or moving silently about
> their work. A boy carrying a bedpan and soiled bandages;
> a sister hurrying to a bedside; two young men crouched
> over a prostrate form, tenderly dressing a wound. Daylight
> shafts through the barred windows like rays of hope that
> fade and grow bright and dim and disappear.

Yes, this is where it all began. This is the place which calls you
back. Today, I am told, is Novices' Day. The young men are
probably from the Missionaries of Charity or from the Christian
Brothers' Novitiate in Bow Bazaar. I thought to myself: 'What a
tough initiation this is, for those young boys preparing to enter
religious life. No one can ever say that they were not exposed to life
in the raw.'

As we filmed, in the space of ten minutes, they carried out a
corpse, and carried in someone on a stretcher from an ambulance.
Filming inside is still a problem because of the light, but, like
Malcolm Muggeridge, we carried on, more in faith than in the
expectation of good results. Only time will tell. But even with
perfect lighting conditions, how can one convey visually the
Presence which is undoubtedly there – what the ancients might
have called the Genius of the Place and we Christians refer to as the
Holy Spirit?

The throb of a motorcycle is heard outside – Father D'Campo
arrives to say Sunday Mass. The altar is set up on a low platform
between the 'wards' – a score or so of patients and staff gather
around and Kevin and myself are invited to concelebrate. What
surprises us (I almost said shocks) is that the work for the patients

continues unabated throughout in full view of the altar. It took me some time to come to terms with this on-the-spot fulfilment of our pledge to love one another as the Lord had commanded. 'And a certain man went down from Jerusalem to Jerico and fell among robbers…'. The Good Samaritan.

I find it difficult to keep my mind from wandering. I thought to myself – here in this little space (about a hundred square feet) something happened and is still happening which has changed this world of ours. That small, insignificant woman, Mother Teresa, by what she started here, has influenced the minds and hearts of millions of every nation, tongue and creed of this planet. She has become a sign to the nations. Wave after wave of love has gone out from this place over the oceans of the world and gently lapped the shores of many lands, awakening people to the imperatives of Christ – 'Love one another as I have loved you'.

My wanderings are interrupted by the voice of the priest reminding us that this is the Feast of the Epiphany – the manifestation of Christ to the Gentiles. He is quoting the response to the Psalm: 'All nations shall fall prostrate before you, O Lord.' 'That prophecy,' he tells us, 'is being fulfilled before our eyes. Even in this little group around the altar are representatives of every continent – all have come to worship in unison – but not only to worship, but to serve the poorest of the poor – to put your love into action … and you have brought gifts, the gift of yourselves, and you are the bearers of love of your countrymen and women to this Place of the Pure Heart….'

8.00 a.m.

We leave the Home for the Dying in haste but with the promise that we will be back. We were due with the Missionaries of Charity at Howrath and that meant a frantic rush across the city and over the notorious Howrath Bridge. 'Notorious for what?' you ask. For crowds, for traffic jams, for some of the worst slums in the world, which lie beneath its arches. Maura Russell from Ballinaslee, County Laois, is our guide and we battle through, not daring to attempt to film or even let the camera be seen. I know of photographers who have been accosted and some even arrested by the vigilant police. It does not take much to start a riot. It is too early in the day to take the risk.

Maura had informed us that our destination is a convent of the Missionaries of Charity situated in Rosemary Lane. What a lovely name for such an ugly place. At least that is how it looked from the outside – a narrow, dingy, crowded, evil-smelling backwater. And this is perhaps a very superficial view. In reality it was the abode of love. Yes, indeed, those sisters certainly share with the poorest of the poor.

From Rosemary Lane to Shishu Bhavan is about ten minutes – the first part by rickshaw, and then on foot. It was here, in this home for children, that we captured quite an unusual manifestation of love in action. I am always impressed by the love in little mites. They seem to be completely without fear or shyness, and when we remember that many of them were picked off the streets where they were abandoned, this is quite extraordinary and very moving. Those who were big enough to walk had followed us to the roof where we were getting some shots of the surrounding Pilkhana slum. Maura was getting them organised into a play group when one of the sisters appeared. As she bent down to help one of the little ones, the whole group suddenly erupted and literally enveloped her. She actually disappeared from sight beneath a heap of little bodies – all vying with each other to show their affection. When eventually she emerged, still bravely smiling, I felt I had captured something which, without any need of commentary, would go a long way to tell the story.

11.30 a.m.

Back in the very heart of Calcutta in Pren Daan, 'Gift of Love', so named by Mother Teresa herself. The two or so hours we spent there were amongst the happiest and most fruitful of that long day. Here practically all the filming can be done outside. Most of the patients are mentally ill and so they wander out from an enormous building into the bright and pleasantly warm mid-morning sunshine. A few things impressed me. As always with the Missionaries of Charity there was joy in the midst of pain.

Amongst the three hundred or so men and women who had found a home here there was surely pain and depression and even despair. Yet, as we watched them emerge from the semi-darkness into the light of day and observed how they helped each other and responded to the smiling attentions of the sisters and volunteers, I could see that even here was an undercurrent of love. I listened to an amazing story, almost too far-fetched to believe. It was about a patient who was referred to as the 'Jungle Lady'. She looked about fifty years old, moved about on her toes in a stooped position and there was a wild look in her eyes. This I observed through the lens of the movie camera. Later I heard her story. She came to Pren Daan two years before, having been found in a jungle living with wild animals, described by my informant as 'bears'. When found she was going around on all fours and grunted and behaved like bears. Even though she now walks upright, her actions are animal-like. That I can witness to. But the rest of the story seems beyond belief.

Then there was 'the blind leading the blind' – a pathetic yet comforting sight. Roti had been taken off the streets two years before and Shackabati some time later – both are blind and inseparable. Their manoeuvres to get in and out, and up and down the steps, would be comic almost to the point of laughter, were it not for the underlying tragedy.

And so they come and go, the lame, the blind, the weak in mind – while the sisters and volunteers systematically treat their broken bodies and bring comfort to their disturbed souls. Such is Pren Daan. We met Noreen Delahunty from Ballacolla, County Laois, administering tender loving care to a very sick girl. Noreen was a lively character, full of joy, and laughter, radiating love in action.

2.30 p.m.

It is a far cry from crowded, noisy Calcutta to the relative quiet of Titargarh, the location of the home of the leprosy patients. It lies some twenty miles north of the city and the home itself straddles the railway. This takes some getting used to, and I learned very fast the necessity of being ready to jump at short notice. We were greeted most cordially by the Brother Superior of the Missionaries of Charity, and given the freedom of the home. It was but still early afternoon and as we shared a frugal meal with our host he told us the story. The site was given to Mother Teresa by the railway authorities. It is a long strip of land on both sides of the railway track. The buildings are on both sides – the administration on one side and the dormitories, workshops and hospital on the other. The workshops were so close to the railway that one could stretch out a hand and shake hands with someone leaning out of the passing train. There are 127 resident lepers and the centre caters for 27,000 outpatients from the surrounding areas. The Brothers are there in a supervisory capacity – the lepers do the rest. The Brother Superior was very emphatic about this – that it is an entirely self-help operation, and, apart from medical services, everything else we would see was the achievement of the lepers themselves. And what a series of achievements. Everyone has a paid job and there was even a blind man guarding the gate.

As soon as the sun began to dip westwards, giving us some light in the workshops, we began to film. The weaving fascinated me. Not only the elegantly designed and perfectly finished cloth, but also the speed with which it was accomplished. I had seen weaving in many places in Africa and Bangladesh, but I had never witnessed faster action on the loom. One particular pattern of cloth attracted my attention. Yes, it was the blue and white from which the sisters' saris were made. We heard the story.

When the first cloth was produced at Titargarh and put on the market, the word went around that it was made by lepers, so no one would buy it. Mother Teresa stepped in and gave an order for the saris for her sisters. Judging by the rapidity with which her congregation is growing, the lepers will be in business for a long time to come.

There are two vegetable gardens, and a huge pond in a colourful setting of flowers and shrubs in bloom – a thing of beauty in this place of joy.

All this and much more has been accomplished by a group of people whose fate might well have been that of outcasts of society. No wonder so many are knocking at the door.

5.00 p.m.

The train which brought us back to Sealdah Station was so overcrowded that we had to cling to each other to survive, and then we had our precious equipment to protect. When we finally arrived in Calcutta the sun had already set, but it had left its warm afterglow in a rose-tinted sky to calm our spirits into a mood of meditation. There was, indeed, much to ponder after that day's experience. However, the good sisters in Loreto House still awaited us for Mass at 6.00 p.m. There, high above the noise and bustle of the great city, we joined in prayer to express the thanksgiving that welled up within us. It had been an unforgettable day.

Postscript

You may wonder why I have not mentioned Mother Teresa herself in this story. We did meet her several times. At Green Park, near Dum Dum airport, we were lucky to find her on a Sunday morning. This was a place I had been quite familiar with since 1971. In fact, when we were working with Caritas India in Salt Lake Camp I frequently said Mass here, at Mother's request. The work had expanded enormously since then and we found Mother busily directing arrangements for the sisters' retreat, which was about to begin. She received us most cordially and we discussed our idea of making a short film. She had reservations about this and was adamant that it should not be used for direct fund-raising for her work. We were able to give her assurance on that point and so she graciously gave us permission. 'But I must give it to you in writing,' she added. She was obviously most solicitous that her sisters should not be pestered or unnecessarily encumbered in their work. We did, indeed, appreciate that. We asked her about an interview and she explained that she would be on retreat for a week and therefore incommunicado, but that we should return after that.

Bright and early on the following Sunday morning we were back in Dum Dum. With the sisters still on retreat, Mother Teresa was obviously preoccupied. 'We would like to film the work at Dum Dum?' she asked. Yes, of course, she would ask Sister Maureen to help us.

The Interview

It would be better at the Mother house; she would be back there tomorrow. Today it is not possible.

Kevin Began – 'I know you are very busy, Mother...' 'No,' she interrupted, 'I'm not busy, I just have to be around to meet the sisters.'

I said to myself: 'How absolutely typical. This lady who carries on her shoulders the responsibility of an organisation that is rapidly becoming world-wide and the inspiration of it all, is not busy.'

When we finally did get the interview it was quite unhurried. Mother Teresa conveys the impression that while she talks to you, nobody or nothing in the whole wide world matters. She is yours.

It is that extraordinary gift of serenity which has impressed me from the very first time I met her.

The film should deal with the rest of the story.

Michael Doheny CSSp
Firoda Films
31 January 1984

CHAPTER 19

INTERNATIONAL REFUGEE TRUST

When the Pope visited the Philippines about 1980 he used the occasion to highlight the problem of refugees. He said, 'Of all the tragedies in the world, the greatest is that of the refugees.' He made an earnest appeal for the Catholic Church to take a more active role in reaching out to the refugees of the world. At the time of writing, there are about sixty million refugees and displaced people in the world, and Father Mark Raper SJ, Head of the Jesuit Refugee Service, estimates that there are about a hundred million if we include the migrant workers who are forced away from home to earn a living for themselves and their families. The task of coping with such a large displacement of people is enormous. With this in mind, I decided to concentrate more on refugee work. In order to test the degree of interest in refugees in Ireland I organised a three-day meeting in Gort Muire, Dublin, in October 1988.

John O'Loughlan Kennedy, the founder of Concern, was asked to be chairman of the organising committee, and he did a magnificent job. The conference brought together a large number of religious congregations and was attended by the President of Ireland, Dr Patrick Hillery, his wife Maeve, and Cardinal Tomás Ó Fiaich. It was a great success and provided us with a lot of information, along with the reassurance that Ireland was very interested in helping the refugees. A spokesperson from the Department of Foreign Affairs gave an address at the conference. Other speakers included Father Frans Timmermans CSSp, representative of the Bishops' Conference of South Africa (IMBISA); Brian Neldner of the World Lutheran Federation; Father Aengus Finucane, Director of Concern; Father Bob Vitillo of Caritas Internationalis; André Van Chau of the International Catholic Migration Commission in Geneva; and a representative from UNHCR, Mr H. Hutson.

Among the resolutions passed was a decision to establish a committee in Dublin to follow up on the findings of the conference and to establish a structure for the future work among refugees. John O'Loughlan Kennedy was appointed chairman of this new committee, which met once a month. Religious congregations and NGOs were asked to send representatives to the meetings.

At the same time, Aloysius Donnelly, director of Concern Universal, had come up with the idea of celebrating the thirtieth anniversary of the First Refugee Year, by having another Refugee Year, to create a wider awareness of the problems of refugees. Arrangements began in London to prepare for a national launch of Refugee Year 89/90. Free office accommodation was provided by Sister Mary Coleman of the Sisters of Namur.

The launch took place in November 1989 in the Hilton Hotel in London, with speeches from Arthur Dewey, UNHCR, Geneva; Frederick Forsyth; myself and others. A similar launch took place in Dublin in the hall of Stokes Kennedy Crowley, chaired by Olivia O'Leary of RTÉ. The original name of the organisation was Refugee Year Trust, but later it was changed to International Refugee Trust.

The focus of John O'Loughlan Kennedy and his committee was concentrated on the plight of the refugees in Ireland, and the protection of asylum seekers. There were about four hundred refugees in this country, but they were undergoing great difficulties. The committee called itself the Irish Refugee Council set itself up first in John O'Loughlan Kennedy's office, and later in Arran Quay, Dublin.

The International Refugee Trust focused its attention on the millions of refugees abroad, and opened offices at 4 Dublin Road, Stillorgan, County Dublin. Father Norman Fitzgerald CSSp became its first executive director. Father Norman played a major role in building up the infra-structure of the organisation from its small beginnings. Working closely with the head office in London, the Trust grew gradually, and started programmes in the Middle East, in Kenya for the Somali refugees, in Cambodia for the returnees from Thailand, in Sierra Leone for the Liberian refugees.

The Middle East
Our first big campaign was in the Middle East, for the Kurds who were fleeing in their thousands from Iraq. Seán O'Dwyer and Father Gerry Murphy served in the disaster brought about by this exodus.

It was Mother Teresa who asked me to go to Baghdad on a peace mission on her behalf. When the crisis came to boiling point after the invasion of Kuwait, I rang Mother Teresa from London and asked her what we should do. She said, 'You must pray and pray and pray.' When I pursued it further, saying I was thinking of going to Iraq myself she said, 'You must go there without fear as Jesus would.' So I decided to go first to Calcutta, to get a briefing from Mother Teresa, and then to Baghdad. I spent three days in Calcutta discussing and praying with Mother Teresa. She wrote letters to King Hussein of Jordan and to President Saddam Hussein of Iraq, and asked me to deliver them in person. She also wrote to President George Bush. The substance of her letters was that they should avoid war at all cost and try to settle their differences peacefully by dialogue.

I met King Hussein of Jordan, a good friend of Mother Teresa, for half an hour and he received me very cordially. He was very concerned about the situation, and refused to join the Allies, much to the disappointment of the US and Britain.

I then went into Baghdad with Danny Lillis, consultant to International Refugee Trust. Travelling to Baghdad in the build-up to war was difficult. There we were received cordially by government officials and taken to the Melia Mensour Hotel. We later found that it was the same hotel which housed the international hostages. The hostages were on the top floor under arrest whereas we were in the second floor. The Melia Mensour Hotel was advertised as 'a hotel with a difference'.

The Human Shield

About eight hundred international workers, technicians and professionals were being held by the Iraqi government, who intended to send them out to the military locations to protect them against the Allied bombing. These people were known as 'the Human Shield' by the media. The women could leave if they wished but some wives opted to stay with their husbands. They were brought mostly from Kuwait and locked in the hotel.

I decided to visit the hostages as pastor. One night at about 7.00 I took the lift to the tenth floor. When I got out of the lift, I was surrounded by security men who could not speak English. They tried to put me back on the lift, but I kept talking about going to see my brothers who needed a priest. I asked for a seat as I was an old man. I got further into the hallway and sat down, saying I would wait till an English-speaking security officer came. I opened my breviary and began praying. They did not know what to make of me. Eventually an English-speaking guard arrived and fortunately, he was sympathetic to me. He allowed me to go to the eleventh floor, where the prisoners were. They were amazed to see me. I spoke to them and said I would pray for them and with them. I went to the far side of a very large dining-room and sat there saying my prayers. Gradually I was joined by two, then six, and eventually about twenty collected around me. I had chosen a suitable text of scripture which I read. I prayed with them. One man on my left hand said, 'I don't believe in God, I am an atheist, but you must pray very much for us.' I turned to him and said, 'Hold on a moment. You say you are an atheist and now you want us to pray for you. You had better begin praying yourself since you believe in prayer.'

I went to see the prisoners regularly, and passed on messages for them. The crucial time to be with them was when they assembled in the foyer and were being organised to go out to the military locations. I used to talk with them, encourage them, and pray with them. I met some heart-rending cases. One Welshman had an Arab wife, and they had a child, Alexander, about three years of age. I met them in the foyer of the hotel waiting under strict security to go out to a military site. Alexander was tired and running wild about the place, crying but unaware of the situation. I spoke to the father and mother in turn. They were devastated. We prayed together for their safety – they were determined to stay together. The mother told me that they did not know where they were going, but had been told to prepare for a journey of four-and-a-half hours.

There were many others like them. One sixty-three-year-old man in need of an operation was with his wife of the same age. I had met them previously, and had pleaded for them on humanitarian grounds, but in vain. Some business people had taken asylum in the British Embassy. I used to visit them and pray with them talk with them, and counsel them. It was a period of great tension and anxiety.

A group of wives of the hostages travelled to Baghdad to see their husbands and to plead for their release. They were from the UK and in fact they succeeded in meeting the president, Saddam Hussein, who was very gracious to them. He released their husbands and turned their sadness into great joy.

I used to say Mass with some of the hostages in their rooms. We became close to one another and I could see once again the importance of the role of the pastor with displaced people. We read in the Old Testament of the captivity of Babylon, when the Israelites were taken there by force as refugees: 'By the waters of Babylon we sat and wept...'. Babylon is fifty-six miles from Baghdad and I visited it during my trip to Iraq. It is a truly historic place, dating back to 6000 BC.

I was lucky to be accommodated by the government in the same hotel as the hostages. Putting me in the Melia Mensour enabled me to visit them on a regular basis and to help at least some of them. Danny and I had been put there for other reasons which I gradually became aware of. A car from the government was also at my disposal. It was the government's way of controlling us and watching our movements. We were virtually prisoners with a minder to watch us, to bring us everywhere we wanted to go.

The prisoner of Baghdad

One British hostage had been held in prison, in Abe Graebe, outside Baghdad. His name was Ian Richter, and he was taken in reprisal for the imprisonment in London of the Iraqi assassin of the country's former prime minister. Shortly after that happened, Richter, a chemical engineer, was at the airport, going on leave, when a security guard tapped him on the shoulder and asked him to stay behind. Without questioning, he was put into solitary confinement for three months. His wife Shirley did not know where he was, and the officials would not tell her whether he was alive or dead. Eventually she found out where he was, and each month she used to leave her three young children in London and travel to Baghdad to see him.

In the build-up to the war, Shirley was not able to get into Baghdad and so she asked Danny and me if we would try to see him. We eventually secured permission to go to Abe Graebe Prison. In the beginning they refused to allow Danny into the cell, saying that the permission was for one person only. I argued with them, because Danny had known the family better than I, and I wanted him to meet Ian. Eventually they asked me if Danny was a priest. I replied that he was not yet a priest but he had been in training, which was true. On that score we were both allowed to see Ian. I had told the guards that I would be praying with him, and I brought the vestments to say Mass. They allowed me to say Mass, although we were carefully watched. Mass took an hour-and-a-half, as we used the pauses between the readings to talk to Ian about Shirley and the three children, whom he had not seen for five years.

During the Mass the guard would fall asleep, and this gave us the opportunity to ask Ian about life in the prison. He had managed to keep himself very busy. He used to jog for about fifteen miles each morning in the prison grounds in a very limited area. He prayed a lot and used to write one letter each day to his family and friends. I used to bring his letters home for him, after passing through the security checks of course. He was living in reasonable conditions with a small cell to himself, and had the use of a radio. He used to get the news of the war from the BBC each morning. He was even able to cook his own food. I visited Ian five times in all – on two occasions after the war.

I was the first to break the news to his wife that he was alive after the war. There were fears that he might have been near a chemical plant which could have been blown up, spreading the poisonous gas into the prison, but it did not happen and he survived. Ian had problems getting clean water, but he had managed to boil it in the prison. I found the prison guards very courteous and kind. They admired Ian, and were hoping that he would be released. He was eventually released in December 1991, just as many other hostages such as Terry Waite, John McCarthy and Brian Keenan were being released from Lebanon. It was not politically wise to hold innocent men in prison, and had brought angry reactions from many states in the West. I was able to celebrate Ian's release with his family and Danny Lillis in Richmond in London just before Christmas 1991.

The Parc Hospital
The Parc Hospital was one of the best hospitals in the Middle East. It was built by the Iraqi government for two reasons: to provide a medical service for seriously-ill patients, so as to eliminate the need

for travelling to Europe and elsewhere for treatment, and to train Iraqi nurses and overcome the taboo which prohibited Arab women taking up the nursing profession.

Saddam Hussein was introducing western standards into Iraqi society. He was very interested in upgrading the status of women, and was succeeding gradually, unlike other Arab states. He was particularly interested in educating Arab girls.

Ireland had the contract for the running of Parc Hospital and the nurses were mostly from Ireland. Iraq was setting a lead for Arab countries in many ways, and it was the most progressive Arab administration in this respect.

I became familiar with the personnel of the hospital, and used to go there nearly every day. It was a way of escaping from my security guard. I made arrangements with the matron, Marian Noone, to give me an appointment for every day, and in fact I got a complete medical check-up. The nurses and doctors were extremely worried in the build-up to the war. Their parents wanted them all out, and home. They loved the work there, and it was good employment for hundreds of nurses. But now they were upset and frightened by the prospect of war. Gradually their numbers dwindled, and the last of them left a week before the outbreak of war. The Irish did great work in the hospital while enjoying the many benefits of Baghdad, including its climate and leisure facilities.

One incident stands out in my mind when I think about the Parc Hospital. The story began in Kuwait after the invasion by Iraq on 2 August 1990. The European residents of Kuwait were told to report to the government in Baghdad. Many obeyed the instruction, but some debated going underground in Kuwait in the hope that a settlement would be reached. Bruce Duncan, his wife, two young sons and two daughters decided to remain in Kuwait. As things got dangerous, and war became imminent, they decided that the mother and two daughters would return to England. The two boys, Rory and Alexander, were minors and could go if they wished, but they decided to stick by their father.

Later on, as the difficulties increased, Bruce asked the two boys to consider leaving. He himself had no alternative but to stay. The boys set out from Kuwait, secured their exit visas, and were being driven to the airport by an Iraqi driver when they had a dreadful accident; the car turned over, killing the driver and Alexander. Rory was badly wounded and was taken into the Parc Hospital. I was told about the tragedy and I went to see him. His father was called up from Kuwait, and I met him in the room with Rory. Bruce was very angry. He had taken the picture of Saddam Hussein from the wall and put it on the floor. I told him to put it back at once – he had committed a criminal act for which he could lose his life. He obeyed. I became close to him and his son. Rory called me aside and whispered to me that his father was very bitter, and asked me to try to help him.

I found they were good Catholics and I told them I would say Mass in the hospital room. Marian Noone informed me that it was forbidden to say prayers or to have Mass in the hospital. When we were alone she told me to bring everything for Mass and she would lock the door under the pretence of changing Rory's dressings. I arrived quietly one morning at about 10.00 and had a reconciliation service for Bruce and Rory before Mass.

I visited them many times afterwards, and one day Bruce said, 'If the death of my son Alexander brings peace to Iraq I would be fully reconciled. I offer his life for peace.' Rory said, 'I will go back to England to bury my brother, and I hope to return to Iraq and work for peace for the country.' It is a beautiful story of the workings of grace in the soul of an embittered man. He was ready to forgive. I brought Bishop Michael Kenny, from Alaska, who was on a mission of peace, to see them. He said afterwards that if he had achieved nothing else other than meet Bruce and Rory, his trip to Iraq would have been worthwhile. Bruce and Rory left shortly afterwards and I have not heard of them since.

The countdown to war

In reply to Mother Teresa's letter Saddam Hussein invited her to come and bring her sisters to work in Iraq. I returned to Rome in December 1990 to report back to Mother Teresa, but she was not ready to go to Iraq at once, as she had committed herself to going to her native Albania.

Mother Teresa had been praying for years to get into her own country, but the atheistic president had not invited her. At last the invitation had arrived and she had to give it priority.

I was invited to appear on the *Terry Wogan Show* in London, where I launched a Christmas Record for Refugees. The St Winifred's Choir from Manchester also appeared to sing 'A Better World'. The lead singer was an Iranian refugee. I brought a special message from Mother Teresa to Terry Wogan, which I read out to the audience.

I returned to Baghdad on Christmas Day 1990 with supplies of much-needed medicines, which were permissible under the terms of the sanctions against Iraq. I remained in Baghdad until 16 January 1991 – the day after the deadline for war declared by President Bush. I tried to convince as many people as possible to leave Baghdad on or before 15 January, but my advice was ignored – the residents did not think the Allies were serious, believing that they would not go to war with Iraq and that Bush was bluffing. I argued that there were 300,000 Allied soldiers with the most up-to-date equipment in Saudi Arabia, which was an indication of the seriousness of their intention to strike with a mighty force.

I will never forget the night of 15 January 1991. I was alone in my room, reflecting on the horrific war that would break out at any moment. I knew it was coming, but I could not convince the government officials or the people of Baghdad to leave the city before the bombs would begin to drop. These and many such thoughts flooded into my mind, and I broke out in a cold sweat – I had to change my clothes several times even though there was a light frost on the ground outside. I have never felt such fear, which was almost beyond my control. I thought of Jesus in the Garden of Gethsemane, but of course I could not be compared to him in his mental anguish.

I prayed as never before, but I did not sleep during that long night. Although nothing happened that night, the suspense was almost more than I could bear. The ominous silence was frightening, the tension in the air was at explosion point. There was nothing left but prayer, and it was prayer that carried me through. God was present to me and with me that night for sure. Some good friend must have been praying for me.

Next morning a car came to take us to the airport. We waited for a flight all day – one moment we were told to get ready, the next we were told the flight was cancelled. It was 5.30 p.m. when we boarded the last plane from Baghdad for Amman, where we landed about one-and-a-half hours later. I had been in bed for about three hours when Danny Lillis called from London to say that the war had started with the bombing of Baghdad. We had left Baghdad just five hours before it started. I turned on the TV and saw the planes dropping bombs on the beautiful people I had just left a few hours earlier. I turned it off in disgust. Our mission of peace to Iraq had failed, but at least we had tried.

Danny asked me to get back to London as quickly as possible, and so I decided to go to the airport. But it was virtually deserted, apart from a few of the staff. Earlier there had been a radio announcement that the airport was closed, so neither passengers nor staff had turned up. Rumour had it that the airport might be attacked by the Israeli airforce.

One man saw me in the hall and shouted abuse at me: 'What are you doing here – who do you Americans think you are? Get out of our country and leave us alone – we do not want you here…'. His abuse went on for some time, but I kept silent. He eventually said to me in an angry tone, 'What do you want anyway?' I replied politely, 'I want a cup of coffee, please, but the restaurant is closed.' I took the wind out of his sails. 'For your information', I continued, 'I am not American – here is my passport – I'm an Irish priest and I have just come out of Baghdad where I have been working for several months on behalf of Mother Teresa, trying to stop the war.'

His attitude changed completely – he got me a cup of coffee and a few slices of bread. Coffee has a great significance in the Middle East as a sign of friendship and peace. It is a ritual. Abdulla asked what he could do for me. I said I was trying to get to London by any means. He offered me the use of his office and telephone. He found telephone numbers in the Arabic directory, and could not have done more for me. How could I travel to London with the airport closed? Should I go through Syria by road, though it could be dangerous, as I would have to pass between the lines of Baghdad on my right and Israel on my left? Should I go by road to Aquaba, and by boat to Egypt, to Cairo where I would get a flight to London? At about 2.30 p.m. I decided to go back into the city of Amman.

The whole country was in a state of shock. I tried to get a taxi but in vain. I told Abdulla of my difficulty and he offered to bring me into Amman. On the way he was still very angry about the war, which he blamed on the Americans. He said many derogatory things about them. 'Am I to teach my children to hate Americans for all time?' he fumed.

He asked me if I would honour him by coming to his house, meeting his family and blessing his house and children. He lived on a hill, and as we got out of his car he pointed over towards his native Palestine and said to me, 'Each morning when I get up, I have to look across at my homeland where I should be living.'

I spent half an hour in his house drinking coffee, and looking at the school homework of his little children. His wife spoke excellent English. He asked me to bless the household, which I did. I then asked him to pray according to Islam, which he did. After this, he drove me to my destination. I met Abdulla a few times afterwards, on some of my return trips to Amman, and he promised to assist me in my work if he could.

A very sad occurrence that remains in my memory is of a Dominican student who had been studying for the priesthood in France during the Gulf War. He was so worried for the safety of his family that his health began to deteriorate. He could not eat or sleep or concentrate on his studies. One morning he got the good news that all his family had survived the war. He was overjoyed and called his fellow students together to celebrate. The celebrations continued into lunch. After lunch he decided to go for a swim. He jumped into the pool and lost consciousness. He was taken out of the pool, but was already dead. His body was taken back to Baghdad for burial. I attended the huge funeral – one of the saddest I ever witnessed. I visited the family afterwards and found them very distressed. They had survived the war, but their son had lost his life in the security of Europe. How strange are the ways of God. May his dear soul rest in peace.

Iraq after the Gulf War

I returned to Baghdad on 9 March 1991, about two weeks after the war, with a truckload of food supplies. Our aim was to carry on our mission of peace and reconciliation and respond to the needs of the suffering, irrespective of the politics. Mother Teresa would always say: 'Do not get involved in politics, because if you do you cannot love all people, and we must love everyone.'

The journey to Baghdad was a difficult one, especially as I was travelling on my own, with a driver who did not speak a word of

English and with long delays caused by security checks, broken-down trucks, etc. We travelled for two and a half days across some 600 miles of pure desert. At midnight on 8 March we crossed the border from Jordan at Ruweished, into no-man's land, where we slept for the night in the truck. On Saturday morning at 6.00 we arrived at the customs post where we spent two hours getting clearance. Once over the border into Iraq there is a very good flat road, without a blade of grass, a shrub or a tree. There is nothing but desert on the road to Baghdad. The road had been bombed in about fifteen places and a few vehicles had been blown up, including a civilian passenger bus.

Near Baghdad a bridge had been destroyed, but small vehicles were able to cross. However, we had to take a diversion via Ramadi. We made it to Baghdad at about 8.00 p.m. Unfortunately, when getting down from the large truck, I fell awkwardly and twisted my knee. I was hospitalised in St Raphael's in Karada. All the windows of the hospital had been blown out by bomb blasts and the patients had been sent home. I was alone but very well cared for by the Dominican Presentation Sisters and the doctors. My leg was in plaster for ten days.

The city was like a morgue, in total darkness. There was no electricity, no pumping of water for domestic or sanitary purposes. There was little or no fuel and the streets were empty of cars. The entire phone system had been knocked out. There was raw sewage in the streets. The people were in a state of shock, anger and depression. Most of the shops were locked up, business was at a standstill and food was very scarce. Many buildings, though not hit directly by bombs, were, like St Raphael's, damaged by blasts.

Far more damage had been done than was admitted by the Allied forces. In Falluja, near Ramadi, about 250 people had been killed by bombs which missed their target, a bridge, and had exploded in an open market. In Samawa on the Euphrates 350 civilians were killed by bombs in an open market far away from any military target. In Nasiriya a bridge had been knocked out of action for traffic but was bombed again, killing about 100-150 pedestrians.

The estimated number of deaths in the Iraqi army varied from 100,000-150,000. It all added up to a very sad and grim picture. Of the seven bridges crossing the Tigris in the city, four were damaged and this caused great difficulties for traffic crossing the city.

As I lay in bed in St Raphael's a lot of people came to visit me, including several Church leaders, delighted to see me back. All advised me that it was a very dangerous time, and that I should lie low.

Many people who visited me were worried about their relations overseas, and asked me if I would phone them when I returned to Amman to let them know they were safe and well and that they should not worry about them. I received hundreds of letters from frightened people in Baghdad. From Amman, I telephoned all over the world to reassure people that their loved ones were safe.

A civil war broke out in Iraq after the Gulf War. The Kurds were moving southwards from the north, and the Shiites were moving north, and were only sixty miles from Baghdad. Anything could happen – I was in God's hands. There was a house-to-house search for weapons in Karada. Many arrests were made and the people were very frightened.

The medical situation was extremely serious and many people were dying because of the destruction of the infrastructure throughout the country as a whole. The loss of telephones, elecricity supplies, proper sanitation and clean water supplies had brought the health services to a standstill. The acute shortage of medicines brought about by seven months of sanctions, and the growing shortage of food, had weakened the population beyond acceptable standards.

Dr Marcus of the Ministry of Health was very angry about the sanctions, saying that although medical supplies and baby foods were not included, in practice it was impossible to bring them into the country – even the medical supplies that were bought and paid for before 2 August 1990, the date of the invasion of Kuwait, were sent back from the border. 'Our medical standards were the highest in the Middle East, but now they are unacceptable and even below the standards of the Third World,' he said bitterly. 'Sixty cases of immediate deaths were recorded in Medical City alone when the electricity plant was blown up. These people were dependent on life-support systems.'

Dr Marcus complained of the military attacks on the hospitals in Basrah, which caused millions of dollars of damage. He asked for medical supplies and gave me an extensive list. He also asked for nurses, and three sisters of the Divine Motherhood in Jordan offered their services. They were Sisters Brigid Kennedy, Juliana Chin and Caroline Granil.

The Christian Churches had remained in Baghdad during the war, sharing the great sufferings and frightening experiences of the people, who lived in fear under the massive bombardments day and night. Though all the ambassadors had left, the Apostolic Nuncio remained in Baghdad during the war. The Ministry of Religious Affairs and Endowment (AWKAF) is responsible for the religious affairs of the state, and it has given much greater autonomy to the Christian Churches than any other Arab state.

The ICRC had an office beside St Raphael's Church and were trying to assist in the tracing of soldiers at the front. Long queues of people lined the street looking for information about their brothers or sons who had fought in the war. It was sad to see parents waiting for days for an indication that their sons were still alive. There was a great sense of frustration and suffering, with only the slightest glimmer of hope.

I returned to Amman with my leg still in plaster and using crutches. The taxi broke down on the way, so the journey was long and painful. I was invited to stay with the De La Salle Brothers in Amman. Thanks to Salim Saad, the Irish Consul, I got an office in the centre of the city. Salim Saad, himself a Palestinian refugee, understood what it was to suffer. From my office I began to organise more convoys of food for Baghdad. Soon many refugees from Iraq came to me for assistance in getting refugee status, so that they could go abroad. It became extremely difficult and dangerous to manage, as I was constantly watched by Iraqi security. Furthermore, there was no sympathy for Iraqis in any of the embassies – all countries had closed their doors against them.

An Iraqi woman with five teenage daughters approached me and asked if I could get them out of the country. She was in despair and pleaded with me to take them anywhere in the world. She wanted to save her daughters at any cost, even if she would never see them again. She was only one of thousands. I tried Germany, the US, Britain and others without success. The doors were solidly closed against nationals of Iraq.

Later there was a great exodus of Palestinian refugees, estimated at 300,000, from Kuwait into Jordan. Palestinians and Jordanians were being expelled from Kuwait because of their support for Iraq in the war. Refugee Trust set up a medical programme co-financed by the EU, and implemented by Father Patrick Flanagan. It saved many lives and helped many people.

Father Flanagan also ferried food into Baghdad. In September 1993 he reported the gravity of the situation in Baghdad and Iraq. He said food was like gold dust. He told the story of a young boy who went to school very agitated and depressed. The teacher asked him what was wrong with him. Did he not have any breakfast? The boy replied that he did not have any breakfast and his father told him that he must wait his turn for his next meal. He had his family to feed in rotation, and this boy's turn would be in three days' time. 'It is a simple story,' wrote Father Flanagan, 'but it illustrates the condition of things for most families in Baghdad today.'

Father Flanagan took another convoy of supplies into Baghdad in 1993 and yet again in March 1995. His last report makes disturbing reading:

> On arriving in Amman I found an air of pessimism as far as news of Iraq is concerned. I talked with many people who said the situation had deteriorated ... robberies by armed gangs were alleged to be commonplace ... The Missionaries of Charity told me that the Sisters in Baghdad feared for their safety, and were afraid that if they continued to keep large stocks of food in their compound the people would simply storm their stores to get food. Such is the desperation of the people. Hospitals have little or no medicines and children and old people are seriously at risk.
>
> Father Baffro, head of Caritas Iraq, told me how his house had been invaded by a gang who kidnapped him, and stole money and valuables from his house, including his car. His brother had been arrested and thrown into prison for changing American dollars on the black market. Father Baffro was afraid to return to Baghdad, wondering if something worse was in store for him.
>
> Father Louis Sako told me that the situation in Mosul was very bad. There was a constant influx of people from

Northern Iraq, where he said law and order had broken down and armed gangs ruled as they pleased.

Father Adeli informed me that there was a constant exodus of Iraqis to Amman. Most of the estimated refugees arrived in Amman with nowhere to go. Many were sleeping in the streets in downtown Amman.

Father Flanagan continued:

The journey to Baghdad with Sister Josephina of the Missionaries of Charity went according to plan. On arrival at about 6.00 p.m. in the fading light, people, and particularly women in their long black robes and head-dresses, were crowding around the gates of the convent, begging the Sisters for food. It was a pitiful sight and was repeated all the five days I was there. Archbishop Dahdah was as usual very gracious and did everything possible to make me feel at home. There was an anxiety in his face, however, which had not been there before. He told me the situation was very bad and getting worse on a daily basis. 'We are living,' he said, 'THE ULTIMATE TRAGEDY.'

He also said there had been a rise in anti-Christian feeling from some fundamentalist pressure groups and this was one of the reasons why so many Christians had tried to get visas to other countries. Christians find themselves constantly intimidated by Muslim fundamentalists, though not, it must be said, by the Government as shown by the fact that Government had given back many schools that they had previously taken over from the Church. Saddam Hussein has himself always favoured the Christian Community. The Chaldean Patriarch, it seems, has always enjoyed favoured status with the President. It is said that all the President's household staff are Christians. He trusts them more than his Muslim brothers.

I had a long discussion with Father Vincent Von Vossel, a Redemptorist priest who spent all his priestly life in Baghdad. He said he never remembers the situation being as bad as it is now. He felt they were descending into a situation of social anarchy. He had just visited a woman whose husband had been killed, with six children to care for, who was living in a small house with no visible means of support. She was depressed and mentally unstable at this stage. She was dependent on Father Vincent to bring her some food.

Prostitution has increased at an alarming rate. This, of course, was unheard of in a Muslim society but because of the need for food, and the fact that there are an estimated eight females of marrying age to every man of the same age, the practice has increased considerably.

Father Vincent would like to get more milk, especially, as all his work nowadays was taken up with visiting families and bringing them food. People, he said, had sold all their valuables, including their furniture, to get money to buy food. 'Desperation' was a word he often used to describe the overall situation.

Visiting Baghdad today is a disturbing experience. It means listening to, and experiencing a constant story of despair and hopelessness.

While in Baghdad I took the opportunity of visiting the Humanitarian Headquarters of the United Nations based in the Canal Hotel. The message from there was simply that they did not have enough food to meet the needs of the people. Surrounded by a bank of computers, short-wave radios and numerous telephones, one man told me that they were meeting about five per cent of the needs of the people. Any food they received was distributed to three refugee camps of Palestinians, Iranians and Kurds.

Before I left Baghdad our convoy of food had arrived at the Archbishop's store. The convoy of sugar was due to arrive a few days later.

Finally, all I can say is that something needs to be done, and done quickly.

20 March 1995

Mother Teresa goes to Baghdad
By 11 June 1991 Mother Teresa was ready to go to Baghdad. I had prepared the way for her and she invited me to accompany her. We

travelled by air from Rome to Geneva, and from there we went by a United Nations plane – the only way into Baghdad by air. The sanctions imposed by the Allies included the grounding of Iraqi aircraft. The UN would not normally take civilian passengers, but they made an exception for Mother Teresa. We arrived at a military airport in the desert, about sixty miles from Baghdad, where a large delegation which included officials from the Ministry of Health and leaders of the Church was waiting for us. As we landed, Mother Teresa asked the hostess if there was any food left which she could give to the poor. The hostess brought a lot of parcels of food to her.

The officials presented me with their programme, which included a state banquet. They had also booked Mother Teresa into the Rasheed Hotel. I told them she would stay in a simple convent and would not agree to attend a banquet. They altered the plan of her visit. We left for the city and went to a convent of local Sisters – the Sisters of the Immaculate Conception in Zafarania. Next day the Minister of Health came to see Mother Teresa in the convent, a visit which was unprecedented in an Arab country. During this meeting Mother Teresa got down to business quickly, and asked the minister for two things – a house for her Sisters who were waiting in Rome, and an audience with Saddam Hussein. Two days later the ministry invited her to see a number of houses. She got a choice of three, and picked the one which suited her best, near St Raphael's Convent and St Raphael's Hospital. In fact, the house was formerly part of St Raphael's and was used as an orphanage until it was confiscated by the government about fourteen years earlier. By Friday she was cleaning the empty house, and many Christians came to give her assistance. They brought furniture, food, paint, etc. In a short time the house was transformed, and I said the first Mass there. One Christian man and his wife began to strip their house of carpets and furniture to give to the Sisters.

Mother Teresa sent word to Rome through the United Nations satellite station for the Sisters to come by road via Jordan. When they arrived, Mother Teresa spent a few days with them before she left for Rome. The government had asked her if she would open another house outside Baghdad and, when she agreed, they took her to Kerbala, a town that had been devastated by the war against the Shiite Muslims after the Gulf War. She agreed that she would work there if they provided her with a house, which they did. When she brought this news back to Baghdad the Christians would hardly believe her. Kerbala was a sacred city for Muslims, second in the world to Mecca, and no Christian was even allowed to live there. Yet Mother Teresa had been invited to set up a relief programme in the midst of the Shiite Muslims. However, they would have to wait until Mother Teresa got the first home for disabled children off the ground.

Mother Teresa met the vice-president and on Monday, 17 June 1991 she met Tariq Aziz, the deputy prime minister, the only Christian in the Cabinet of the strongly Muslim government, for about an hour. The minister stressed the needs of Iraq in one phrase: 'Remove the sanctions.' 'We cannot export our oil,' he said, 'Our foreign assets are frozen and we cannot buy food – we are dependent on others for everything. The embargo is crippling our country.'

Before leaving, Mother Teresa met the leaders of the Christian Churches, the Red Crescent and the UN. On 26 June she left on a UN plane for Rome via Geneva.

The expansion programme

In August 1997 I went to New York in the hope of setting up a branch of International Refugee Trust. It was very providential in that I was assigned to Father Joseph Hickey, parish priest in Elmont. He was very interested in my work, and became the first Chairman of the new organisation. Before leaving Elmont, I had a Committee, with Fr Hickey as Chairman, Joe Messina as Treasurer, and Edward Abrosario as our legal adviser. I was invited to appear on a television chat show hosted by Mgr Thomas Hatman, Director of the Telecare station, to discuss refugee issues.

I then decided to go into Europe and I contacted some friends including the following:

> Dr Georg Specht, Director of Caritas Germany for many years, with whom I worked very closely in Ethiopia, in Sambia and elsewhere for many years.

> Mrs Netty Muller Grosse, whom I met in Baghdad on a mission of peace. A very devout Christian, and dedicated

worker for the poor and underproviledged, she works tirelessly to improve the conditions of the poorer classes. Mrs Maria Oost de Boer, Urk, Holland, whom I had known in Ethiopia for many years. She was leader of a team of Relief workers in Ethiopia.

Mrs Mona Mullerup was a leader of DanChurchaid in Biafra during the Nigerian Civil War. She worked with her husband, Reverend Pastor Mullerup in the relief of famine victims, and saved a lot of lives.

Mrs Elizabeth Bicknessl was a volunteer in Ethiopia, and secretary at the Ethiopian Catholic Secretariat for about two years.

Father Claude Galmiche, a Missionary of Africa whom I knew in Zambia, who was responsible for the foundation of the Cheshire Home for handicapped children in Chipata.

Mr Edward de Brandt was Director of Caritas Belgium. I worked with him over the years in famine and war situations. An excellent man, he is now retired.

Almost all have have offered their services to establish branches of Refugee Trust in their various countries.

CHAPTER 20

UNDERSTANDING THE REFUGEE

Refugees speak out their needs
Refugees need not only our sympathy,
They need our understanding.

Refugees do not want our pity,
They want our practical assistance.

Refugees do not appreciate our long speeches
    and fine words,
They prefer our silence and our sincerity.

Refugees do not value our pride and arrogance,
They look rather for our respect and dignity.

Refugees are angered and enraged by our rejection,
They need our total acceptance.

Refugees do not appreciate our interference,
They appreciate being left alone and to themselves.

Refugees do not value our condescension and patronisation,
They rather prefer our love and our prayers.

Refugees do not want our anger and bitterness,
They crave our kindness and forbearance.

Refugees do not want our discrimination and segregation,
They love unity, peace and solidarity.

Refugees do not like pious talk and platitudes,
They prefer genuine spirituality and real sanctity.

Refugees do not ask for special attention,
They prefer to be treated like ordinary people.

> Refugees are not beggars,
> They are our equals, if not our betters.

I was caught in the earthquake in San Francisco in 1981. Danny Lillis and I had been doing business with the US branch of International Refugee Trust. We were packing our bags to leave for London when the earthquake struck. Suddenly the house began to dance around us. Danny shouted to me to go to the back of the house, but we were blocked by the water from the swimming pool. The pool became an angry sea, overflowed onto the lawn and came into the house. We went out the front door instead, and in the streets there was pandemonium

We left for the airport, but were unable to get into the terminal building. The roof had fallen in and the passengers were all gathered outside, waiting for news of their flights. After about two hours we were brought by bus straight onto the airstrip, where the British crews had prepared everything on the tarmac at the foot of the plane. We went through customs, emigration and passport control without difficulty, and we were soon airborne.

In London we were surrounded by journalists and TV crews looking for the news from the first passengers to reach London. We were invited onto Sky TV for a commentary on the events in San Francisco.

It was an interesting but frightening experience for us, but more so for the people of San Francisco. Some were killed on destroyed motorways or caught under falling houses, and many were afraid to go on living in the centre of the city. It knocked the complacency out of the population. Some changed their jobs, afraid to go into the city again. California was once considered a paradise, but no longer. It has a beautiful climate all the year round and is inhabited by some of the wealthiest people in the world, but God spoke to them, saying not to take all their pleasures for granted any more. 'The Lord cast down the mighty from their thrones and raised up the lowly.' God draws good out of everything in his infinite wisdom.

In the long history of the Church, stretching back into the Old Testament, God spoke to his people through disaster. Sometimes it was the only way in which he could make contact. Amos said that if small-scale disasters don't work, large-scale disasters are necessary, that they are very effective, though unpleasant methods of divine catechesis of stubborn people, who, because of their social injustice or idolatry, have sinned against God who brought them out of the land of Egypt and the grip of the Pharaoh of Egypt (2 Kings 17:7).

Jeremiah gave voice to the agony and misery of the refugee. He foretold the destruction of the beautiful city of Jerusalem by the Babylonians, and the carrying off of the Jews into exile and bondage. His prophecy was not popular and sparked off a great controversy, many believing that Jerusalem was indestructible. His supporters quoted Micah 26:18:

> Zion will become ploughland, Jerusalem a heap of rubble, and the mountain of the Temple a wooded height.

Perhaps we should view disasters and the agonies of exiles and refugees as fitting into God's mysterious plan, carrying a very significant message, destroying our apparent religious securities to purify our faith and strengthen our love for him. God replaces our false security with the genuine security of faith. The Babylonian captivity demonstrates how the Jews went into exile as a nation and emerged as a Church. Such a providential achievement could not have been foreseen by us. In the Christian faith there must be the challenge, the reality of the desert, and ultimately the arrival in the promised land.

We have to look at modern catastrophes in the same light, and both human-made and natural disasters must somehow be seen as God's plan in the history of salvation.

The plight of refugees

If I have devoted much of my life to refugees, it is for a very good reason. It all goes back to when I lived in exile with the Biafrans for nine months, and I tried to understand what it is to be a refugee. It was a tough school, but there was no better place to learn the real truth about the bald realities of being displaced, of having lost everything. It produced profound effects in me.

The anxieties and sufferings that refugees have to endure are beyond our understanding. Their greatest sorrows are inside them. A woman was sitting beside a bowl of rice in a camp in the Philippines, just staring in front of her and ignoring the meal.

When the commander of the refugee camp was asked why she was not eating, he told her story. A boatload of people escaping from Vietnam was surrounded by pirates. There were fourteen on board, including a woman and her two small children. The pirates told them that the woman must give over her two children or they would sink the boat and all in it. The woman had no alternative but to comply. Her children would be used for slavery and possibly for prostitution. Think of the anguish of that poor woman – her remorse for having given away her children, her guilt for the rest of her ruined life. The grief would not go away because she loved her children and they would now haunt her for the rest of her days. She was devastated.

Many people think of refugees as people with empty stomachs, but that may well be the easiest of their sufferings. They have lost everything, including their past, their future hopes and dreams. They suffer from the greatest poverty of all, their insecurity. They don't know where they will be tomorrow, where they will get food for their families. They are at the mercy of others, totally dependent on them for everything that they get. They are prisoners, and the women are often the victims of rape and violence. They can't go back, they can't go forward, they are in a limbo of non-existence.

When the Frelimo attacked a village in Mozambique, the people scattered in all directions. One woman picked up her four children and ran away from the gunfire, only to find herself in the famous Kruger National Game Park in the Transvaal. It was fifty miles wide, and when the woman reached about half-way across she found she could not cope with the four children. She had to abandon the two weaker ones and make her way through the wild animals into South Africa. She arrived in a Catholic mission outside the game park, exhausted, with her children on the point of death. The priest looked after her, and she and her children regained their strength. She had to report to the police, who put her in a refugee camp. Think of her mental anguish – her guilt for having left two children to die in the wilderness in the midst of ferocious wild animals. She will be haunted by actions for which she cannot be blamed.

I was in Malawi working with Father Conor Kennedy at the Mission of Ntendere in the diocese of Dedza, when a boy of eighteen or twenty years of age came into the compound. He was one of a family of twelve – mother and father and ten children. When his village was attacked suddenly the family fled into the bush and got scattered in the confusion. He found himself in Malawi, and was hoping that his family would also flee in that direction. He had spent a year looking for them without any success, going from one refugee camp to the next. He called to many police stations and missions in his search, but no one had heard of or seen them. He now presumed they were dead, and yet he was afraid to go back home. So he came into the mission to ask for help. He would have to live his life with the memory of that family he loved so much. He was devastated. If anyone could help him it was Father Conor Kennedy, who had a great relationship with refugees. Conor had also been involved in peace initiatives, and in reconciling the warring factions in Mozambique.

Atrocities are, unfortunately, part and parcel of war. In Mozambique a man was accused of siding with the government. The people were assembled and his wife was given a knife to cut her husband to pieces in a public square. Such atrocities are familiar to refugees.

Research into atrocities is being done in a clinic in Los Angeles in California. There is a concentration of Vietnamese in Los Angeles and many of them suffer from blindness. In the Doheny Clinic these blind people were examined and it was discovered that their eyes are perfectly healthy. There is nothing physically wrong with their eyes. They suffer from psychosomatic blindness. The clinic is trying to devise means of curing it. The patients are made to live a normal life, to go shopping, to use the buses and do everything that normal people do. It is said that the blindness is the result of seeing atrocities such as that in Mozambique. Gretchen van Boemel, who carries out the research, has sent me some of her findings. No doubt much of the sickness among refugees originates in stress, and there is need for much more research into their condition, especially their mental behaviour.

The sufferings of refugees go very deep. The emotional distress, psychological trauma and mental anguish are scarcely touched in the anxiety to relieve their hunger. More must be done for these aspects of refugee work and more research is called for, to address the hidden sufferings of refugees and displaced persons. The spiritual needs of refugees is an important factor for those working among them. Their sufferings bring them closer to God. They must be given the opportunity of practising their faith, of praying to God in the religion and culture that they know. It is very wrong to use their vulnerable situation to force religion on them, or to proselytise them.

The refugees must be left free from intimidation of any kind. When Mother Teresa went to Albania she asked the government there to allow her to open not only Catholic churches but also mosques for the Muslims, thereby respecting the religion of all. We must be open to the voice of the Holy Spirit in bringing God's message of love and reconciliation to our devastated, war-torn and sick world. In Leviticus 19:33-34 we read:

> If foreigners live with you in your land, do not harm them. You must count them as fellow citizens and love them as yourselves. For you too were once foreigners in a foreign land.

The desolation of exile

To be in exile is to experience total and absolute desolation. To be uprooted from your home and transplanted in foreign soil produces the deepest form of poverty and human suffering. It is a shattering experience which should never be underestimated.

We are often inclined to look on such an experience as a loss of material things and possessions, but that is a very superficial and inadequate assessment of the reality. It is far more than that. The material restoration can be effected in a short space of time, while the scars of uprooting and separation are deeper and often permanent. A religious sister once expressed her feelings when she fled from Eastern Europe into Austria:

> We had all the material help we could wish for, food, blankets etc. but these did not compensate for what we had lost – our homes, our loved ones. We needed help of a different kind, we wanted leadership, guidance, spiritual help, we needed a priest, a shepherd, one we could trust and talk with and express our fears and emotions, our total desolation.

The refugee in exile experiences a desolation of mind and spirit that demands urgent attention and serious consideration, while people are rushing around bringing food, blankets and clothing. It is a complex problem with many aspects – it cannot be broken down and categorised, since the trauma affects each person differently. The problems of the young differ from those of the old, those of the educated from those of the illiterate, and so forth.

People may be very poor, with bad living conditions and inadequate food, but if their surroundings are stable they know how to get what is needed for survival. We must therefore distinguish between 'static' and 'mobile' poverty – the poverty of the refugee on the run. The refugee is not only materially destitute, but has no idea of how to get survival rations – he or she is lost, alone. A refugee does not know where to look, whom to trust, whom to ask, or how to go about it. Enforced mobility leaves people with no friends or neighbours. When someone has to flee into the bush or take to the roads, the ensuing events take on a new dimension, resulting in remorse and even despair.

Deciding to become a refugee is a tortuous process. Should I move? How imminent is the danger? How serious is the threat to my life and my family? What does the future hold? What are my chances of survival if I remain? What are the consequences of being separated from the family?

Very often the decision is not rational, but is based on emotion or is the result of sudden panic brought about by an often irrational and uncontrollable fear. The decision to move is often based on the judgement of others, the herd instinct, without due consideration being given to reason. Once such a decision is made there is generally no turning back, and remorse may result when it is too late to reverse the course of action taken.

Moving means abandoning your home, and grabbing a few material possessions, usually in the form of food rations. There is generally no time for a planned, orderly withdrawal, where essential things take precedence over short-term rations. I have met many refugees with professional qualifications in countries of first asylum who could not prove that they were nurses or doctors and consequently could not get jobs. Although they have the skills and means to earn a livelihood, they are prevented from doing so by the absence of proof of identity and qualification. In refugee situations, doctors and nurses are in great demand, but without proof of competence they are rejected. How useful their knowledge of the language, culture and medical taboos of their own people could be. A highly educated person with professional competence becomes a nonentity overnight and people with identical qualifications are often flown out from Europe at great expense, to do what could be done by a local qualified refugee.

One of the major effects of disaster situations is the creation of deep mistrust in the victims. Fear, often of imaginary things, is a characteristic feature. So often people are expected to be loyal to two parties or more, all of which are opposed to one another. Some are betrayed by their own, others are made to confess to crimes they never committed. During the civil war in former Rhodesia, the rural population was accused by the government security forces of harbouring freedom fighters, while at the same time they were accused by the freedom fighters of giving their support to the government forces. They were caught in the crossfire of split loyalties. Unable to trust anyone, they took refuge in the large cities.

It is a long and painstaking process to rebuild trust in people. The restoration of confidence may take years to accomplish, even when the conflict is over.

One of the greatest agonies of refugees is the realisation that they are unwanted everywhere they go, by everyone they encounter. They feel rejected by their own country, and they take refuge in the first available country of asylum, where they expect sympathy and understanding. Instead they encounter hostility and rejection. The feeling of rejection constitutes a major part of their sufferings. They have run away in search of security, but find themselves in an alien country, listening to a foreign language, experiencing a strange culture, often in the midst of a people of a different religion. All of the sudden changes in their lives aggravate acute feelings of loneliness and of being lost in a hostile world, where no one wants to know of their plight.

Most people don't want to understand the suffering and the trauma of refugees. They tend to be uncomfortable in their presence and can even blame the victims for their misfortunes. They don't want to think about the possibility of such pain, especially when it has been inflicted by other human beings.

Not all countries are hostile to refugees. Julius Nyerere, former

President of Tanzania, opened his doors to all refugees and gave national Tanzanian citizenship to thirty-five thousand refugees from Rwanda. Zambia took in refugees from six neighbouring countries, and is still hospitable to them. Ethiopia was open to the Sudanese. Malawi welcomed refugees from Mozambique.

It is difficult to get into the rich nations of the world. Europe has almost closed its doors to refugees, and the EU has joined hands in so doing. A refugee who has been refused entry to one EU country cannot apply to another country within the EU for asylum.

The struggle for survival

The main preocupation of uprooted communities is survival. By taking to the roads they lose the support of their neighbours. They become a mobile, insecure and confused community, lost and leaderless. This sudden change is characterised by several kinds of deprivation, including total economic loss, imminent famine, serious health problems, especially for the very young and the very old, and the status of unwanted minority in an unfamiliar environment. The reality of this uprooting affects motivation and produces shock, frustration, resentment, apathy, inability to plan and a sense of hopelessness.

The natural instinct to survive is so strong that people will go to extreme lengths and explore all possibilities before abandoning the will to survive. When so many normal supports are removed, many fail to win the battle for life, while others just make it at tremendous cost. The biological survival instinct is very powerful but it also varies according to will-power. There is no lack of evidence to show the extent of suffering which people are prepared to endure in order to keep alive. Self-preservation is the strongest human instinct.

Closely linked with this biological survival is the aspiration to eventually establish economic security. This is where the provision of aid by international donors should be selective. It should aim at keeping all alive and healthy, but should not create permanent dependence. Assistance should stimulate the production of food and the provision of shelter by the refugees themselves and the creation of conditions where the uprooted community re-establishes itself by its own efforts. The planning should aim at balanced integration and always avoid over- and under-assistance. The aim should be to get the community out of the disaster zone to subsistence level and gradually to dependable self-reliance by reducing the level of dependence before withdrawing.

The needs of the actual community affected should be assessed, taking into account all aspects, including its past and present production and consumption, its own special food needs, its resilience in the face of different kinds of deprivation, cultural taboos affecting food, medicine etc, its present and potential ability to cope with change, alternative diets, and so forth.

An uprooted community is one which has been forcibly pushed out of the local environment and which is trying to settle in a new place. It carries with it its social system and maintains its values and attitudes. It keeps its systems of leadership, its micro-politics, its hierarchical order. This should not be interfered with, as these values are almost as sacred as biological survival. Relief workers must try to study these social aspects, rather than impose their own system.

It is important to note that a community is not just a collection of individuals. It must be considered as an organism, a unity. It has its own characteristics which may differ from one area to another, from one tribe to another. Communities display varying degrees of resilience, susceptibility to stress and innovation, weak points, capacity to recover and rebuild.

Uprooted communities carry with them remarkable powers of survival and recovery and relief workers must approach them as active communities, using the various elements to the best advantage. Even in the midst of crisis, natural leaders emerge, and these are the foundations on which the communities in exile can be built. Leadership must be developed and the social structure should be reconstructed as soon as possible. Uprooting often produces multiple-leadership patterns, occasionally in conflict with one another. Patience and caution are necessary to avoid serious blunders. It is vital to identify the real leaders, who will reorganise the disrupted community and activate it in its new surroundings. Everywhere in Africa there exists a sophisticated social system for governing the community and this should be maintained in the new situation. The elders usually play a prominent part in decision-making, which is generally based on long-standing conservative lines. It is therefore necessary to make an evaluation not only of the needs but also of the potential of an uprooted community. Its own organisation can be mobilised to great advantage.

Studies of survivors in similar circumstances at refugee camps reveal the principal behaviours shown by the victims are attachment ideation, drive to survive, modelling, prayer and hope. Research shows that, in disasters, the most conspicuous behaviour is the victim's preoccupation with principal attachment figures, such as parents, wives and children. Separation from family and loved ones is the highest form of loss. The existence of strong social bonds between refugee and kin provides effective sustenance and acts as a strong force towards reunion. The attachment provides a coping mechanism for the victims and separated members of a family will not rest until a reunion is somehow effected. The attachment ideation provides the most powerful motivation for enduring extreme hardship, long starvation and otherwise intolerable living conditions. A typical answer by survivors of terrible ordeals is 'I just kept thinking of my wife and family – that was all I had to live for.'

People love their own culture and will rarely abandon it. It is as much a part of them as the language they speak. Uprooted people hold onto it and refuse to adopt another culture in the country of first asylum. International agencies sometimes believe that transporting uprooted people to countries where economic conditions are better solves the whole problem. In fact, it creates a lot of unhappiness and even bitterness. Transplanting people where they do not fit in and where they are forced to live very unhappy lives provokes frustration, resentment and occasionally mental and physical disorders. It is virtually impossible to substitute one culture for another in a short time.

Several Africans spoke to me on this topic. One refugee employee of a UN organisation in Europe said she would prefer to return to her country, which was at war, in order to be with her husband. She was living with two children in comfortable surroundings and had a good job, but the separation from her husband and the strange culture in which she was living were too much for her. She suffered acute loneliness and isolation in exile which could not be compensated for by her so-called free environment and material security.

Language also presents a major problem and further isolates refugees. They cannot express themselves, their emotions remain locked up inside them, their needs are misunderstood and there can be no exchange of ideas with their hosts. The Angolan who crosses into Zambia cannot make himself understood and so tensions and frustrations accumulate. The adult refugees are generally too old to learn a new language, but allow their children to attend local schools in the host country. The children quickly learn a new language, but become, as a consequence, more isolated from their parents and culture. Psychologists have claimed that survivors of catastrophes who stayed among those speaking the same language have needed less psychological treatment than those who fled to a foreign country and learned a different language.

Survivor syndrome commonly affects refugees. It is characterised by feelings of guilt and depression, guilt not only at having survived when others died, but also intense guilt about what had to be done in order to survive. It can manifest itself in physical illness and anxiety paranoia. Such people need far more than physical help.

Learning from refugees

Donor agencies generally restrict their assistance to the provision of clothes, food, medicine, drinking water, etc. Then they withdraw. They often pride themselves on having been the first to take action, but they fail to mention other basic needs which have not been met. Too much emphasis is placed on the quantity of aid, rather than the quality and type of service provided. Relief workers often create great suffering and generate bitterness in spite of their good intentions. Their lack of sympathy and empathy with the victims, their obsession with getting things done, their eagerness to be efficient, their unwillingness to spend time sharing some of the sadness of refugees, leaves hurtful scars and deep antagonism. There is often an absence of real love and genuine care.

We run the risk of treating people as animals to be fed and ignoring the far more important aspects of their psychological and spiritual make-up. We do not always respond to the craving for love and affection inherent in every human being. The greatest disappointment for any person is to feel unwanted and unloved. It is the source of much of the deviant behaviour in youth and generates a sense of hopelessness leading to despair in adults and elderly people.

International Refugee Trust aims to assist refugees from every point of view, aware that their needs are individual and special to each one. This has been a clear indication from our experience of working closely with refugees, in Biafra, Zambia or wherever. The Vatican is most interested in the pastoral aspects of refugees, and has invited the Trust to do more in this field. In fact it has asked us to start a religious institute for this purpose, so that the spiritual aspects of the refugees will not be neglected. Mother Teresa worked on the pastoral dimension, all the time seeing the image of Christ in everyone, irrespective of their station in life. As she expressed it:

> When you touch the wounds of the poor, you are touching the body of Christ.

We must see the goodness in others. I have learned this in my work over the years with the handicapped. The refugees likewise teach us courage, patience and endurance. They are unwanted and unloved, driven out of their homeland into a foreign country where nobody wants them. They pose a threat to the local people among whom they expect to get a welcome, a place of safety and security. They have nothing and they get nothing.

Refugees are totally dependent on others – they are exploited and abused because they are most vulnerable. The women are the hardest hit – they are weaker and so open to abuse and violence. They quickly lose their self-respect, and are reduced to total beggary, with no human rights. There are roughly sixty million refugees on our planet, fleeing for their lives, going nowhere, having left behind the security of their homes, which they may never see again.

During a recent visit to Bosnia and Croatia I visited a camp outside Split, where 850 refugees were crowded into makeshift tents. They were mostly women and children, mainly Muslims who had been driven from their homes near Sarajevo. They were in a state of mourning, lamenting what they had lost, worrying about their elderly relatives left behind. It was pitiable to see them, and yet they were courageous. They welcomed us and prepared coffee for us. Their fragile tents would serve them another month, but the cold weather was coming and then they would have to move again.

The first exiles we hear about in the Old Testament were the Israelites, who were taken by force to Babylon.

'By the waters of Babylon we sat and wept....'

The weeping continues as more and more refugees flee from their homes today. Never in the history of humankind have so many been on the move on our disturbed planet.

Gene Dewey

A long-standing friend in the world of refugees is Arthur Gene Dewey, from the US State Department. I first met Gene in Biafra with Clyde Fergusson, a special envoy from the State Department, when they came to negotiate ways of bringing relief to the stricken people. They were investigating the possibilities of making peace, and how the United States could bring about a settlement of the civil war. Gene Dewey actually returned to Nigeria after the fall of Biafra and brought food to the priests and sisters in prison in Port Harcourt, before they were expelled.

I lost touch with Gene for many years, until the launching of International Refugee Trust in London in 1989. He was representing UNHCR, where he was serving as Deputy High Commissioner. He always spoke positively about refugees and his Christian attitude came across clearly. I quote an extract from his presentation on a strategy for refugees and peace in the 1990s:

> 'The next decade offers a chance to begin this vital next step – the peace-building step that logically follows the emergency response and peace-making steps I have just discussed.
>
> To take this step, however, we must put to rest many of the damaging myths surrounding refugees.
>
> • The myth says that refugees just need emergency care and maintainance; the reality is that refugees are the most suitable candidates for self-reliance and development-related projects.

- The myth assumes that refugees are so disadvantaged that they should have everything given to them while they regain their strength and self-respect; the reality is that refugees would very quickly lose their strength and self-respect, their ability to survive and to compete, if they are just handed everything.
- The myth suggests that refugees have lost everything and can contribute nothing; the reality is that refugees bring new skills, new ideas and creative energy to the development of their new countries.
- The myth states that host countries should keep refugees out of their national development plans because they would be a drain on programmes benefiting nationals; the reality proves that, when development funds are provided for countries hosting refugees, they can be and are additional to normal donor contributions, and they benefit nationals as much as, if not more than refugees.
- The myth portrays refugees as destroyers of the environment – trees, rangelands and water resources; the reality demonstrates that refugees can be the replenishers of what they have consumed, and leave much more behind for the host country in terms of trees planted, water systems installed and environmental restoration undertaken.
- The myth implies that refugees are the tragic losers in the international system and can therefore be written off in the quest for development contributions; the reality is that the refugees are the true winners – if we ignore them in development strategies, it is at our own peril.

The fact is, of course, that given peace, refugees themselves are great builders for the future. They are themselves a great asset for the world of the 1990s. Refugees like the Vietnamese girl who clambered ashore from a boat in Australia at the age of fourteen, speaking not a word of English, and who has now graduated at the top of her class with a state-wide prize in English.

We read of the Lao refugee resettled in France, who worked as a factory hand by day and studied pharmacology by night, and who is now a successful and licenced pharmacist in Paris.

We heard of a Ugandan Asian girl who fled to Austria a month before her school leaving exams, found her education going down the drain and who fought back to achieve an excellent Austrian degree that led to her recruitment by the Austrian Interior Ministry in Vienna.

We know of the Eritrean teenager who walked barefoot through the battlefields to Sudan, studied hard, got settled in Sweden and returned with an awesome string of qualifications to help the world's refugees as a senior UNHCR expert.

These, and many hundreds more, are epitomised for me by one of the most remarkable posters issued by UNHCR. Surrounding the familiar photograph of an old man with an unruly shock of white hair, the slogan on the poster reads:

'A bundle of belongings isn't the only thing a refugee brings to his new country. Einstein was a refugee.'

Gene concluded his presentation by reminding his audience that as we approached Christmas we must not forget that Jesus Christ was a refugee when he was driven into exile by King Herod, who sought to kill him. Christ wanted to share the deepest sufferings of humankind while he was on earth. We must see Christ in the refugee.

Frederick Forsyth once wrote about refugees:

When I first saw them I was not quite certain what they were. They came towards me down the narrow jungle track, single file, black eyed, carrying what humble artifacts they had been able to salvage from their abandoned villages, the women toting their children on their backs, heading they knew not where. Beyond them I heard the crackle of gunfire at the fighting front.

Hundreds and hundreds of thousands of them, uprooted by fear as the fighting swept through their farms and hamlets, impelled by no logic of decided destination but simply by a blind panic that drove them from everything they once had, into a limbo of rootlessness and occasional charity.

That was Biafra 1968. With luck most of them would one day go back home and rebuild again when the war finally ended. For millions of others since then there has been no such luck.

At the last count there were forty-five 'small wars' on this planet. They may rank as small wars to us, seated comfortably in our prosperous north-west European fortress. But for the peasants, farmers, herdsmen, stall-keepers and their families, they are not small wars at all. They are endless and often lethal. Landscapes which, though never rich, were once life-sustaining become barren vistas of burnt houses, destroyed crops, slaughtered livestock, poisoned pools.

So they run, trot, then walk and finally collapse. By then they have reached another land, often just as poor as the one they have left, unable to sustain them and resentful of their arrival.

The official count of refugees stands at twenty million, a great underestimate. Add in the 'internal refugees' (those who have not crossed an international border) and those too frightened or weak to register and we are looking at sixty million. Not all flee from wars: droughts, crop failures, diseases and tyrants play their part. The four horsemen have never been busier while our food surpluses escalate into expensive mountains.

Many agencies try to help, most target specific groups – children, the old, the hungry – but not all these categories are refugees. I believe International Refugee Trust is the only agency that targets refugees as a group, the truly most 'wretched of the earth', because they suffer all the scourges plus that of having no home of their own.

CHAPTER 21

THE BOSNIA CRISIS

When the Bosnia crisis broke the International Refugee Trust turned its attention there. The Irish branch of our Trust organised convoys of food, blankets and medical supplies and sent them by road directly to Bosnia. They used the Franciscan Fathers and Caritas to do the distribution in the beginning.

I went with John Whalley, executive director of the London office, to see how the distribution was going. We flew to Zagreb and met Cardinal Kuharic, who received us warmly and invited us to stay with him. He briefed us in detail on what was happening. He had made a survey of the damage that the Catholic Church had suffered. He had a book of photographs, with pictures of many damaged churches and presbyteries thoughout his diocese. By then, September 1992, about four hundred churches had been damaged. One priest spoke to us of his own sufferings and the torture he had endured. He asked that this information be kept private as he feared reprisals. As we travelled through the country we could see the damage for ourselves. In Ravno near Split we were taken by a priest to see his church and presbytery, which had been damaged beyond repair. The retreating soldiers had blown it up with a phosphorus bomb. We then travelled to Medjugorje where we met Father Slavco.

The following is an extract from our report from Split, dated 21 September 1992:

> John Whalley and myself visited a refugee camp just three miles outside Split where 856 refugees, mostly women and children, were taking shelter under canvas tents – an average of six people living in each tent. Fortunately the weather is warm at present but in one month's time the winter will begin, bringing temperatures down as low as minus fifteen to minus twenty degrees in the mountain areas. The tents will become totally inadequate.
>
> The camp is inhabited predominantly by Muslim women and children who had fled from the countryside and villages around Sarajevo – the worst-hit city in the

country, still under mortar fire. The women gave us a warm welcome, preparing coffee for us. The children crowded around and they too were very friendly. The women spoke of their terrible ordeal, walking to safety for days and nights and eventually getting a lift on any form of transport to Split. They have been here now for four months, desperate for news of their elderly relatives left behind. They are desperate to go back home – their husbands have gone to fight in the war. They spoke with emotion of relatives who died on the way and of the elderly who were too weak to travel and so were left at home. They spend their time grieving for home, in an atmosphere of great frustration, knowing it is impossible to return as yet. They feel forgotten by the outside world. The children have nothing to do as there is no school, and no teachers to occupy them or teach them.

They are just another example of what is happening to the 1.5 million people left homeless and destitute by the war. As the winter approaches the cold may kill more than the war, because 'winter kills'. The refugees' plight is grim, their future uncertain and their hopes are in the balance.

They were grateful for our visit and for the help we were bringing. Their needs are more than material – they need peace above all. At the Caritas distribution centre in Split, which we inspected this morning, supplies were running very low – because of the shortage only half rations are being distributed. The director of Caritas is asking for more food as soon as possible, with a special request for baby food, tinned meat and fish, flour and sugar.

We have followed up on the convoy of food sent out from Ireland by Refugee Trust, and met the people responsible for the distribution at the various centres. Father Leonard Orec sent the food to Medugorje for distribution by Father Slavco Barbaric, who divided the convoy into six consignments, sending three trucks to Mostar, two to Stolac, and one to Neum and Ravno. We were within ten miles of Mostar but unable to go there because of shelling. From Neum we toured the surrounding villages which had been damaged and destroyed by the fighting. Some were totally abandoned while in others, a few people were trickling back to ruined houses. The devastation had been great, except in Medugorje itself which was untouched. We visited many refugees who had fled from the fighting in Bosnia-Herzegovina.

We spoke with representatives of UNHCR in Zagreb and Split who described the situation as getting worse. Chris Thorn in Split spoke of 'working in an atmosphere of quiet desperation'. He was frustrated because he was moving only half of the requirements to prevent starvation, not to speak of the additional burden of providing clothes and shelter to cope with the winter. Red Cross representative Jakov Kovac is of the same opinion regarding the deteriorating situation, especially due to oncoming winter. Every priest, sister, and layperson we met was consistent – the missionaries expressed their aspiration very clearly: The first and most important need is peace, the international community must stop the war, the boundaries must be respected and the people protected – the war of aggression must be stopped.

John Whalley & Kevin Doheny CSSp

In 1993 a St John of God Brother, Thomas O'Grady, volunteered his services to work in Bosnia. He opened an office with Caritas in Split. He visited many interior villages, penetrating into Sarajevo in February 1994. He was invited to set up a Refugee Trust Office in that city by Archbishop Vinco Puljic, who stated: 'The presence of Refugee Trust in Sarajevo would be a great moral support and material help for the Church and the people of Sarajevo.'

Brother Thomas's visits made a great impact and he was able to link the Bosnian refugees in Ireland with their families at home. He tells the story of Muris Masic, a patient in Cappagh Hospital in Dublin, who was recovering from injuries received during the civil war. Masic had heard that his home had been destroyed by a bomb and he was not sure whether his family was alive or dead. He had asked Brother Thomas to investigate the truth. He reported that:

On the morning of February 15, Caritas Office had a queue of relatives to receive the letters I brought from Ireland. I was overcome with emotion when I received the news that the wife and two children (aged three and six) of Muris had shown up.

I was so pleased to speak to them and give them first hand news of Muris. The little boy, Kenan, said to his Mama – 'Can we go now and see Tata [Croatian for Dad].' Narmina, the mother, said – 'Not just yet. We will soon come to Dublin, but first we must get a visa.'

The family are now living in the Muslim Theological Seminary until they are given a new apartment....

Brother Thomas continues to relieve the hidden human sufferings of the refugees, as well as the physical needs, in line with the objectives of Refugee Trust.

The tremendous response to the Bosnia appeal in Ireland was wonderful. The generosity of the Irish is unsurpassed anywhere in the world. Mr Ismet Ovcina, a member of the Executive Board of Sarajevo City Council for co-operation with the UN and NGOs, had this to say:

Refugee Trust has been in Sarajevo for one year now. They have made a magnificent impact on our city and have won the hearts of all those who are fortunate to be in contact with them.

They have developed major rehabilitation programmes for the visually impaired and the blind, senior citizens, disabled and traumatised children.

They are very professional and work in full co-operation with the ministries of Bosnia and Herzegovina, the civil authorities of Sarajevo, and have a special place amongst the sixty international NGOs here in Sarajevo.

The Refugee Trust team lead by Peter O'Grady OH, has alleviated sufferings of life here in Sarajevo without complaint, proudly. It is not an organisation which is demanding, on the contrary they endure the same problems as the Sarajevan people – the shortage of water, electricity and gas, the continuous shelling, and the snipers. They simply live the spirit of Sarajevo and they are working hard for the better future of our people.

Refugee Trust does some very special things. I have witnessed their support to the Bosnian families who have relatives in Ireland. I have discussed the possibility of forming an Irish Bosnian Club here in Sarajevo.

I express my personal gratitude to Peter O'Grady and his local team, to the Board of Trustees in Dublin, to the Irish people for their generosity and to the Irish Government for their continual concern for Sarajevo and the people of Sarajevo and Herzegovina.

Cardinal Vinco Puljic wrote this letter from his residence in Sarajevo:

On the occasion of the first anniversary of Refugee Trust Ireland's arrival in the city of Sarajevo, and the launching of their first bulletin, I wish to congratulate them on their year's exceptional work for our people.

The presence of Refugee Trust, Ireland, amongst the senior citizens, the visually impaired and blind, the intellectually disabled and the 335 refugees from Eastern Bosnia engaged in processing herbal medicine has heightened the awareness of Irish people to the needs of our people in this terrible conflict in our country.

We wish to express our gratitude to the Irish people and their unfailing support to Refugee Trust which enables Brother Peter O'Grady and his local professional team to assist the most needy people in our city.

Brother Thomas O'Grady published the first copy of *Sarajevo News* on the anniversary of his arrival there. I quote an extract from his editorial:

For more than three years Bosnia and Herzegovina has been exposed to a brutal assault.

The goal of this aggression would seem to me to have been to destroy the multinational, multicultural and multireligious state of Bosnia and Herzegovina, a territory which has long been part of European territory and history.

Bosnia has been saved specifically by a succession of superhuman efforts and the courage of its citizens.

In its defence, Bosnia has suffered over 200,000 dead, more than 1.5 million people have been displaced and are forced to live in all corners of the world. For more than three years now, citizens of Bosnia and Herzegovina have existed on humanitarian aid, which has been delivered in quantities below the minimum necessary for survival.

Sarajevo, the capital city of Bosnia and Herzegovina, a city which for centuries enriched European culture and civilisation, has been besieged for three years. The name of this city in the heart of Europe used to be pronounced with respect and pride. For three years now it has been strangulated in front of the eyes of the entire European and world community.

Refugee Trust has been motivated by the people of Ireland to respond to the people of Bosnia, to show solidarity with them since the beginning of the war. Refugee Trust has taken humanitarian aid from Ireland to Bosnia and Herzegovina. Right now, we are coming to the end of the first year of our rehabilitation projects designed in co-operation with the Bosnian and Herzegovian authorities.

As far as human resources are concerned, Bosnia has both – the people and the ingenuity. If you decide to be involved in the process of rehabilitation, you will be creating the conditions for the greatest numbers of Bosnian refugees to return home. Amongst those displaced there are distinguished scientists, university professors, engineers, economists etc. They will become your partners in co-operation, something that will present for each of us a unique challenge. Co-operation with Bosnia and Herzegovina is a challenge for civilisation.

If you become a partner with Refugee Trust in the rehabilitation for Bosnia and Herzegovina, you will become a part of Refugee Trust's success story.

Refugee Trust wishes to acknowledge the generosity of

the Irish people, the concern of the Irish Government and our friends in the United States. Without your support, our mission to Bosnia and Herzegovina could not be realised.

Peace came to Bosnia in 1996. Brother O'Grady had built up a very impressive programme for the alleviation of suffering in the city of Sarajevo, Mostar and other towns. He opened five 'living centres', providing day-care services for the elderly, bringing Croats, Serbs and Muslims together for meals, and to socialise, play games, read the papers or watch TV. Brother O'Grady also opened a centre for the blind, with a blind man in charge. I visited all these centres in October 1996, and I was very impressed by the work. Brother O'Grady and his team were helping a lot of elderly people who were living in high-rise flats, without water, electricity or heating, and very little food. One woman I visited had no feet and no family. She was sitting on her bed, with a smile on her face, and she said: 'I dream of Brother Thomas.' She was almost totally dependent on the assistance of Refugee Trust.

The Refugee Trust team puts great emphasis on reconciliation, as evidenced in the 'living centres', which bring various ethnic groups together in an effort to build up peace and forgiveness.

CHAPTER 22

WAR IN RWANDA

Four hundred years ago, a group of people called Tutsi established feudal kingdoms in the lands now known as Rwanda and Burundi. They formed a land-and-cattle-owning aristocracy, ruling over a larger group of farmers, the Hutus. In return for their labour, the Hutus were granted the use of land and cattle and the protection of their overlords. Tutsi controlled the three main sources of power: the cattle economy, the monarchy, and religious life. Their rulers taught that Tutsi are inherently superior and that their dominance was ordained by God.

An ancient fable told of a mythical king of Rwanda, Gihanga, who had three sons, Hutu, Tutsi and Twa. He gave each son a jar of milk, and instructed them to keep the jar safe till the next day. However during the night Twa became thirsty and drank the milk. Hutu fell asleep and knocked over his jar and the milk was spilt. Only Tutsi succeeded in keeping his milk safe until morning. The king decided that Twa, who had clearly disobeyed him, should be punished by never being allowed to own cattle, and from time to time he should suffer starvation. Hutu, who had been careless, would be allowed to own cattle only if he worked for Tutsi. The worthy Tutsi was to be rewarded by possessing all the cattle, and by being allowed to rule the others, for only he could be trusted with the jar of milk.

Europeans reached the area during the nineteenth century, with the Germans taking over the region in 1885. Rwanda was ceded to Belgium after World War I and remained under its control until 1962. Under the Belgians the minority Tutsi continued to rule the majority Hutu. This, in many ways, is the root cause of the present conflict between the two ethnic tribes. A recent letter sent to the secretary general of the UN by the major seminarians who are refugees in Goma underlines this point: 'We touch here an ideological point – the Tutsi feel they are born to rule and the Hutu to serve.'

In 1959 the Hutus revolted and overthrew the Tutsi minority. It is estimated that up to one hundred thousand Tutsis were slaughtered and approximately two hundred thousand fled to Burundi, Uganda, Tanzania and Zaire. This was the first of the recent periods of slaughter in Rwanda.

On 1 October 1990, a force of Rwandan refugees living in Uganda invaded Rwanda to join in an attempt to topple the government of President Habarimana. They were repelled, but it began a kind of guerrilla warfare that ended in the killing of the presidents of Rwanda and Burundi on 6 April 1994. This led to an explosion of hate and resentment that had been building up since the fifteenth century. Colette Craven, a native of Rwanda, summed up the situation as follows:

> I am a native of Rwanda and we come from the South of Rwanda, Butare. The area you come from is very meaningful, because the Northerners are known as hardliners, and the Southerners as moderate. The late president was from the North and he enjoyed giving favours of any kind to the Northerners. The latter enjoyed these privileges for the past eighteen years and they did not want to share their power with any other political group. This fact was the cause of the conflict.
>
> We were a family of ten children, seven girls and three boys. My father was a Hutu and a bank manager. He died in 1991 from a long illness. My mother was a Tutsi, an extended relative of the last Queen. As far as I can remember, I have never heard any dispute or problem caused by the fact that our extended family was comprised of both Hutu and Tutsi people.
>
> I got my university degree from the University of Brussels and in 1985 I went home and got a job with the Resident Mission of the World Bank in Rwanda as project manager. I met my husband, who is Irish, in 1987 in Kigali, where he was working as a technical assistant, in an Irish-funded government project.
>
> The civil war started in October 1990 and the attack by the rebel movement was located in the north-east. In other parts of the country we could perform our activities safely. The negotiations were going on and an agreement was signed in August 1993. The implementation was due

to start in December 1993 by the UN peace-keeping force. But since January 1994 everyone could feel the atmosphere was tense and unfriendly. You could guess something unusual was going to happen, because the president, under pressure from his entourage, kept delaying the setting up of the new coalition government. That government was to confirm the power-sharing for the benefit of the rebel movement and the inside opposition. Some persons of his own entourage used to talk openly about the planned massacres, but no one believed that a human being could dare execute such atrocities. The president's plane was shot down on 6 April and the killing started that night, door to door by the Presidential Guard. Ourselves, we hid in the house for four days, after which the French troops came to evacuate the nationals of the European Union. On the way to the airport we could see bodies lying along the streets, soldiers with guns and militiamen with machetes going into houses.

We arrived in Ireland in May, after a week's break in France. We now live in Tullamore, County Offaly. Since I left Rwanda I followed news bulletins closely to find out the whereabouts of my family. I was informed that my brother and all his family were killed the first day of the killings. Although Hutu, he was killed because he was an educated man of the South and therefore he belonged to the opposition.

My cousins, two nephews and two brothers-in-law were killed as well. Although my mother was a well-known Tutsi, she escaped the genocide. She was to be shot in July 1994, when the rebel army took control of the country. Apparently some elements of the army undertook some savage killings as a revenge and my mother was one of their victims.

The future of Rwanda is bleak and it still needs external assistance. To achieve the revival of the economy and the reconstruction of the country, they need all the people from outside who left, back again so that they can start a new era. And the culprits of the genocide have to be judged and condemned, so that the people carrying out their own revenge can stop. The arrests, disappearances and vengeful actions have to be taken care of by the independent judicial system. And then the reconciliation process can start, which will lead to a lasting peace and a long stability for Rwanda.

An estimated half a million people were murdered in Rwanda in about three months, beginning in April 1994. Most of the bodies were disposed of in the rivers.

I met a priest in Kigale who brought me into a church to show me the terrible fire damage and also the destroyed sacred vessels. The congregation had been burned alive. Many of the killers were so-called Christians, most of them Catholics. How could a convinced Christian kill his own brother and sister in cold blood? There is a great contradiction in it, and the Churches must accept responsibility for the shallowness of the faith.

I was told of another massacre which was perpetrated against a congregation in another church just outside Kigale. The people were saying their prayers when the guerrillas arrived. They pleaded with the guerrillas to allow them to at least finish their prayers. They agreed, but immediately afterwards went in and shot the kneeling congregation. Two bishops and about 115 priests and religious sisters were murdered. It has been said that a priest called a meeting of the bishops and clergy, and informed the guerrillas of the time and place. All those attending the meeting were massacred.

There were atrocities everywhere. Makuramanzi, a girl aged thirteen, survived a massacre in the church in Nyamata, a small town in Bugesera, south of Kigale. Her story is heart-breaking, but typical:

> I tried to get up but in vain. I was very weak from my injuries and there were so many bodies everywhere that I could hardly move. A few children, perhaps they were unaware of the dangers, stood up. I called one of the children to help me. She was a girl of about nine. She replied that she could not help me because they had cut off her arms. I struggled to sit up, but I could not stand

up. I tried and tried but could not do it. Finally I saw a young woman whom I recognised. I called to her. At first she did not answer. I insisted and eventually she responded. When I looked closely I saw that she had her arms cut off.

But now I do not know if what I am feeling and seeing is real life or a nightmare. She confirmed that it was real life.

Ninety per cent of Rwandese call themselves Christians, according to a 1991 census. Before the Catholic Church was, after the government, the single most powerful institution, through its network of social, educational and medical institutions run by the many religious groups attracted to a peaceful country with a good climate. Rwanda is a very beautiful country and its infrastructure and the quality of life enjoyed by most of its citizens before the war would have been far higher than those of most other developing countries. They had a highly developed system of farming that made use of every acre of available land. The overpowering presence of the Church created a certain anti-clericalism among the educated class.

Father John Skinnader CSSp, of the Justice and Peace Department in Rome, spent about three months in and around Rwanda in December 1994 and January and February 1995. He made some very interesting points:

> My overpowering memory of Rwanda is a sense of evil that I experienced on entering the Churches of Gyseni and Kibeho. Here were some of the Churches that had been viciously attacked during the war and the occupants inside either hacked to death or blown apart by grenades. In the Church of Kibeho which is the 'Medjugorje' of Africa, we discovered two young girls in the burnt-out confession box, sitting reading their bible. As one aid worker remarked to me: 'Religion may have taken a battering here but it is still the faith that sustains them in their hour of need.'

Many of the people responsible for the killings and the

desecration of the churches were members of their own congregation. So, what went wrong?

A Church built on sand

Most journalists and aid workers were shocked by the total failure to give religious rites to the dead. As a UN Ghanaian worker said to me: 'Surely the first human right we have is the right to be buried with dignity.' But sixty to seventy thousand people were buried in Goma with bulldozers, with no dignity. When I asked one of the Hutu Rwandan priests why none of them were going out in the evening to give a blessing to the dead, he replied that, apart from the practical problems of getting to the grave sites, there was also the problem that 'we do not know who is Catholic in the mass graves and who is of another faith'.

For most of us this seems like an extraordinary statement, but it is necessary to understand the prevailing mentality. The people are profoundly Catholic – Catholicism pervades every aspect of their lives. In the refugee camps there are holy pictures everywhere, people wear rosaries around their necks, the Bible is widely read, and there is a high expectation of morality. Many families or groups will try to have their own private altar in their makeshift tents, with pictures venerating the Sacred Heart or the Blessed Virgin Mary. Churches are filled every Sunday to overflowing – even after all the massacres. The Catholic Church is the centre of their lives. Hence the problem of blessing people in a mass grave where there is nothing to indicate that it is a 'Catholic' grave.

We have to question ourselves as missionaries when we deliberately set out to make a country 'Catholic'. What are we actually aiming to achieve? Rwanda is profoundly Catholic. The people are very devout and sincere. But how much of Jesus' message is found in this kind of Catholicism? Have we, as missionaries, not tended to catechise as regards the sacraments and neglected the weightier matters of the law, such as justice, mercy and faith (Matthew 23:23)? There is no profound sorrow over the events that took place in their country. There is a feeling that they did what had to be done – namely, the effort to annihilate all the Tutsi people so that they could overcome their fear of becoming slaves again.

The Hutus would seem to have a filial faith and obedience to priests and bishops. This explains in part why Radio Mille Collines could gather and incite so many ordinary people to carry out so many mass killings. Both Church and State seem to me to have had a strong grip on the emotions and feelings. There does not seem to have been any effort to allow people or priests to have the space to analyse the situation for themselves.

The implication of Church leadership being too closely aligned with the government was another major factor in the Church's failure to speak out against the atrocities. From the beginning, the Catholic Church had cosy relations with both the colonial administration and the royal house. Before independence, it began to support the emancipation of the Hutus. During the second republic, the late Archbishop Vincent Hsengiyumva was a member of the Central Committee of the ruling party (MRND) and for years remained close to President Habyarimana.

The church pulpits provided an opportunity for reaching almost the whole population with a strong moral message that could have played a vital role in preventing people being manipulated by political authorities. But it would seem that, for the most part, the Church stayed silent. Even now, most of the priests and seminarians from the Hutu side will still not acknowledge that any large-scale genocide took place. Part of their reason for not admitting this is because they feel that the outside world would focus on this aspect of the killings and not acknowledge the Tutsi role.

As the AMECEA bishops celebrated Mass with the seminarians at Nyakibanda, there was no reference during the prayers of the faithful to the twelve thousand men, women and children who had been butchered and bulldozed into a mass grave outside the seminary wall. At Ruamba I refused to say a requiem Mass for a dead parishioner, because the people refused to acknowledge the mass grave behind the church. The historical and present realities of people's lives must be faced if the liturgy is to have any true value and meaning. This will be one of the big challenges for the Church in Africa in the future. How is it that for the most part the Church in Africa is gathering momentum all the time, yet the political, economic and social reality for the people is disintegrating rapidly? Have we created a two-tier system? Is the Gospel message a leaven in society, or the icing on top of a hollow cake?

Given the stance of the Church leadership, it is no surprise that some priests and others associated with the Church have been accused of actively participating in the massacres and the killings. Fortunately, the number of priests turned killer is small. But in the case of the Church, the symbolism is huge.

At Kibeho in Gikongro, where I spent six weeks, the African Rights Organisation claim that a priest was implicated in the massacre of almost a thousand Tutsi schoolboys and schoolgirls. They also claim that in the massacre at the parish of Ndera in Greater Kigale, many witnesses confirmed that a priest of the parish of Ndera played an active role in organising the killers. Both Catholic and Protestant leaders seem to have been implicated in the genocide of the Tutsi. The vehemence against Tutsi domination in religion, politics and economics is so deeply rooted that it is impossible for Hutu people, bishops, priests or laity, not to be tainted with it. However, there are those priests, nuns and lay people who rose above ethnic background and historical programming to redeem the Church by their acts of heroism.

Why were so many church buildings destroyed in one month of ethnic genocide? As one bishop was heard to declare, 'It is as if the churches did not belong to them.'

Perhaps this could be part of the problem. Most of the money for the building of the large, elegant churches that flourish all over Rwanda came from overseas. There seems to have been little input from the people themselves in their construction. While the people have a great allegiance to the faith, perhaps there is a feeling that the Church as institution does not belong to them. Having access to foreign currency for projects, many Church leaders are accused of developing lifestyles that alienated them from the struggles of the common people and made them appear part of an exploitative upper class.

All over Africa, the Churches have put a lot of their time and energies into developing infrastructures in the educational, medical and social fields. The huge effort involved does not seem to have brought about a genuine evangelisation. As Father Wolfand Schonecke points out, 'The experience of the Church in Rwanda puts serious and urgent questions about the model of Church Africa has inherited from the missionaries and continues to follow. The powerful institutions in Rwanda covered up a lack of rootedness in Rwandese culture.'

We need to redress the whole problem of development and under-development from an African perspective and not from a purely Western one. Society needs to be built up on principles of political and economic justice and respect for human rights – not on foreign aid with foreign perspectives.

What lies behind the fact that the two countries which have experienced the most ruthless ethnic cleansing are places where apparitions of Our Blessed Lady have been reported – former Yugoslavia and Rwanda at Medjogorje and Kibeho? Are these to be seen as apocalyptic prophecies or religious escapism from harsh realities? Is it because our liturgies do not answer the emotional and creative needs of the people? Certainly the liturgy in Rwanda has an element of creativity, but still it is not allowed to flow with a natural African rhythm. It is controlled by Western rational patterns and movements.

The tradition of carrying identity cards which define the bearer as either Hutu or Tutsi needs to be done away with immediately. It was through their identity cards that many people were identified for killing. The Church should take a lead here in demanding change.

I had the benefit of spending some time in Buturae Diocese, which has one of the most active pastoral commissions in Rwanda. They have been coming together since the tragedy to tease out a way forward. In one of their reports I read:

> This crisis must give rise to a new way of being Church. A crisis, patiently borne, gives way to a spirit of creativity. The so-called Christian Communities of the hills have proved their inadequacy. Should they be rehabilitated? Would it not be better to let them die peacefully, to give place to more authentic forms of communities? Should we rehabilitate these enormous parishes which are so costly and difficult to manage? Must we take up again all our social, health and education works? It became clear that they burdened the Church and prevented it from carrying out its real apostolate. Their broad scope led the Church to think that its roots were deeper than they are. The African Synod with its emphasis on inculturation, dialogue, justice, could provide the basis for a new start.

The national debt

The national debt is a huge problem in most African countries. Money that should be going to support the infrastructure in many of these countries is being used to repay debts accumulated by governments trained in colonial mentalities. Monies are being taken from their countries, without anything being given back. During the 1970s many countries in the Developing World were forced to accept loans from Western banks, at low interest rates which have trebled over the past twenty years. 'In concrete terms this means that for every £1.00 in aid received by developing countries £3.50 is returned in debt repayments to First World countries' (*Intercom*, September 1994).

It is truly frightening to see the number of young people carrying arms in Africa today. Whereas it is difficult to get food supplies, there does not seem to be any problem getting arms. It is those countries who come to the aid of the starving nations who also furnish the arms with which they can kill each other. There is a great need for coherence in Western attitudes towards developing countries. If not, all we are achieving is 'Band-Aid' all over again.

Aid workers in Rwanda

I spent a week in Rwanda in December 1994. The purpose of my visit was to visit Refugee Trust volunteers – nine in all, doing medical work in two rural clinics. They are doing really wonderful work, not only in the medical services, but in the reconciliation and reunification of families. One nurse, Eugene, went underground to escape the war and atrocities. He remained in hiding until he heard that the Irish had taken over his clinic. He found the courage to return to his job. He also found his wife and children, whom he presumed had been killed, safe and well. The presence of the volunteers is of vital importance – they give confidence and security to the people in a hidden, but most effective war.

The first team to go to Rwanda consisted of Dr Don Colbert (Galway), Sister Dorothea Murphy (Glanmire, Cork), Sister Finola Kidney (Cork City), Sister Brenda O'Neill (Galway), Sister Eileen Byrne (Beaufort, Killarney, County Kerry), Ann Malone (Greystones, County Wicklow) and Cliona Cronin (Dublin). The beginnings were very difficult, starting from nothing, but the team was excellent. Four of the nurses were sisters of the Congregation of the Franciscan Sisters of the Divine Motherhood, and Sister Brenda was a Little Sister of the Assumption. The Franciscan Sisters had widespread experience of Africa and could adjust easily to the situation, though they had never seen poverty like this before.

We in Refugee Trust are deeply indebted to the Franciscan Sisters for releasing the Sisters, and to the Sisters for their great generosity in Rwanda during the first three most difficult months of our programme. We are indebted also to the Little Sisters of the Assumption for releasing an excellent nurse in the person of Sister Brenda O'Neill.

The first team of volunteers was replaced by an excellent team of lay people, all nurses, including Cleo Watson (Mayo), Brenda Harkin (Carlow), Laura Tighe (Roscommon), Paul Gilsenan (Dundalk), Eileen O'Leary (Thurles), Carol Desmond (Bantry) and Ann Malone (Greystones). They work, with Sister Finola (formerly of Zambia) and Sister Rita FMDM, as a close-knit group with love and dedication, bringing reassurance to the local population, and attracting the refugees to return home again from the refugee camps.

The team began with nothing except damaged buildings, both in Kiyanza, in the Province of Mugambesi, and in Rusero. Kiyanza Clinic had previously served about forty thousand people. Of these, twenty thousand had lost their lives in the massacres – half of the population was wiped out.

Sister Finola expressed her feelings:

> It was so eerie. I am so used to African villages and the surrounding countryside being so full of people – here we did not see a soul – not a soul. After an hour's wait a small boy appeared looking very frightened. However, he overcame his fear and then went off to look for the Headman. That Headman proved such a good friend. He helped us in every way possible to get the clinic going and to allay the people's fears of approaching us. He was just wonderful. The clinic building itself was a sight to behold – damaged and looted.
>
> We went back to Kigale and contacted MEMISA, a Dutch organisation, and asked for medical supplies,

which they gave us. Ndense, who was our faithful helper during the time we were there, listened as we said we wanted to meet the people and hear what they had to say. They soon told us what the main diseases were – malaria, scabies, malnutrition, dysentery and many, many more things. But where to start? So, we started right there and then working out of boxes and returning to Kabale in Uganda every day in the beginning – three hours there and three hours back and so much to do in the clinic!

Eventually the team moved to Kigale, thus reducing the travelling time to about forty-five minutes.

There were no staff in the clinic – all had fled the slaughter. One man whom we met up with later in one of the camps became a great help to us, caring for the orphans, and he told us that when the militia arrived with machetes, he ran one way and his wife ran the other. It was only after agonising weeks that they found each other – amazingly, both were unharmed.

The stories we heard as we worked in the clinic would have been unbelievable, but for the evidence of our eyes which bore out the truth of them. I was standing there one morning, just feeling overwhelmed by the whole horrific misery of it all. There was not a corner where you could put your eyes to get a moment's respite – not a corner where you could bend your ear, where you could hear something even vaguely nice.

A passage from Jeremiah came into my mind at that moment: 'A voice was heard in Rama – it was Rachel weeping for her children – because they were no more.'

I wonder how many Rachels we met in Rwanda? Some women had lost everything, just everything – all their children, their husbands, brothers and sisters, parents – they had absolutely nothing left. They came in sorrowful, bedraggled lines, back from the camps, having heard there was a clinic, and hoping for some help. Most of them were covered in scabies, with a bit of torn clothing wrapped around their thin bodies. And these were people who had lived in good conditions really, before this terrible thing happened.

Many times I heard myself saying in my heart – God, where are you? Where are you in all of this? Where were you when it all started happening? Had I listened I might have heard him say – I was here and I am still here, being hacked to death by the machete.

We did what we could, even to giving them hoes and seeds, hoping they would have enough heart to start cultivating again – and the amazing thing is, that they did.

I heard so many stories. One I still remember so vividly was that the authorities called all the religious of the area together, both local and foreign, and once they had them all in a large building, the doors were bolted and every single one of them was slaughtered.

I heard about a Canadian Brother who had worked for thirty years in Rwanda and when his confrères had returned to Canada, he asked to stay behind. He was in his house when the militia called in. He was taken to his room with his hands and feet tied (this was all witnessed), and told to kneel down. He was told he needed prayers because he was going to die, and then a huge hammer was brought down on his head. I could only be glad that it was done quickly.

There was another story of a White Father, who was sheltering Tutsis in his house and was told to release them. 'Over my dead body', he said. 'That's okay,' they said, 'it will be over your dead body.' They shot him dead and took the people away. Yet in the midst of it all there were so many incidents of bravery and compassion. One woman, Agnes, who had lost every single one of her children except the smallest one who suffered from Down's Syndrome was coming to the clinic one morning with this child when she heard a noise in the grass. It was a discarded baby. She lifted it and tried to feed it from her shrunken breast. She then brought it all the way up the mountain to the clinic, in her arms, together with her own child, who was dragging heavily on her, and asked us to try to save it. It was about two weeks old and wizened like an old man.

We saw many children, no more than nine or ten, trying to care for their younger brothers and sisters because their parents and older members of the family were all dead. These children should have been out playing and going to school. There were many, many more incidents like this.

The day I was preparing to leave Rwanda, they sent for me saying they had a surprise. I sat there and speeches were made – their thanks to Refugee Trust for sending us out from Ireland. There was dancing and singing and one refrain kept being repeated, thanking me for the work in the Nutrition Centre.

'Sister, you told us that you had no children of your own, but would help us with our children – but we want to tell you that you have been a model mother to us.'

I was overcome. This from people who had no idea when the next massacre would come, and yet they found space in their hearts to reach out to me, to affirm me and to tell me I had made a difference in their lives. I hope that mercy will come into the hearts of all Rwandan people. I am sure it is mercy the Lord wants from them and all of us.

Beside the Rusero Hospital where Refugee Trust was working there was a seminary for about six hundred seminarians, beside a beautiful lake. It had a fine church. I heard that half of the students had fled and half of them were killed. Not one of the teachers escaped – all were slaughtered.

Apparently, whole families, on seeing their friends and neighbours being hacked to death jumped into the lake where they drowned *en masse.* I visited the seminary and was saddened to see the buildings empty and the grass growing up all over the compound.

My niece, Nora Doheny, spent over two years working as a volunteer with Concern Worldwide in Rwanda. She sent me this report:

I work on the Rwanda/Tanzania border in five refugee camps. Concern has responsibility for the procurement of food, the education and the camp management in all five. We do the distribution in three camps. We have a total of 175,000 refugees in all and there are five to ten volunteers running the show. For the first five months I was very busy between all the camps, doing everything from registration to food distribution. The refugees crossed the swamp from Rwanda, arriving in terrible conditions, hungry, frightened, exhausted, many of them very sick, even on the point of death. Organising them means many meetings with camp leaders, and international donor agencies, including UNHCR officials. So I was very busy, but it is all so interesting and rewarding. I am responsible for the overall administration and office work for the programme, and I am now doing that full-time.

We are due to open a new camp soon and so I have been working on that for the past few weeks. Concern Worldwide has been given the responsibility for the infrastructure of the camp, with the exception of the water supplies, which is undertaken by Oxfam. There will be twenty-eight blocks and we will be able to cater for forty thousand people. We will also build a distribution centre, much like a hay-barn. The size of the camp is 2 km x 1.5 km. We have two engineers on the job and they have to erect 118 classrooms for schools in the camp. These will be made of mud-blocks and will be fairly durable. They will be used by the Tanzanians, if and when the Rwandese return home.

I have responsibility for the purchase of all the construction materials and for paying the salaries of some eighty-five Tanzanian workers. I also have to organise seven trucks and six landrovers, so I am kept busy, which is a good complaint, as there is not much to do when we don't work. We generally work six days from 8.00 a.m. till 5.30 p.m.

I am very, very happy in the refugee camps. It is totally absorbing and the people are beautiful and kind. They appreciate the help we give them, but they are all pining for home, though they are terrified of returning to Rwanda, after the atrocities they have been through. It is hard to blame them, but what future do they have in exile? At least here they can sleep at night in security. We have no police in the camps but the people are very well behaved. I thank God I am here and I have no regrets about coming. At least I can be of some small service to a people who have suffered so much.

My visit to Rwanda was a sad one but Refugee Trust must continue to stay with the people and be a witness of love and justice among them, hoping that they will be reconciled and live in peace and harmony with one another.

Lessons for the future

During my first morning of visiting the refugee camps in Goma, Zaire, I was introduced as Father John. Immediately there was an cry from the people: 'Why have our own priests abandoned us? Why has God abandoned us?' I replied that I did not know why their own priests had not been visiting them, but I knew that God had not abandoned them. I tried to reason with them. 'Can you not see the hand of God in the relief that is coming to you now? Are not Catholics and Christians from around the world responding now to your desperate cries for help? Like Jesus on the Cross, surely God is present in all your pain and suffering.'

Yet at the heart of this terrible tragedy there was a feeling that somehow the Church, whom they had come to love and trust, had betrayed them. They were not able to articulate it in so many words, but still they knew that their relationship with the Church had been profoundly altered. It will take more than a few months of reflection to come to a deep and clear understanding of what led to the genocide in Rwanda.

The first morning I visited the camps I got some idea of the enormity of the problems facing them. For miles and miles the blue and green plastic sheeting used by the refugees to provide temporary shelter stretched into the misty morning cloudiness on the side of the smouldering volcano that is home to some eight hundred thousand. As we made our way along the road, we were struck by the continuous line of people carrying wood into the camp from the surrounding hillsides. How long could the countryside sustain this denuding of its vegetation? Will it ever recover from the mass influx of people tearing its limbs apart? What alternative is there for the people but to forage for the firewood they need for cooking?

Caritas, Save the Children, Médecins sans Frontières, Assist UK, the UN, the World Food Programme, the Red Cross, the Lutheran World Federation, Concern, the Overseas Development Association, were just some of the aid agencies that met us on their way out of the camp or sped past us with relief supplies. Everywhere there was a buzz of activity, a sense that something was being done, that progress was being made in the battle against hunger and desease. Yet the bodies laid out along the road were a constant reminder that too many people were still dying needlessly and that more needed to be done. Could the international community keep up this constant supply of aid? It was mind-boggling to witness the vast numbers of people who needed to be fed – and this was just one of the many camps spread all around the borders of Tanzania, Uganda, Burundi and Kenya. Where would it all lead to?

I had come to Goma with an Irish aid agency – Goal. They were involved in running two large camps for unaccompanied children and were also the arm of UNHCR for food distribution to all the centres for unaccompanied children – there were an estimated eleven thousand children in these centres. They also collected the dead lying on the road from Goma to the camps. In August, between three and four hundred bodies were collected per day. I went each evening to the mass graves to make a blessing over those who had died that day. Most of the journalists I met, and many observers, were shocked by the total lack of any religious ceremony for those who died. Many of these journalists had been in Ethiopia and Somalia at the height of the famine, where there had always been some type of religious ceremony for the dead. Yet here we were with a people who were profoundly religious but there was no trace of any blessing for the dead. Had everything that they believed in died during the mass slaughter that had taken place in Rwanda? What role had religion played in the conflict until now, and what did this say to all missionaries as we are beginning to launch Evangelisation 2000? What are the lessons of the Rwanda situation and can such a catastrophe be prevented from taking place in the future?

Mary Robinson and refugees
In November 1994, Mary Robinson, then President of Ireland,

made a marathan trip through Africa, visiting such countries as Tanzania, Zimbabwe, Zaire, Uganda and Rwanda. The main purpose of the exercise was to visit the refugees who had fled from Rwanda into Zaire.

She was given a regal reception wherever she went. In Zimbabwe she was received by President Robert Mugabe, who used the occasion to pay tribute to the work of the Irish missionaries who served his country so well during the liberation war. He did not mention anyone in particular, but I'm sure he had in mind the great Bishop Donal Lamont, a Carmelite bishop who fought hard to break the apartheid system. Bishop Lamont wrote a pastoral letter as far back as the late 1950s, which the other bishops refused to sign for fear of the regime, but Bishop Lamont published it. It led him into great trouble and landed him in prison. He had to stand trial for treason, and he took the opportunity of making a lengthy speech from the dock, which was later published in book form. He became a national hero when Zimbabwean independence was achieved. The Jesuit missionaries also suffered, and four priests were shot in Musami Mission, together with four Dominican Sisters. Father Donovan disappeared and was never found. Robert Mugabe was surely justified in paying tribute to the Irish missionaries for their part in the liberation, education and development of his people.

Mary Robinson then went to Goma Refugee Camp in Zaire, where there were about half a million refugees from Rwanda, living in miserable conditions and dying by the thousand. She went around greeting the victims of the terrible atrocities, and shaking hands with the poorest of the poor. She was the only head of state to visit the refugees in Goma. What a message it was for the heads of state all over the world.

She spoke out vehemently on the violation of human rights, on the blight it cast on the whole human race, and she asked, in no uncertain terms, that those responsible should be brought to justice and receive appropriate punishment. The whole world was in some way responsible for these horrific atrocities and we should not rest until justice was administered.

Later the president went to the UN in New York and made her feelings known in an emotional appeal for justice at the highest level. She is a credit to Ireland and an example for all heads of state worldwide for her courageous stand on human rights. All Irish people should be proud of her.

CHAPTER 23

PERSONAL REFLECTIONS

Though each one of us has a personal decision to make regarding our work for refugees, the natural reaction is 'I am no Mother Teresa'. However, let us put first things first. The Gospel of St Luke is a simple yet very sophisticated document, and it is not by chance that the parable of the Good Samaritan and the incident giving rise to the statement that 'Mary has chosen the better part' are placed side by side. Certainly we must seek to play the part of active Christians, but we must also seek the spiritual, contemplative life – what we can all do is pray daily for the displaced people of the world. Some young people may want to go further and actively assist refugees. Each of us has a part to play, according to our ability and position in life.

The authentic way to help refugees is to live with them, travel with them, and identify completely with them. But the front line can only survive if it has the backing of the people behind the lines – their prayers, sacrifices and financial support. We then become a great and powerful team working hand-in-hand for the good of refugees and displaced persons.

The real witness is the person working with the refugees on a one-to-one basis. I was so close to the situation myself that I fully appreciate the difficulties. It was the people of Biafra yesterday, it is the people of Bosnia and Rwanda today. Many have risked their lives to reach the poor, without asking for any reward. Like Mother Teresa, they see the image of Christ in every poor person. As she says, 'When you touch the wounds of the poor you are touching the body of Christ.' We must all live more simply, so that others may simply live.

Let us remind ourselves of a wise saying of Mahatma Ghandi:

> There are enough resources in the world to satisfy all men's needs, but there are not enough resources in the world to satisfy all men's greed.

We should be active contemplatives in this world of turmoil.

We must live in the presence of God all the time. 'St Patrick's Breastplate' expresses it all – Christ above us, Christ below us, Christ around us. In the words of the hymn for the feast of St Patrick:

> Christ be near at either hand,
> Christ behind, before me stand,
> Christ with me where e'er I go,
> Christ around, above, below.

There should be union with God and with people – one mind, one heart, one love. We must try to have faith, trust and confidence – seeing God in ourselves, seeing God in others. We can be at the disposal of God at all times – always doing what pleases him. We must strive to see him in the distressing disguise of the poorest of the poor. Jesus himself was a refugee. As soon as Jesus was born, Joseph had to flee with the Holy Family into Egypt because Herod wanted to kill the child. Jesus wanted to share every form of human suffering, including the dreadful experience of becoming a refugee.

We must see Christ in every refugee to day – they are the truly wretched of this world. The list of their afflictions is endless – the tragic insecurity of their lives, the uncertainty, the mental anguish, the utter darkness, the unknown future, the worry for their children and their dependants... the shadows are endless, the isolation is great, pushed out of home and homeland, unwanted and unloved, friendless, separated from their neighbours, alone but always human, yet suspect, watched and guarded like prisoners, yet innocent, abandoned by their country and now in an alien atmosphere which is often hostile, searching for help, dependent on others, clinging to a straw – looking for someone who understands, someone to talk to, to share their problems, someone who can sympathise and empathise with them, turning to God with spiritual longings, searching for a safe place to go, searching for peace. The Church must be there in their midst, sharing their sufferings. The shepherd must be with his flock, living with them, travelling with them, listening to them, sharing with them, loving them.

The pastor is Christ among them, praying with them, ministering to them – a presence among them, a protection for them.

> The Good Shepherd lays down his life for his sheep.
>
> *John 10:15*

Mother Teresa was once asked, 'What must we do to transform the world?' Her answer was simple, 'We must begin with ourselves.'

> We must act justly, love tenderly and walk humbly in the sight of God.
>
> *Deuteronomy 24:17-22*

Moses said to the people:

> You must not pervert justice in dealing with the stranger, or an orphan, nor take a widow's garment in pledge.
>
> Remember that you were a slave in Egypt and that the Lord, your God, redeemed you there.

The story of humankind, from Adam's fall, is one of injustice. The first real act recorded was the murder of Abel by Cain.

Refugees are the real victims of injustice, oppression and ostracism, being ignored and forgotten for the most part.

A refugee is a kneeling person:

> Kneeling in front of the captain of a ship to ask for a reduction in his/her escape price;
>
> Kneeling in front of pirates to ask for mercy, to be left in peace;
>
> Kneeling in front of the international agencies to ask for food and the bare necessities of life – just to keep alive;
>
> Kneeling in front of the police to ask for permission to move outside the camp, as if it were a prison;
>
> Kneeling in front of a foreign delegation to beg to be accepted into a foreign country;

Kneeling in front of the press begging for a hearing;

Kneeling in front of the Church asking for a pastor, a priest, a guide – just to be accepted as a human being, as a Christian;

Kneeling in front of you and me for spiritual advice, encouragement, above all for justice and fair play.

For refugees all distinctions of wealth, power, social function and role have collapsed completely and evaporated like smoke. What is left? Just A HUMAN BEING WITHOUT A MASK.

Stability and security have disappeared. Refugees are unloved and unwanted by almost everyone, fleeing from an oppressive and unjust regime in their own country, travelling for days, sometimes for weeks, even months, into the unknown, to a country that does not want them, trying to survive while hunted in the forest like wild animals.

Who sees the human cost of oppression in the refugee camp? Who cries out against it? Who speaks for the poor, who have no voice of their own?

Who looks at the young people and sees their rightful, natural belief in the future wither and blow away with the dust? Who sees the old people who were used to a good life once upon a time and now see the awful difference of their children's and grandchildren's lives?

Those of you who are parents of young children – imagine your child now aged eight, born and raised within the confines of a barbed-wire fence. If you are parents of young adults, imagine your son aged twenty-six who was seven years old the first time he fled from war and has been been fleeing ever since. Imagine you have a friend who refuses to speak of the future, because to try to imagine a future makes his present life unendurable.

The injustice that is the source of these questions moves me to anger. The obverse of sadness is anger. If such injustice moves you to pity, I hope it will also stimulate anger – to protest about a world where the 'haves' can blandly forget the 'have nots'.

We should be ashamed that more governments do not speak out with a stronger voice. Ireland's former president, Mary

Robinson, is a great example to others. We must never forget our tragic history, which made us into the generous nation that we are.

Strange as it may seem, refugees are a real gift to us. Through our friendship with them, we can come to enter more deeply into the mystery of God's love for us. We have seen intimations of God's compassion in the lives of those who are so often treated without compassion; we catch traces of salvation among people whose lives are fragmented; through the eyes of those who have been driven outside the human city we have seen the face of Christ, who died outside the city. In the resilience of those who build laughter out of such wholly inadequate materials, we know a little better what it is to be human.

Human dignity is so often ignored in the laws and practices of the international community which we represent. We would like to find modest ways of defending that dignity wherever it is threatened, and so give voice to the voiceless. However tottering our first steps, we should walk in the love that does justice. Our task and our privilege are to build bridges to enable people to cross the gulfs that divide them, by enabling them to take responsibility for their own lives in some measure, by encouraging friendship, by advocacy, by fostering their spiritual growth, and by being available to them in the camps and in the developed countries.

We, as Christians, must be a bridge between old and new, oppressed and oppressor, Black and White, Christian and Muslim, Jew and Gentile, pastor and flock.

A visit to Nigeria twenty-three years after the Biafran War

What a joy it was for Father Pat Dunne and myself to return to Nigeria. What a change, what a beautiful transformation the country had undergone during my absence of twenty-three years. There was peace and prosperity everywhere, and a fast-growing Catholic Church, with an energetic local clergy that was a joy to our hearts. The improvements went far beyond our dreams.

We began in Onitsha, where we attended an ordination of twenty-five priests for the diocese of Onitsha alone. Only sixty years ago all the missionaries were White, whereas today in Onitsha there were only two White priests, and we were passing through. The local Church had come alive in a big way. We attended the beautiful ceremony in the open stadium, where the numbers were great and the atmosphere was jubilant, full of spiritual joy.

My next stop was Owerri, and Bishop Mark Uneghbu of that diocese sent a car for me. Travelling down the road we passed through Uli, famous for its wartime airstrip. For me it was so full of emotional memories, of danger, night-time bombing, taking cover in the ditches, waiting for planes to land in total darkness, and of course those brave pilots who lost their lives bringing food and medicine to the starving population. I got out of the car to ponder these terrible moments of the war, asking God never to let it happen again in Nigeria.

I received a great welcome from the Bishop and stayed with him for a night. The beautiful Owerri Cathedral was visible for about a mile on the Obaku straight road – a true monument to the vision of Bishop J. B. Whelan, who planned and commissioned it, and to Bishop Mark Uneghbu who finished it. I had often seen Father Christy Ring directing the work on the vast site, and wondered was it too ambitious, or would it ever be finished. I had memories of Con Murphy, who put on the perspex in the boiling heat, with the perspiration running down his face, and of Frank who contributed to its construction. We all thought it was too big, too grandiose and would never be filled. How wrong we were. I was there on Sunday and it was packed for several Masses. When it was planned, the site was outside the town, but now it is at the centre of a very large town, grown beyond recognition.

The other church, St Paul's, is a monument to the Kennedy family – Da Kennedy who designed it, and Ray who built it with a volunteer, Don McLeish. Don built several churches and schools, and a two-storey building in Okpala Seminary. He relieved several missionaries by his wonderful work, and undertook to build a rest house for the priests on the seafront at Eket.

The bishop's house brought back pleasant memories of the Irish and American volunteers who served as secretaries in various departments. Peggy Farrelly was private secretary to Bishop Whelan, with Mairead McGrath. Pat Loftus was secretary in the bookshop run by Father George Lahiffe, and there were many others.

The next stop was also an exciting one – Okpala Seminary, where I had been director for ten years, two of which were during the war. I received a rare welcome there, though the students did not know me. It was a wonderful experience just to roam around the compound and admire the many improvements, especially the additional buildings. I was moved to see that one of the new buildings was dedicated to the Doheny Brothers, with a sign clearly marked 'THE DOHENY BLOCK'. I spent a week there and visited all the stations in the parish.

It was wonderful to see the growth of the Church. Achara had a beautiful church and priest's house, while Ibokwe and Alulu also had new churches. I said Mass in all the stations – a sheer joy, and the people were ecstatic in their welcome, expressed in music, song and dance. They were even planning a church in the growing town of Okpala. I was glad to be able to get a donation towards it from Mary Doohan of the Little Way Association in London.

I paid a visit to Aba, eighteen miles along the road to Port Harcourt. More beautiful memories flooded back of the day I knelt in prayer in the church and asked God to help me find someone to put the roof on Okpala Church. I visited Bishop Vincent Ezonye CSSp, who told me of the growth of the Church in Aba. Where there were two churches in my time, there are thirteen now, with more planned. There are three major seminaries in the Eastern Region, where there was only one in my time. These seminaries are full, with about five hundred in the Bigard Memorial in Enugu. It is an unbelievable growth, probably the fastest-growing Church in the world.

I went to see retired Bishop Anthony Nwedo in Umuahia. He had founded a Congregation of Sisters which had grown rapidly and was doing sterling work in education and medicine. The bishop was worried about the political situation – the northerners were determined to maintain complete control and had rejected the results of the recent elections, which had been declared fair. The colleges had been taken over by the government, and so the Church no longer had the same influence on education.

I spent the last two days with a great friend, Father Peadar Dinan CSSp, in Enugu. He is one of the few Holy Ghost Fathers left in the country, among them Father Tim Buckley who runs a parish outside Enugu.

The overall picture is most encouraging. The seed we helped to plant is growing very fast. Many Nigerian Spiritans are ministering in other parts of Africa – Zambia, Zimbabwe, Tanzania, Kenya, and as far away as Papua New Guinea. The same can be said of the

Holy Rosary Sisters, now speading the Gospel in different parts of the world.

It is a fruitful vineyard. May it continue to grow and inspire other parts of Africa in which darkness prevails to accept the message of God.

CHAPTER 24

LOOKING BACK – LOOKING FORWARD

My heart is filled with gratitude for the beautiful life God has given to me. It has been full of variety, joy and challenge, conflict and war, peace and calm. God was always at the crossroads when I was trying to find the right road. It has been a most challenging pilgrimage.

On this road of life, I met some wonderful people, who helped me enormously. Mother Teresa of Calcutta, whom I met for the first time in Ethiopia in 1973, had a major influence on my life. It is difficult to imitate her, but I tried. She had great simplicity, dynamic faith, unlimited generosity and kindness, transparent goodness, genuine charity. I was privileged to work closely with her for more than twenty years, and have seen her influence on so many people in Africa, Europe and the Middle East. A woman for all seasons, she appealed to the young and the elderly, of every race and colour.

Mother Teresa drew good out of everything and everybody. I once visited Calcutta shortly after she had fallen ill, and was struck by the strong reactions of the people to her illness. One wealthy Muslim left his work and did a pilgrimage to Mecca so that God would not take her away. A Hindu boy wrote directly to God: 'Dear God, please do not take our Mother away from us.' The local paper carried a cartoon depicting the Churches' reaction to her sickness. It showed a mosque, a Hindu temple, a Buddhist temple, a Christian church. Outside each building, members of each congregation stood dressed in their respective costumes, with their hands joined together in prayer as they looked to Heaven. The caption underneath was: 'O God, please do not take our Mother away from us.' The cartoon clearly illustrated the respect and acceptance that everyone in the world had for Mother Teresa, irrespective of nationality, creed or colour. Mother Teresa's prayer life stands out as an example to all. She attributed all her success to God's loving intervention. She attributed nothing to herself. God used her as an instrument of his divine power. there in no-one to compare with her today – so weak-looking and yet so strong, so frail and yet so dynamic. She was a woman for all times, all people. Her death, in

September 1997, has deprived the world of a shining light in the darkness.

Another great example was Leonard Cheshire, founder of the Cheshire Homes. He also had a major influence on me and taught me a lot about the handicapped. I loved working with him, as we toured Africa together in search of more facilities for the disabled. Through Leonard, I met his wife, Lady Sue Ryder of Warsaw, the founder of the Ryder Homes, another remarkable person. I was privileged to be able to help her establish homes for the elderly in Ireland.

My brother, Father Michael, was another great source of inspiration in my life. I followed him to Blackrock College as a student, and into the Holy Ghost Congregation. I was appointed to Owerri, in Nigeria, where he was a missionary. Later we developed the same lifestyle in our outreach to the poor. Mike worked on communications, and blew the whistle for the world to hear on many occasions. His great gift was communication through speech, a gift that God asked him to sacrifice for the last six years of his life, from the time he suffered a stroke. We worked very closely throughout our lives. We both worked with Mother Teresa and Leonard Cheshire. Mother Teresa wrote to Mike several times during his illness, asking for his prayers for her work.

During my life I met many international journalists, among them Jonathan Dimbleby in Ethiopia, Mike Nicholson and Fred Forsyth in Biafra. I always helped them, mindful of the power of the media.

I met wonderful people in the refugees, frustrated though they were.

I met many volunteers who have devoted years to alleviating the sufferings of the poor, silently but courageously, often in dangerous circumstances. The demands made on them are great, and they need our support in their frontline struggle in the war against famine, hunger and oppression.

The power of prayer

The power of prayer cannot be over-estimated. 'More things are wrought by prayer than this world dreams of.' One of the most encouraging things about our kind of work is that unknown numbers of unknown people are praying for us all the time. I met a woman in Dublin who said she had been praying for me when I was in Iraq. I had not met the woman before but she had heard of me from my cousin, Eileen Malone. She attended the same prayer meeting as Eileen, who told her about my work and whereabouts.

We must thank God that such good people exist in the world. I certainly needed prayers in Iraq. We can never understand how we overcame such and such a difficulty until we hear a story like this. Eileen gave me this poem on the power of prayer:

> The day was long, the burden I had borne
> Seemed heavier than I could bear.
> And then it lifted – but I did not know
> Someone had knelt in Prayer;
> Had taken me to God that very hour
> And asked the easing of my load,
> And he, in infinite compassion,
> Had stooped down,
> And taken it from me.
>
> We cannot tell how often as we pray,
> For some bewildered one, hurt and distressed,
> The answer comes, but many times those hearts
> Find sudden peace and rest.
> Someone had prayed and Faith, a reaching hand,
> Took hold of God and brought him down that day,
> So many, many hearts have need of prayer,
> Let us pray.

On reflection I know that I was in great difficulty in Baghdad, especially on the night of 16 January 1991, the day after the deadline for war. I fell into a cold sweat of great fear which I could scarcely control because of the inevitable and imminent bombing soon to be inflicted on the people of that city. I thought of Christ in his agony in the garden. Perhaps it was Eileen Malone and her prayer group who helped me through that awful night. 'Someone had knelt in prayer....'

God spoke to me
God spoke to me in many beautiful ways at the turning points of my life. He guided me at the crossroads. He spoke to me through

my early background, my family upbringing, through my dedicated, devoted and devout mother in the struggle against poverty, through the faith and love I received in a good home.

God used my brother, Michael, to show me the way forward – into Blackrock College, into the Holy Ghost Congregation, and eventually to the missions in Nigeria.

God called me into exile in Biafra to teach me what it is like to be a refugee. He also taught me through the displaced people who said to me: 'What mattered most to us was the fact that you stayed with us in our hour of greatest need, when other Europeans abandoned us.' The importance of a pastoral presence living among refugees was their great message to me.

The Lord advised me to take up the cause of the poor, and to use my Biafran experience in a more global sense after the Biafran war, through a confrère, Father Donal O'Sullivan, when he was first assistant to the Spiritan General Council in Rome.

God led me into Ethiopia just before a great famine and revolution, thus inviting me to use my Biafran experience in this new situation. My experience proved invaluable, helping me to unite the Churches and agencies, to deal with the disaster by setting up the Christian Relief and Development Association.

God helped me to use my gifts by setting up a programme for street girls in Ethiopia, by inviting, through me, the Good Shepherd Sisters whose vocation is to care for street girls and prostitutes. It proved dangerous for me as I tried to befriend their clients in order to help them, a work I was not trained for, but God protected me from danger.

God spoke to me again in 1979, through the Bishops' Conference of Zambia, which invited me to set up programmes in Zambia for refugees from six neighbouring countries.

God spoke to me in Maheba refugee settlement in north-west Zambia, through an Angolan refugee who told me that we, as priests, should be living with the refugees in the settlement as 'the shepherds of the flock'. 'The good shepherd lays down his life for his sheep.'

Christ spoke to me through the Zimbabwean refugees in J. Z. Moyo camp in Zambia, when they showed appreciation for their pastor, Father Nigel Johnson SJ, of whom they said, 'He is one of us.'

God invited me to set up an agency, Refugee Trust, to concentrate on the pastoral care of refugees and displaced persons.

Jesus invited me to go into Baghdad, before the Gulf War, through the person of Mother Teresa, who said to me, 'Go, Father, without fear as Jesus would.' When I was overcome with fear on the night before the Gulf War, God invited me to pray as never before to regain my composure.

God spoke through an angry Arab, a Muslim called Abdulla, at the airport in Amman as I looked for information about a flight to London the day after the Gulf War broke out. His abuse turned into love and friendship in a beautiful story of reconciliation.

God spoke to me through Archbishop Emmanuel Clarizio about the possibility of establishing a refugee institute for the pastoral care of refugees and displaced people.

God speaks to me in Psalm 17 on a regular basis, especially when I am faced with failure or discouragement. He gives me comfort through that psalm:

> You, O Lord, are my lamp,
> My God who lightens my darkness,
> With you, I can break through any barrier,
> With my God, I can scale any wall.

God puts thoughts into my head, and words into my mouth, which give me extraordinary courage and the determination to take any challenge on board.

Jesus spoke to me in no uncertain terms from the broken crucifix in the bombed-out church in Namibia, with the words: 'I have no hands but yours.'

God spoke to me through Gene Dewey's deep insight into the plight of refugees, looking on them as assets rather than liabilities in his beautiful speech on 'the myth of refugees'.

There is no such thing as chance. God plans everything – the things we do, the people we meet, the many incidents that make up our everyday lives. Our crosses, our ups and downs, our successes and failures, all have a meaning – but do we listen carefully, do we interpret them accurately? Above all, do we act on them seriously?

God speaks to us through others as he spoke through the two

apostles on the road to Emmaus. The apostles were mesmerised and confused by the sad events of the first Holy Week.

> Were not our hearts burning within us as he explained the scriptures to us? He opened our eyes.... We recognised him in the breaking of bread.

The Lord brought me into contact with Leonard Cheshire, who introduced me to the world of the disabled, for which I am ever so grateful.

God brought me in touch with many elderly people in Ireland through Sue Ryder when she invited me to assist her to establish her Ryder Homes in this country.

God spoke to me so many times through Mother Teresa, with her simple gems of wisdom: 'Let God use your weakness.' 'If there are one hundred people in need, then help one and you will find that you can help more, perhaps ten, perhaps the whole lot, because it is not your work, it is God's work, operating through us.'

God spoke to me through Father Niall O'Brien's Book *Revolution from the Heart,* which described the growth of the missionaries, of the Church, of the Christian communities in the Philippines.

God continues to speak to us, all the time, but are we listening? Do we hear his voice in the silence of our hearts?

> Oh, that today, you would listen to his voice, harden not your hearts.

> *Psalm 94(95)*